Storm over the Multinationals
The Real Issues

Written under the auspices of
The Center for International Affairs
and Graduate School of Business Administration,
Harvard University

Storm over the Multinationals
The Real Issues

Raymond Vernon

HARVARD UNIVERSITY PRESS
Cambridge, Massachusetts
1977

Library of Congress Cataloging in Publication Data

Vernon, Raymond, 1913–
  Storm over the multinationals.

  Includes bibliographical references and index.
  1. International business enterprises.   I. Title.
HD2755.5.V473   338.8'8   76-30790
ISBN 0-674-83875-0

| Preface

Books that deal with the multinational enterprise, the transnational corporation, or the international firm have not been a rarity over the past few years. Indeed, it is a little frightening to observe the mounting flood of words on these subjects coming from the typewriters of scholars, journalists, government officials, and novelists. Why one more such book?

This book is intended to help the reader who is trying to keep his head above the flood. It tries to maintain some sort of large perspective on the nature and consequences of the multinational enterprise. That is not an easy thing to do. Here and there, swept along in the torrent of published words, one can find a revealing fact, a perceptive study, a powerful generalization. But much of the outpouring turns out to be a tide of special pleading or of narrow pedantry. Anyone who tries to filter out the polemic and the propaganda so as to grasp the meaning of what is left is likely to find the task forbidding. That task is what this book tries to perform.

Systematic efforts to grasp the meaning of the multinational spread of large enterprises began at Harvard nearly fifteen years ago. Not surprisingly, I have drawn heavily on the substantial body of research that has been conducted at the Harvard Business School during those years, as well as on the work of my colleagues at Harvard's Center for International Affairs. In more recent years, the network of serious researchers and the output of useful research on the subject have increased astronomically, so that exciting and revealing contributions have been coming from dozens of institutions. Very soon the sheer weight of all the materials will be so great that no individual scholar will be able to keep up with the important contributions. But up to the time that this book went to press, that was my aspiration.

The subject of the multinational enterprise, as this analysis points out, engages the values, the fortunes, and the psyches of some of the most powerful leadership groups in modern society—businessmen, politicians, intellectuals, and poets. Any author who lays claim, as I do, to a position detached from all such leadership groups is likely to generate a predictable reaction. From the perspective of every disputant, the hapless author is classified as belonging to the enemy.

On the other hand, as the reader will shortly see, I regard the subject as much too important to be settled by the parties who so far have led the debate. Most of them, as it turns out, are cast in leadership roles that oblige them to assess the multinational enterprise from special points of view; most cannot stray very far from a predictable set of conclusions without weakening the position of the institutions they are committed to lead or without failing the test of their loyalty to the well-formed ideology with which they are identified.

No one, of course, can quite escape the traps that his training, experience, associations, and interests constantly set for his unwary intellect. Indeed, some social scientists have insisted that the very effort not only is doomed to failure but also is intended to mislead and to deceive. This book, then, entails a risk on everybody's part: on mine in aspiring to an unattainable measure of objectivity; on the reader's in exposing himself to a presentation that could conceivably entrap.

Writing this book has taken a great deal of time, of money, and of institutional support. Throughout the project, substantial support came from the Ford Foundation and from the Associates of the Harvard Business School. In the later stages, the Rockefeller Foundation and the National Science Foundation also made significant contributions, as did the Federal Work Study Program. The National Bureau of Economic Research extended to me the hospitality of its West Coast office for six indispensable months of quiet scribbling.

The support, as usual, came not only from institutions but also from individuals. A number of my colleagues were good enough to play the role of helpful critic, but the contribution of L. T. Wells, Jr., in this role was particularly devastating and creative. William Davidson directed a heroic effort in data collection and bibiliographical search, assisted by an unusual group of students that included Roger Greene, James Hughes, Brian Ike, John Murville, Edward Samorajczyk, and Samson Tu. Rajan Suri broke all precedent by coaxing the needed data out of the computers precisely on schedule. And Joan C. Curhan was responsible for the recruitment, training, budgeting, controlling, and reporting that are entailed in research efforts of this order.

Contents

Storm over the
Multinationals
The Real Issues

1 | The Multinational Enterprise as Symbol

THE WORLD we are obliged to inhabit, it sometimes seems, is managed by a deity with an exceedingly wry sense of humor. This is a century in which technological forces have pushed nation-states together and sharply reduced their autonomy. It is also a century in which national governments have taken on the novel and difficult task of actively trying to promote the welfare of ordinary people. The decline in national autonomy has seemed at times to hamstring governments in the exercise of their new responsibilities, and the rise of the multinational enterprise has epitomized the seeming clash. Created in part as a result of the shrinkage of international space, in part as a response to new opportunities those forces have generated, the multinational enterprise is widely seen as threatening the autonomy of the nation-state.

If scientists and engineers had not found a way to shrink international space over the past century or so, the odds are high that the multinational enterprise would be a rarity today. The international telephone, the computer, and the commercial aircraft have been indispensable to the growth of such enterprises. At the same time, even without benefit of the multinational enterprise, these revolutionary innovations vastly altered the international environment of the nation-states.

1

Communication by voice across the Atlantic first occurred in 1927. Thereafter, for about three decades, a ru-
dimentary radiotelephone service existed, a service that
was plagued by chronic atmospheric interference and in-
terminable queuing. Not until 1956 was the first transat-
lantic cable telephone put in operation. By the early 1970s,
as the price of international telephone calls steadily declined, Americans alone were making over a hundred
thousand international calls every day.[1]

Along with the spectacular improvements in communication came the development of the computer. For
the multinational enterprise, the importance of the computer lay in the fact that the routine data needed for the
direction and control of global operations could be trans-
mitted in vast quantities and could be retrieved and re-
grouped with lightning speed. The information so trans-
mitted was reduced to a series of binary choices, a yes or a
no. The ambiguities of the written and spoken word
shrank drastically. The elimination of ambiguities, which
is important in all routine business operations, is especially important for business conducted over long distances, where error and distortion can go undetected for
long periods. Between 1960 and 1975 the cost of handling
a bit of information in a general-purpose computer fell
more than 90 percent, while both speed and reliability increased over ten times.[2]

Backing up the telephone and the computer has been
the commercial aircraft, together with its ubiquitous adjuncts, the international travel agent and the international
credit card. In air travel and transport, growth rates have
been positively breathtaking. Between 1960 and 1974, for
instance, passenger volume on international commercial
flights rose from 26 billion passenger-miles to 152 billion.[3] From the beginning to the end of the same period,
while industry's costs in general rose about 70 percent,
the operating expenses of aircraft per ton-mile first moved
down, then up, ending at almost the level at which they
began.[4]

Hand in hand with the spectacular shrinkage in space in this century has gone the greatest increase in the output of goods and services that mankind has ever experienced. Almost every part of the globe has been touched by the vast outpouring. The countries that were rich to begin with, such as those of North America and northwest Europe, have become very much richer. New countries, such as Japan and Saudi Arabia, have joined the ranks of the rich. Areas of ancient poverty, such as Korea, Iran, Mexico, and Taiwan, have been pulled out of that category into a new phase of development. Even many of the poorest areas of the world, although still overwhelmed by malnutrition and disease and threatened by new problems of unbridled population growth, have shown modest signs of improved welfare, thus reversing a long decline. Infant mortality rates have fallen nearly everywhere. With a few notable exceptions such as Bangladesh, the poor countries have held their own or have improved their position in the quality and quantity of their food intake.[5] Visible advances in literacy have become common.[6]

The spectacular shrinkage in space created by improved transportation and communication, therefore, is only one manifestation of a vast global change. The implications of the change have touched everyone engaged in consuming or producing, in buying or selling, in projecting ideas or in absorbing them, through the network of a multinational enterprise or through any other means.

One fundamental consequence of the shrinkage in space, affecting all forms of enterprise, has been a rapid movement toward the homogenization of consumer tastes. The universal instinct of curiosity and the widespread propensity for emulation have spread some products rapidly through the world, including not only the markets in which multinational enterprises are present but also the markets in which they are not. Portable radios, Donald Duck dolls, and existentialist novels, for instance, have become ubiquitous items in global markets.

The evidence regarding the homogenization of buyers' preferences around the world is not very systematic.[7] But its purport is unmistakable. The manufactured products that appear in the stalls and markets of Accra or Dar es Salaam are no longer very different from those in Djakarta or Cartagena or Recife. The plastic pail has replaced the gourd, the earthen pot, and the banana leaf; tin roofs are replacing the local varieties of thatch; electric batteries and electric bulbs are taking over the function of kerosene, wood, vegetable oil, and tallow; the portable radio and the aspirin tablet are joining the list of life's universal necessities.

For consumers at higher levels of income, consumption patterns in different parts of the world show the same overwhelming tendency to convergence. Middle-income automobiles, when judged by appearance and performance, are losing their last traces of national distinction; bicycles and ski equipment are universal commodities tailored to a global market; French wines and Italian shoes are sold almost everywhere and copied where they are not sold; the Beatles are a household word not only in London and New York but in Moscow and Budapest as well; McDonald's universal hamburger sign is found on Tokyo's Ginza as well as on the streets of London, Hong Kong, and Melbourne.

Many industrial technologies appear to be going through a similar process of global homogenization. Time was when manufacturers of capital equipment in France, Britain, Germany, and the United States produced quite distinctive lines of machinery—distinctive in the sense that each reflected the special producing conditions of the national economy in which they were created. Accordingly, many U.S. machines tended to be profligate in their use of raw materials while not demanding great skills on the part of their operators; this tendency was characteristic, for instance, of the woodworking and metalworking machines developed by the Americans before

World War I. Concomitantly, U.S. machines tended to be designed for high volumes of output and to be specialized in function. German machines, by contrast, made greater demands on their operators and could be worked to closer tolerances and higher precision.

Today the firms that design and construct large industrial plants and the firms that produce capital equipment for such plants still display national distinctions in certain lines. But in most industries such distinctions have been declining. In the tractor industry, national distinctions have given way to universal norms.[8] In electrical equipment, the same tendency exists.[9] Among firms that build chemical process plants, the trend toward global standardization has gone to such lengths that national characteristics no longer are of much significance.[10]

With national distinctions declining in consumer goods and in industrial products, the chances have increased that a product turned out by a firm in one country will be compatible with the requirements of buyers elsewhere. At the same time, opportunities to sell in foreign markets have been matched by threats that foreigners might intrude on the home territory. The opportunities and the threatened and actual intrusions have not been confined to the marketing end of business. With transportation costs declining and communication becoming more efficient, new opportunities to employ low-cost labor or to acquire low-cost materials have constantly appeared, and, as ever, those firms that do not seize the opportunities are exposed to the possibility that their rivals might.

The reaching out and intertwining of the various national economies after World War II generated a sharp rise in the movement of ideas, goods, people, and money across national borders, a rise that has been much larger than the overall rate of expansion of the world's economies.

As for goods, the striking growth of international

trade in the postwar period has been adequately dissected
in numerous studies. In sum, during the three decades
from 1945 to 1975, international trade grew persistently at
a more rapid pace than the growth of world output.[11] In
the first two decades of the thirty-year period, the outstanding growth rates were concentrated among the
richer industrialized countries, especially among European states. Later on, however, some less-developed
countries and centrally planned communist countries exhibited similar trends. Although extraordinary increases
in the price of oil and other commodities in the early
1970s complicated the interpretation of the trends, the underlying message was unmistakable: goods originating in
foreign countries were taking on greatly increased importance in the economies of most nations.

The nature of the products involved in the mush-
rooming international trade helped to emphasize that
the interpenetration of the world's economies was not
casual or ephemeral. Until the raw materials boom of the
early 1970s overwhelmed other trends, the growth leaders
in international trade included relatively sophisticated
products—chemicals, machinery, automobiles, electronic
products, and the like.[12] In contrast to the unprocessed
and undifferentiated materials of earlier eras, such as coffee beans, coal, and timber, these sophisticated products
were highly differentiated. For instance, while Caterpillar
Tractor's big earth-moving equipment traveled eastward
across the Atlantic, Fiat's little garden tractors moved
westward to North American markets. This kind of traffic required foreign sellers to project some fairly complex
messages to their overseas buyers and to develop elaborate relations on foreign soil with banks, distributors,
government officials, and servicing organizations.

The growing interrelationships of the world's economies have appeared in other ways as well. The interpenetration of techniques and ideas, for instance, can be seen

in the data on patents issued by various national governments. These data disclose the rapid growth everywhere
of patents owned by foreigners.

In principle, of course, the issuance of a patent to a
foreigner is not an infallible indicator that a new idea has
crossed an international boundary. The idea itself is
usually revealed to the world when the inventor petitions
his home government for a patent, whether or not he also
patents abroad. The inventor's decision to file for a patent
in another country is only a measure of his expectation
that the patent monopoly he hopes to secure from the
foreign country may prove to have some added value
there.

The figures on patents seen in Table 1, therefore,
reflect the quickening interest of innovators in exploiting
the full fruits of their innovations beyond their home
markets, an interest that has apparently grown faster than
the innovators' interest in home markets. In the United
States, in reflection of that trend, the patents issued to foreigners rose from 13 percent in 1955 to over 30 percent in
1972. In Germany and the other advanced industrial
countries, the importance of foreign patent holders expanded as rapidly.

One widely chronicled consequence of the pervasive
interpenetration of economies has been a growth in the
amounts of fees and charges that business enterprises
have been able to extract from their licensees in foreign
economies. When licensing fees are paid across an international border, they may have little to do with the movement of technical information; they may, for instance,
represent nothing more than payment for the right to use
a foreign-owned trade name. In any case, payments of
such fees roughly doubled between 1965 and 1973.[13] And
as an indication of the pervasiveness of that quickening
trend, in countries where receipts and payments were
both substantial—in the United States, France, Britain,

Table 1 Patents issued to nationals and foreigners (selected countries and years)

Issuing country	1955	1965	1972
UNITED STATES			
Total number	30,535	62,857	74,798
Percentage			
to U.S. nationals	87.0%	80.1%	68.9%
to EEC nationals [a]	8.9	13.5	17.6
to other foreigners	4.1	6.4	13.5
GERMANY			
Total number	14,760	16,780	20,600
Percentage			
to German nationals	77.8%	59.7%	46.8%
to U.S. nationals	6.0	15.9	22.2
to other foreigners	16.2	24.4	31.0
FRANCE			
Total number	23,000	41,800	46,217
Percentage			
to French nationals	53.3%	34.9%	23.3%
to U.S. nationals	12.0	20.4	24.2
to other foreigners	34.7	44.7	52.5
UNITED KINGDOM			
Total number	37,551 [b]	55,507 [b]	42,794
Percentage			
to U.K. nationals	59.9%	43.7%	23.6%
to U.S. nationals	18.3	23.2	30.4
to other foreigners	21.9	33.1	46.0
JAPAN			
Total number	8,557	26,905	41,454
Percentage			
to Japanese nationals	74.9%	66.1%	70.3%
to U.S. nationals	13.6	17.1	14.3
to other foreigners	11.5	16.8	15.4

Source: For 1955, P. J. Federico, "Historical Patent Statistics," *Patent Office Society Journal* 46, no. 2 (1964). For 1965 and 1972, *Industrial Property*, December 1966 and December 1973 issues, respectively.

a. All nine countries presently members of the EEC.
b. Patents applied for, not patents issued.

Japan, and Germany—both the inflows and the outflows rose at roughly the same rate.

I have been referring to the increased intertwining of national economies without taking much note of the differences between countries. Almost all countries have been exposed to the trend in some degree. By the 1970s, for instance, both the United States and the USSR displayed signs of their increased reliance on the outside world—the United States in a visibly increased use of foreign raw materials and increased sales to foreign markets, the USSR in an increased need for foreign technologies and foodstuffs. Still, the vulnerability of these oversized national economies to outside economic forces was much less, relatively speaking, than that of middle-sized Britain, Germany, France, Italy, and Japan. As for the small industrialized nations such as Denmark, the Netherlands, and Sweden, these were more vulnerable still. But unlike the medium-sized countries these nations had long since come to accept the hard fact that their high standard of living depended on the continuation of an open economy, and they had crossed a psychological divide that allowed them to contemplate their vulnerability without excessive discomfort.

The tendencies toward increased interdependence created most pain in the less-developed countries. As many of these countries viewed the consequences of shrinking international space, "dependency" seemed a more apt description of the outcome than "interdependence." Many of these countries, former colonies of European powers, located mainly in Africa and Asia, had acquired their national identity only within the preceding decade or two. Others, such as the Latin American nations, had a longer national history and had just begun to develop the first glimmerings of hope for an independent economic existence. The bizarre gyrations in raw materials that occurred in 1973 and 1974 had briefly kindled those hopes into a roaring flame of expectations, but the cold realities of dependence took hold again as the demand for raw materials fell off and their prices weakened. In oil, OPEC's seeming dominance over the market began to be recognized as a fragile position, whose long-term continuation depended on a working relationship with the international oil companies and the tolerance of the principal importing governments for continued high prices in the product. In commodities for which such conditions did not exist or were not operational, such as copper and bananas, the vulnerability of the less-developed countries was easier to see.

Nor has the vulnerability been limited to the raw-material industries. Virtually all the developing countries have found themselves reaching out through one channel or another to acquire more foreign technology. Reflecting that fact, a U.N. study found, for example, that "payments for technological transfer" in a group of developing countries grew during the 1960s two or three times faster than did the countries' total manufacturing output.[14] Some countries, like India, have strongly preferred arm's-length licensing arrangements between Indian firms and foreigners and have resisted the establishment of foreign-owned subsidiaries.[15] Others, such as Brazil and Mexico, have been more eclectic. Whatever the choice of channels has been, however, the increase in the technological linkages between developing countries and the outside world has been pronounced.

The increased ties in the developing countries have been apparent not only in the import of technology but also in the export of goods. In the more industrialized of the developing countries—notably in India, Mexico, Brazil, and South Korea, as well as in Israel and Singapore—the composition of exports has steadily shifted toward manufactured goods and, among such goods, toward products of increasing sophistication.[16] Ironically, the shift in exports from raw materials toward sophisticated manufactures has not reduced the need of the developing countries for intimate links with importing countries. Developing countries have had to confront the fact that sophisticated products generally require the establishment of distributors' networks, trade names, banking connections, and various other ties that reduce flexibility of movement and reinforce a state of seeming dependence. Partly in order to hold down that trend, some developing countries have made special efforts to build up their trade with socialist countries.

India, again, is an important case in point.[17] Its cultivation of trade with socialist states has altered the form of its dependence from one expressed through the multinational network and foreign distributors to one expressed in the give-and-take between governments. From time to time, for example, the Soviet Union's capacity to put pressure on India has been unmistakable. But the fact that foreign socialist governments have not insisted on maintaining their own enterprises inside the Indian economy has been regarded as a major advantage. In this respect, India has exhibited a preference that is widely and strongly held throughout much of the world.

By one means or another, then, interdependence has grown. That growth has created tension and anxiety on the part of many nation-states and national institutions. When the growth has been accompanied by an expansion in the role of multinational enterprises, the tension has been especially apparent. The link between the expansion of multinational enterprises and the growth of tension has been more evident in host countries than in countries where multinational enterprises are headquartered, but the problem has been apparent in some measure almost everywhere. This book is devoted largely to exploring the reasons for that tension.

If I am right in my analysis, the question has to be addressed at several quite different levels. Many of the problems that have engaged the disputants in the debate over the multinational enterprise stem directly from the fact that the enterprises operate simultaneously in a number of different national territories and are not confined to one national jurisdiction; issues in the fields of taxation, competition, disclosure, and labor relations often fall into this category. But many of the problems involved in the debate—often the most basic and most compelling problems of all—are very much broader, going to the very structure of contemporary society. These underlying problems need to be identified and sorted out, lest they befog the analysis of problems more explicit to the multinational firm.

Perhaps the most basic issues with which the multinational enterprise is linked in the debate are those grouped under the heading of economic hegemony and economic dependence. Throughout history, powerful nations have tried to create international economic systems according to their own tastes and in harmony with their own interests. If the leaders of such great nations have thought about the subject at all, they have had no great difficulty in persuading themselves that the systems they were promoting also served the interests, if not the tastes, of the rest of mankind. In the past few decades, one power that has been pressing hard for the creation of an international system in its own image has been the United States. At the same time, of the larger firms in manufacturing and extraction that have developed on multinational lines, more have had their headquarters in the United States than in any other country; according to one count, about 250 such firms are headquartered in the United States, 150 in various countries of Europe, 70 in Japan, and 20 in all the rest of the world. In banking, the same concentration is evident, with 20 multinational banks headquartered in the United States, 13 in various European countries, 9 in Japan, and 3 in Canada.[18] That the United States has generally supported an international environment in which multinational enterprises can flourish is widely seen as solid evidence of the tie between the propensity for hegemony and the operations of such enterprises.

Another reason why the multinational enterprise is so high on the political agenda is its close identification with the industrialization process itself. No one needs to be told that the world has been experiencing some disturbing second thoughts regarding the benefits of industrialization. Although the industrial growth of most nations in the past few decades has been spectacular by any historical standards, in much of the world poverty persists alongside conspicuous wealth, while many of those above the poverty line follow a pattern of living that often seems vulgar, self-centered, and vacuous. Meanwhile, in most countries, ordinary people are exposed to the frenetic efforts of hawkers to fill their eyes and ears with empty messages; to an unending stream of trivial changes in food, clothing, and household goods, changes whose cost is passed on to the consumer; to the self-serving insistence of many firms that their befouling of the environment is in the public interest; and to persistent acts of bribery and extortion that taint the commercial transactions of modern industrial society.

The widespread social concern over these developments has been building up at the very time when the multinational form of enterprise has been growing in importance. In the United States, for instance, large firms that could reasonably have been classified as multinational in 1950 accounted in that year for only 17 percent of total U.S. sales of manufactures. By 1967, the U.S. firms that were then multinational in scope accounted for 42 percent of U.S. sales and, by 1974, for 62 percent.[19] In the noncommunist world at large, the firms classified as multinational in 1950 reported annual sales that amounted to about 8 percent of gross overall product, but by 1967 the figure was 17 percent and, by 1974, 22 percent. The same trends could be discerned in commercial banking. By 1975, U.S. banks had outstanding loans to foreigners of about $30 billion and outstanding deposits from for-

eigners of about $24 billion, both figures being two or
three times as high as they would have been ten years earlier.[20]

Nevertheless, a study that uses the multinational enterprise as its focus proves to be a poor vehicle for analyzing these fundamental social issues. Hegemony, corruption, inequity, pollution, and indifference to consumer
interests were endemic in mankind's history long before
the multinational enterprise existed. Moreover, nations
that have placed severe limitations on the subsidiaries of
multinational enterprises operating in their areas do not
seem to have escaped these ills; at best, such countries
have only altered the source and form of the problem.
Take the cases of the USSR and India. Although not using
multinational enterprises as their vehicle, these nations
seem unable to resist the temptation to try to dominate
their neighbors; they have had to wrestle with corruption
in their bureaucracies and with indifference on the part of
their producers to the interests of consumers; and they
have shown strong indications of a markedly unequal distribution of privilege and power inside their economies.

China provides still another test of whether industrialization can be achieved while yet avoiding some of
the major perils that most industrialized countries seem
to have experienced. Some observers see China as a fundamentally new phenomenon, capable of developing
along lines that avoid these problems; others are much
more skeptical. So far, the available record of China's performance at home and of its policies abroad is fragmentary and impressionistic, too thin for any serious judgment on issues of such transcendent importance.

Moreover, China's policies with regard to foreign-owned
enterprises are only a minor feature of a vast and ambitious scheme for reshaping Chinese society. These policies alone can hardly be assigned much credit for China's
successes or much blame for its failures.

Accordingly, a study of the multinational enterprise,
however exhaustive it may be, cannot be expected to deal

effectively with one of the basic worries of our time: whether mankind in the process of industrializing can avoid the vacuousness, the pain, the ugliness, and the destruction that most existing models seem to generate. Regardless of a nation's choice between suppressing the multinational structure of enterprise and encouraging its growth, it still must address these endemic problems of contemporary society.

Much more closely tied to the multinational enterprise as an institution than these pervasive social problems is a set of anomalies and ambiguities surrounding the national identity and national affiliation of such enterprises. In modern societies, the political leaders of any nation commonly find themselves dependent on the nation's enterprises to perform tasks that these leaders think critical to their country's well-being or to their own political survival. Whenever the loyalty and commitment of a substantial enterprise in the economy seem ambiguous, tension is unavoidable. Given the present structure of world business, it is clear why such tension arises. Well over one-third of the world's industrial output comes from large business enterprises whose producing facilities are spread out over several countries. And any list of the world's business leaders, ranked according to their power or their status, would be headed mainly by the leaders of multinational enterprises.

The anomalies created by this situation can be seen from the first moment that an enterprise decides to operate beyond its own national boundaries. Any enterprise that determines to set up a business in a foreign territory ordinarily is obliged to create a separate unit in that territory, under terms determined by the host government. Entities of this sort, endowed by the host government with the rights of an artificial person, are generally seen by the government as national subjects, indistinguishable from other nationals.

As an enterprise spreads across international boundaries, therefore, it comes to consist of affiliates of many different nationalities, each with its own juridical personality, its own responsibilities, and its own loyalties. Yet even though enterprises of this sort are a polyglot mix of national units, they are ordinarily bound together by powerful unifying forces. They are generally owned by a common parent, with its headquarters located unambiguously in some explicit country, such as Japan or Switzerland or the United States; only a few exceptional enterprises, such as Royal Dutch/Shell, make any effort to obscure that point. And they are ordinarily bound by a common strategy—the strategy of IBM or Volvo or Club Méditerranée or Citibank. Some hauling and pulling between the multinational enterprise and the nation-state, therefore, has been inevitable and unavoidable.

To be sure, that kind of stress, as history suggests, is not necessarily intolerable. Since the beginning of time, society has managed to build up its institutions in patterns that are refreshingly disparate, inconsistent, and confusing. Without turning more than a hair or two, individuals have commonly assumed multiple obligations: to be faithful to their kin, obedient to their church, loyal to their country, and responsible to their employer. And then, as if the latent contradictions of their various commitments were not enough, they have supported the Sierra Club, campaigned for a political party, and joined the Masons or the Elks. The contradictions have occasionally led to disaster, to the tragedies of Romeo and Juliet and of Benedict Arnold. But these have been aberrant exceptions. Accordingly, the fact that the multinational enterprise and the nation-state are in some senses inconsistent in goals and outlook does not of itself suggest that they are doomed to mortal conflict, with one institution ultimately prevailing over the other.

Yet the threat of such conflict seems to be growing. And one basic reason for that growth is the emergence of new political and social forces that depend for their success on building up the power and autonomy of the nation-state, not on reducing it. In a fascinating reversal of historical roles, the new nationalists tend to come from various sectors on the left of the political spectrum, while the internationalists tend to come from the center and the right.

In the industrialized countries, the reversal of histori- cal roles is especially apparent. On the left, the national communist parties of France and Italy, sensing the possi- bility of acquiring power by legitimate means, want des- perately to preserve what is left of independence of action for their respective countries. The national labor move- ments that operate in relatively conservative national set- tings, such as Sweden and Germany, see their first chances for real participation in the management of in- dustry. And bourgeois socialist and center parties in many countries throughout the world see themselves closer to the goal of achieving a modern welfare state.

In the developing countries, the leaders with a stake in building up the nation-state cover an even wider polit- ical spectrum, from active revolutionaries on the far left to businessmen and government leaders of a more conserva- tive stripe. For numerous reasons that later chapters will identify, nearly all of them, irrespective of their ideology, see benefits in building up the autonomy and decision- making strength of the states in which they play a leader- ship role. Yet, even as these emerging political elements see the need to build up national autonomy, more en- terprises become multinational in structure and account for an increasing share of the world economy.

All the elements for a confrontation between two powerful sets of forces seem to be present. But the sources of strength of the multinational trend and the sources of tension within the national institutions cannot be fully understood without taking a much closer view of some of the key characteristics of the multinational enterprises themselves.

2 | The Multinational Enterprise: A Close-up View

THE MULTINATIONAL enterprise has come to be seen as the embodiment of almost anything disconcerting about modern industrial society, and it has not acquired this role by sheer chance. Certain attributes of multinational enterprises have increased the probability that the enterprises would be singled out for that dubious distinction. One such attribute is size; another is the kinds of business activities in which the enterprises have specialized; and a third is the patterns of their management and control.

Multinational enterprises have always been distinguished in the public mind by their sheer size. They are, for the most part, the giants of modern industry, commerce, and banking: the big oil companies such as Mobil, Shell, and Gulf; the leading chemical companies such as BASF and Du Pont; the major electrical-machinery producers such as AEG and General Electric; the largest drug companies such as Pfizer and Hoffmann–La Roche; and so on through the upper ranks of *Fortune*'s various lists of the world's leading firms. The average firm of this sort reckons its annual sales in billions of dollars and its annual advertising and research budgets in hundreds of millions of dollars.

To be sure, enterprises of more modest dimensions

19

have been known to develop a multinational structure. Japanese firms, in particular, have been able to develop such structures despite the restraints of limited size. But on the whole such cases have been relatively infrequent.[1] It also has to be noted that a few very large firms, big enough to appear on *Fortune*'s lists, cannot be correctly dubbed multinational enterprises. These few have chosen to place their production facilities almost entirely on home territory. In the aircraft industry, leaders such as Lockheed, McDonnell Douglas, and Boeing have confined their operations largely to the United States. In steel, most of the leading producers, including U.S. Steel, Japan Steel, and Vereinigte Stahlwerke, have confined their producing interests principally to the home market. Aside from a handful of such deviants, however, most of the world's largest firms are multinational in structure.

For the past decade or two, the firms that we have called multinational enterprises characteristically have seen their foreign sales grow faster than their sales at home. As a result, by the mid-1970s many of these enterprises were relying on their foreign subsidiaries for more than half the aggregate sales of their multinational network. In fact, in 1974, for the 179 largest multinational enterprises headquartered in the United States, about $200 billion of their aggregate sales of $540 billion were garnered through foreign subsidiaries.[2] Although multinational enterprises headquartered in small countries such as the Netherlands and Switzerland have long since learned to live with such heavy dependence on outside markets, that dependence represented a very new situation for enterprises headquartered in relatively big countries such as the United States, Germany, and France.

Wherever big enterprises exist, the odds are high that there also exist formidable barriers impeding the entry of new competitors. A number of studies confirm the concentration of multinational enterprises in industries where such barriers are present.[3]

The obstacles to entry take several different forms. In some cases the entering firm needs an organization capable of mastering complex tasks, such as designing, producing, assembling, and selling a large computer or an aircraft engine. In some cases the entry barrier is created by the technical advantages that large producers or distributors have over small; this is the situation, for example, in the oil, copper, aluminum, and automobile industries. In still other cases newcomers are up against the preference of buyers for firms with established trade names. Finally, as in the case of the banking business or the pharmaceuticals industry, the barrier may be due not only to the advantages of an established name but also in part to government licensing or to patent grants.

The typical multinational enterprise characteristically draws its strength from a number of different sources. A hint of the diversity of its sources of strength is provided by the fact that most of these enterprises operate in many product lines. Occasionally, as in the case of the automobile giants and IBM, a multinational firm has confined itself to a relatively narrow line, but such cases have been comparatively infrequent.[4]

A few decades ago the tendency of large enterprises to diversify by product lines was confined largely to firms based in the United States. But by the 1950s the tendency was beginning to appear among the Europeans as well, and by the 1970s it had become a powerful trend.[5] In the case of the Japanese companies the situation was a little more obscure, complicated by the fact that the prototypical multinational enterprise of Japan has been a so-called trading company, an entity that even in its earliest form was already involved in handling the products of many different manufacturers in many different industries.[6]

In any event, as Table 2 shows, large multinational firms do not ordinarily "belong" to just one industry. We no longer think of ITT as merely an electrical-equipment company, in view of its commitment to food products and

Table 2 Principal industry and product lines of 376 multinational enterprises, based on a classification system of 158 product lines [a]

Country of parent and principal industry	Number of product lines [b]					
	Inside principal industry			Outside principal industry		
	Skill lines	Advertising lines	Standardized lines	Skill lines	Advertising lines	Standardized lines
U.S.-BASED ENTERPRISES [c]						
63 skill-intensive	219	27	8	219	74	270
53 advertising-intensive	51	140	34	118	79	125
64 standardized	13	15	165	245	62	261
180 total	283	182	207	582	215	656
EUROPE- AND U.K.-BASED ENTERPRISES						
36 skill-intensive	146	28	9	104	36	141
26 advertising-intensive	6	70	15	30	24	50
73 standardized	9	7	145	206	43	234
135 total	161	105	169	340	103	425

JAPAN-BASED ENTERPRISES

23 skill-intensive	35	6	2	10	3	23
10 advertising-intensive	0	5	2	33	24	81
28 standardized	0	1	50	16	7	29
61 total	35	12	54	59	34	133

ALL 376 ENTERPRISES IN SAMPLE

122 skill-intensive	400	61	39	342	113	434
89 advertising-intensive	57	215	51	181	127	256
165 standardized	22	23	360	467	112	524
376 total	479	299	450	990	352	1,214

Source: Harvard Multinational Enterprise Project.

a. Principal industry classification is based on S.I.C. two-digit categories. Product-line classifications are based principally on Standard Industrial Classification three-digit categories, from data generated by the National Science Foundation, the U.S. Department of Commerce, and Leading National Advertisers, Inc., for the early 1970s. Skill-intensive and advertising-intensive categories reflect unusually high inputs, respectively, of skill-related and advertising expenditures; the "standardized" category is the residual.

b. Each entry represents manufacturing activity by one multinational enterprise in one of the 158 product-line categories.

c. Data for U.S.-based enterprises are provisional for 1975; others are final for 1970.

hotels; nor of Pechiney as an aluminum company, given its acquisition of a large chemicals empire; nor of Pfizer as a drug company, in view of its stake in cosmetics and industrial chemicals.

Not only do the different products of individual enterprises have markedly different technical and economic characteristics at any moment; in addition, the different products alter their characteristics in the course of time. Until World War I, for instance, the production of steel required high technological skills, but that characteristic has long since evaporated.[7] Something like the same pattern can be seen in the petroleum industry. Until the 1920s the technology of refineries changed rapidly; by the 1950s, however, the refining industry had lost much of its technological drive.[8] Similarly, the burst of technological development that produced a family of consumer electronics a few decades ago—radio, television, and high-fidelity recording—appears to have spent its force.[9] The steam also seems to have gone out of the great innovative push that characterized the pharmaceuticals industry in the 1940s and 1950s.[10]

Multinational enterprises, then, often preside over a broad range of products with vastly different technical and strategic requirements. That range adds to the complexity of the managers' problems, but it also constitutes a source of considerable strength. While one line of business is being pressed hard by competition, another may be discovering new and greener pastures. While some of its activities are making great demands on the resources of a network, others may be providing a supply of funds. In short, a new generation of nuclear reactors may be financed from the profits generated by an old line of dishwashing machines.

The strength of many multinational enterprises is sometimes drawn from yet another characteristic, geographical diversity. When enterprises take their first plunge into foreign waters, they ordinarily move with some caution. Once committed to a multinational pattern, however, enterprises expand their geographical reach with great rapidity. For example, during the years from 1960 to 1975, the average multinational enterprise in a group of about four hundred such firms was adding to its network about four foreign manufacturing subsidiaries per year.[11]

The great geographical diversity of the typical multinational enterprise is illustrated by the figures in Table 3. As the table indicates, the typical enterprise in the group covered by the table maintained manufacturing subsidiaries in more than ten countries; only the Japanese-based firms had a narrower geographical reach. Moreover, most had established producing facilities in both industrialized and developing countries in all the main regions of the noncommunist world.

Although Tables 2 and 3 cover only the activities of multinational manufacturing firms, multinational banking networks have also grown at a rapid rate over the past decade, propelled outward from their home bases by many of the same factors that pushed the extractive and manufacturing industries. Between 1969 and 1974, the thirty largest U.S. banks raised their assets in foreign branches from $39 billion to $133 billion, bringing the foreign-asset component to about one-quarter of their total assets.[12] Meanwhile, the leading European and Japanese banks plunged ahead on a similar course. By 1975, for instance, foreign-owned banks held $56 billion in assets in the United States,[13] adding to a network already prominent in London and other capitals.[14]

The great strength of the forces behind the multinationalizing trend, however, is even more dramatically exhibited by another development. A considerable number of multinational enterprises have begun to develop out of <u>bases</u> in India, Mexico, Brazil, Iran, Taiwan, Hong Kong, and other countries heretofore thought of only as host countries. Out of 572 foreign-owned projects

Table 3   Locations of foreign manufacturing subsidiaries of
391 multinational enterprises [a]

Location	180 U.S.-based enterprises, 1975 [b]	135 Europe- and U.K.-based enterprises, 1970	61 Japan-based enterprises, 1970	All 391 enterprises in sample [c]
In fewer than six countries	10	31	37	87
In six to ten countries	43	30	15	90
In eleven to twenty countries	86	46	8	143
In more than twenty countries	41	28	1	71
In Europe only	0	17	1	19
In North America only	0	1	0	1
In Latin America only	0	0	2	2
In Asia only	1	0	12	15
In industrialized countries only	9	15	0	27
In developing countries only	0	0	30	32
In both industrialized and developing countries	170	114	20	313

Source: Harvard Multinational Enterprise Project.

a. The U.S. group of multinational enterprises in the sample includes all those on the *Fortune* 500 list for 1967 which at any time had manufacturing subsidiaries located in six or more foreign countries. The rest of the sample is based on the *Fortune* 200 list for non-U.S. companies for 1970, but includes twelve others not on that list.

b. Provisional data.

c. Includes 15 multinational enterprises based elsewhere than in the United States, Europe and the United Kingdom, or Japan.

reported in the countries of the Central American Common Market in a recent survey, 43 were identified as
owned by enterprises in other Latin American countries.[15] And out of 360 foreign firms in Thailand covered
in a survey of Thailand for the years 1966 to 1973, 15 came
from India, 10 from Malaysia, and 93 from Taiwan.[16]
Moreover, the rate of spread has been remarkably vigor-
ous. For instance, of the 65 projects that Indian firms had
in operation in foreign countries at the beginning of 1976,
nearly half were less than two years old,[17] and 63 more
such projects were in the process of implementation at the
time. The ubiquitousness of the multinationalizing trend
suggests that the underlying forces behind the movement
are pervasive and strong and raises the possibility that
nation-states will have to accommodate themselves to the
continuation of the trend. With that prospect in view, the
question, Who controls such enterprises? takes on height-
ened interest.

To understand the tensions that multinational enterprises have been known to generate, we have to bear in
mind that such enterprises, as a rule, are conspicuously
endowed with money and with knowledge; they are en-
trenched in industries difficult to enter; and they are
foreign in the eyes of most governments with which they
deal. For all these reasons, their existence constantly
raises the question of the locus of their control.

Because polemic is the usual mode of discourse on so
delicate a subject, the answers to the question of control
have characteristically been extraordinarily simple. On
one side, the critics of multinational enterprises depict
them as tight, quasi-conspiratorial organizations, aloof
from governments, devoted solely to the well-being of
their masters and responsive only to their commands. "By
what right," ask Barnet and Müller, "do a self-selected
group of druggists, biscuit-makers, and computer de-
signers become the architects of the new world?" [18] On

the other side, the defenders of multinational enterprises vacillate. Sometimes they paint multinational enterprises as institutions that operate on a global plane, above the fray of national rivalries. At other times, in a mood of greater caution, they describe such enterprises as loose affiliations of independent units, linked only to the extent to which each of the units finds the linkage useful and even more responsive to national pressures than an indigenous national enterprise would be.

In order to choose knowledgeably among these caricatures, we have to know a great deal about the goals, the strategies, and the limitations of the multinational enterprises themselves, a subject that the next three chapters address. But even before we plunge into that labyrinth, a few large generalizations are possible.

First of all, if a firm ventured abroad with no particular source of strength to distinguish it, its capacity to survive would ordinarily be very much in doubt.[19] Picture the position of a U.S. firm in Italy or Brazil, or a Japanese firm in Indonesia, or an Indian firm in Thailand. Foreign-based firms bear special costs, ranging from the obvious costs of communication and control to the subtle costs that traditionally hinder the foreigner in an alien land.

In many cases the countervailing source of strength is fairly evident. Multinational enterprises appear and flourish mainly in those industries in which the multinational structure imparts some kind of advantage. To exploit the advantages of a multinational structure, however, the units of the enterprise must operate in accordance with some common elements of strategy or must draw on some common resources or both.

These generalizations point insistently to a conclusion that, although trite in its substance, yet is profound in its implications. Some degree of coordination and control exists in the network of any multinational enterprise that manages to survive. Individual units in the network may have some voice in shaping the network's goals and influencing its operations. They may also kick up their heels at times and slip out of the network's constraining guidance. But unless the advantages of the multinational structure are somehow brought into play, the future of the enterprise as a multinational organization is in doubt.

It is extraordinarily difficult in practice to determine just how central guidance and central control are actually applied. Because influence can be exercised in many different ways, there is no necessary correspondence between the formal structure of a multinational enterprise and the method of control. In some structures that seem highly centralized, the subsidiaries may, in fact, vastly influence the center, and in structures that seem decentralized, the center may still effectively control the subsidiaries. Moreover, a multinational enterprise that operates in many different product lines—say, from exotic chemicals to pulp mills—must simultaneously pursue a wide range of strategies, according to the requirements of each product. Casual observation of any multinational enterprise, therefore, is likely to be unreliable.

Despite all these pitfalls associated with observing the multinational enterprise, studies of the locus of control in the internal decision-making process do produce some consistent patterns. Particularly consistent are some of the generalizations that describe decision-making patterns by the usual functional divisions of enterprise—finance, marketing, production, government relations, and labor relations.

Money as a rule is a fungible resource in the multinational enterprise, capable of being used anywhere in the system. Accordingly, the center tends to exert fairly tight control over major money flows; it may do so by individual decisions, by formal internal rules, or by the conditioning and acculturation of the finance officers in the network.[20] On the other hand, the problems of personnel administration, and even more generally of labor relations, tend to vary from one national regime to the next;

as a result, the day-to-day decisions on these subjects are characteristically left to the discretion of local management.[21] Of course, when a multinational enterprise confronts a strong international union that coordinates its negotiations across national borders, the strategy of the negotiations perforce becomes a problem for the center; this is the case, for instance, when Philips of Eindhoven or Saint-Gobain confront their respective unions. As for marketing and production decisions, the location of these is responsive to the same implicit principles. When a marketing strategy demands uniformity of price or product in many markets, decisions on price and product are pulled to the center; otherwise, this centripetal pull is weaker.[22] And when the strategy of the firm requires a uniform level of quality, then quality control in the production process becomes a subject for the center. Similarly, if the materials produced by an affiliate in one area become a critical input for affiliates in other areas, production scheduling is pulled to the center.[23]

These generalizations represent visible tendencies rather than inflexible rules. Some of the reasons for deviations from such tendencies, however, are quite straightforward. One is that the structure and practice of an organization commonly adapt themselves to the strategy of the organization, not the other way around. Accordingly, when the strategy of an organization is in flux, formal structure and standard practice may be some time in adapting themselves to the real change.

Many European-based and Japanese-based enterprises exhibited this structural lag as they developed their multinational networks during the 1960s and 1970s. European enterprises commonly were building on structures that had been in existence before World War II. The strategy of these earlier organizations, however, had typically been framed at a time when the interactions between the units of the network were loose and infrequent. Because national differences in consumer preferences and in industrial standards were then considerable, and because national barriers to trade and payments were high, the units of these enterprises operated in relatively watertight compartments. Accordingly, communications among the units could be limited to occasional contacts among the barons that presided over each.

But by the early 1970s organizations of this sort, known as mother-daughter structures, were on the way out. A study of sixty large multinational enterprises based on the European continent, for instance, shows that ten had abandoned the structure before 1968 and twenty-nine more had abandoned it by 1971.[24] By that time, only about one-third of the sixty firms still retained the mother-daughter structure, the others having adopted organizations more appropriate to the exercise of tight controls over the field. Those that still clung to the mother-daughter form were largely firms whose industries and product lines suggested that the need for central coordination was comparatively slight.

The tendency toward global coordination and global control associated with the multinational trend is mirrored in the results of a number of studies.[25] These indicate that over the past few decades an increasing proportion of the world's largest firms have tended to favor an organizational structure that breaks down the enterprise primarily by product divisions, with each such division having the world as its domain.[26] With the global status of the product occupying the top strategic echelon of the firm, differences based on national factors have been obliged to take a second place.

These changes, however, are unlikely to obliterate the organizational differences that arise out of distinctive national histories and national cultures. From all the signs, the Americans can still be counted on to develop unusually elaborate tables of organization, job descriptions, and operating procedures and to feel uncomfortable in the presence of more ambiguous systems of control; the

Germans can still be expected to approach strategic decisions as if they were the sum of a series of technical questions and to give unusually large scope to the technicians to provide the definitive response to their portion of the problem; [27] and so on.

Japanese MNC's Case

The case of Japanese-based multinational enterprises offers another variant of the principle that the structures of organization have tended eventually to mirror changes in strategic needs. In Japan's case, as noted earlier, many of the firms that were operating as multinational enterprises in the early 1970s had evolved from an earlier phase as giant import and export houses, exporting goods acquired from semi-independent Japanese manufacturers and importing materials acquired from foreign-owned factories and mines. In that phase, the trading houses usually conducted their transactions with foreign suppliers and foreign distributors at arm's length and usually had no need to direct or control substantial production units abroad.

As long as that was the case, Japanese firms had no great difficulty in organizing themselves for their job. As a rule, the formal structures of Japanese organizations have even less bearing on how they operate than is true of, say, U.S. organizations. For the Japanese, one important purpose of the formal structure is to provide titles and rank, the importance of which is mainly to reflect the acknowledged pecking order and status in the organization, rather than to determine a division of functions and a chain of command. The decision-making process itself is more diffuse. It is usually designed to involve those most likely to be affected by the decision and is achieved by a great deal of informal consultation. [28]

As long as those likely to be affected by the decisions of the enterprise were all located at a headquarters in Japan, the requirement for extensive consultation among affected parties could readily be satisfied. However, when Japanese firms began to own and operate mines and factories in foreign locations, adequate consultation among key personnel began to be more difficult; some of the key personnel were not physically in Japan, and a very few were not even Japanese.[29]

One result has been the appearance of considerable stress in Japanese multinational organizations, with no clear indication as to how the stress eventually will be accommodated. Whatever the nature of the accommodation may be, it will surely permit the Japanese to maintain control at the center wherever such control matters critically to the strategy of the enterprise.

Although multinational enterprises typically feel the need for some measure of control over their networks, they are often prepared to enter into relatively ambiguous relationships with other firms in which they own an equity interest, relationships that do not connote much control. In Europe, for instance, firms commonly hold minor interests in other firms that are seeming rivals. The motivation for such trivial holdings is hard to establish, but the odds are that such holdings are sometimes intended as tokens of mutual loyalty, tolerance, and forbearance, not as means of control.[30]

Apart from such token holdings, however, Table 4 tells us that in a much larger set of cases multinational enterprises share the ownership of their foreign manufacturing subsidiaries with others, mainly with local partners in the areas where such subsidiaries operate. The prevalence of these so-called joint ventures seems to obscure the real boundaries of any multinational network. But various closer studies indicate that joint ventures are generally linked to the multinational networks according to a few well-defined patterns. And those patterns by and large conform to the principle discussed earlier: the degree of control exercised over a subsidiary depends upon the character of the strategy the multinational enterprise is pursuing.[31]

Consider the case of a multinational enterprise whose

Table 4 Foreign manufacturing subsidiaries of 391 multinational enterprises, classified by ownership patterns [a]

Country and ownership patterns	180 U.S.- based enterprises		135 Europe- and U.K.-based enterprises		61 Japan-based enterprises		All 391 enterprises in sample [c]	
	No.	%	No.	%	No.	%	No.	%
IN ALL COUNTRIES								
Total subsidiaries	5727	100.0	4661	100.0	562	100.0	9601	100.0
Wholly owned [b]	3730	65.1	2278	48.9	34	6.0	4907	51.1
Majority-owned	1223	21.4	1320	28.3	74	13.2	2177	22.7
Minority-owned	723	12.6	712	15.3	431	76.7	1537	16.0
Unknown	51	0.9	351	7.5	23	4.1	980	10.2
IN INDUSTRIALIZED COUNTRIES								
Total subsidiaries	3603	100.0	3207	100.0	46	100.0	6060	100.0
Wholly owned	2612	72.5	1788	55.7	6	13.0	3634	60.0
Majority-owned	657	18.2	802	25.0	8	17.4	1260	20.8
Minority-owned	302	8.4	404	12.6	30	65.2	626	10.3
Unknown	32	0.9	213	6.6	2	4.3	540	8.9
IN DEVELOPING COUNTRIES								
Total subsidiaries	2124	100.0	1454	100.0	516	100.0	3541	100.0
Wholly owned	1118	52.6	490	33.7	28	5.4	1273	36.0
Majority-owned	566	26.6	518	35.6	66	12.8	917	25.9
Minority-owned	421	19.8	308	21.2	401	77.7	911	25.7
Unknown	19	0.9	138	9.5	21	4.1	440	12.4

Source: Harvard Multinational Enterprise Project.

a. Data for U.S.-based enterprises are provisional, as of 1975; others are final, as of 1970.

b. Subsidiaries of which the immediate parent in the system owns 95 percent or more are classified as wholly owned; 50 percent or more, as majority-owned; 5 to 49 percent as minority-owned.

c. Includes 15 multinational enterprises based elsewhere than in the United States, Europe and the United Kingdom, or Japan.

producing subsidiaries operate in separate isolated markets, shut off from one another by import restrictions.
Multinational enterprises that operate on this basis generally derive their strength from their capital, their technology, or their strong trade name. The isolation of the
various subsidiaries, however, means that variations in
the price and quality of their products between one national market and the next can be tolerated. Accordingly,
the multinational enterprise can accommodate the views
of local partners in such matters. As long as the subsidiary
is dependent on a flow of money or technology from the
foreign parent or on the use of the parent's trade name,
the parent's control is sufficient for its strategy.

Even when subsidiaries are not isolated from the rest
of the system, multinational enterprises sometimes find it
possible to tolerate the presence of an independent local
partner. Consider the case of the vertically integrated
multinational enterprises that produce and process oil or
nonferrous metals and then fabricate and distribute a line
of products drawn from the materials. Many of the networks have been prepared to accept local partners in the
subsidiaries that do the fabricating and distributing. In
such cases, effective control can be maintained through
supply contracts and through the provision of capital.
Where that is the case, the parent may be prepared to accept the risk of an occasional squabble with local partners
over the remaining critical questions, such as the prices
charged by the network when selling to the subsidiary,
the markets assigned by the network to the subsidiary,
and the declaration of dividends out of the subsidiary's
profits.

The correspondence between the strategy of the multinational enterprise and its tolerance for joint ventures is
constantly being reaffirmed in various ways. It is not a coincidence, for instance, that the continental firms that are
content with the loose mother-daughter structure described earlier also display a relatively high proportion of

joint ventures among their subsidiaries; [32] both positions
are symptomatic of a strategy that does not demand tight
day-to-day coordination from the center. Neither is it co-
incidental that since 1970—the date of the data reflected in
Table 4—Japanese-based multinational enterprises have
been turning away from their earlier preferences for joint
ventures and have been setting up an increasing proportion of their manufacturing subsidiaries as wholly owned
subsidiaries. Various factors have pushed them in that direction. One is an increase in the sophistication and complexity of the products handled in the multinational networks, a shift from textiles and food products to
electronics and industrial equipment. That shift has demanded greater quality control and more elaborate distribution systems. Another factor is the spread of Japanese multinational networks beyond the insulated
markets of South and Southeast Asia toward the more
open and more interrelated markets of Europe and North
America; that, too, has called for tighter integration of the
day-to-day activities of the units in the network.

A critical generalization emerges, important in
illuminating the sources of tension between multinational
enterprises and national institutions. Most multinational
networks need considerable interaction among the affiliates of the network as well as some measure of control
from the center. From the viewpoint of government, the
existence of that control from the center is not always a
drawback. Governments often make demands on the
center which can be fulfilled only because the center does
have some measure of control over units in the territory of
other governments. At the same time, however, the existence of a central control weakens the influence of the national government on the multinational network's performance. Whenever the government is made aware that a
remote control center may be acting in ways that will not
serve the government's interests, the tension is palpable.

But there are various important variations on this key theme.

In the product lines in which multinational enterprises control some important technological capability, governments often have some very distinct worries. Here, for instance, the strategy of the multinational enterprise can be seen as affecting the national security or the production processes of the country in disconcerting ways. This relation of technology and enterprise strategies is the subject of Chapter 3.

When the strength of the multinational enterprise rests on its ability to assemble and maintain large organizations and large quantities of capital, the focus of official concerns shifts a little. This kind of strength is associated with a cluster of problems that relate to market control and competition, a consideration of which provides the core of Chapter 4.

Finally, some of the government relations with multinational enterprises are best understood as problems associated with waning strength in the enterprises, not with growing power. The reaction of these firms to the powerful pull of entropy, therefore, provides yet another focus, to which Chapter 5 is devoted.

3 | Enterprise Strategies: The Technology Factor

THE BUREAUCRACIES that govern multinational enterprises, like the bureaucracies that preside over most creative and prestigious institutions, have generally gone about their business without very often questioning the rightness of their purpose and the importance of their task. In particular, the bureaucracies of such enterprises have rarely doubted the inherent usefulness of developing and introducing new products and new processes. Accordingly, when nations have felt aggrieved by the consequences of such activities, their complaints have generally produced in the leaders of the multinational enterprises that special quality of irritation and impatience typical of self-assured and creative men.

Multinational enterprises see special virtues in innovation partly because that activity tends to go hand in hand with a rapid increase in sales and profits. The correspondence is, of course, far from perfect; there are other ways to grow than through innovation. But the tie between innovation and increased profits is sufficiently strong to be visible in the data.[1]

The exact role that multinational enterprises play in the process of industrial innovation has been a subject of considerable debate among scholars.[2] Such enterprises have not had an especially strong record in the advancement of scientific concepts, that is, in inventing the ideas that are usually the necessary forerunners of innovation.[3] Neither have they been outstanding in the introduction of run-of-the-mill innovations; these often have come from firms with more limited resources. A Harvard Multinational Enterprise Project study of 703 innovations introduced in the United States after 1945 found, for example, that only 133 innovations were introduced by multinational enterprises. Of 492 innovations introduced in Europe and Japan in the same period, only 107 were introduced by multinational enterprises.

But multinational enterprises _are_ closely identified with the introduction of wholly new products, especially products whose introduction has demanded a long gestation period and a great deal of financing. Copiers, computers, earth movers, reactors, and turbines are examples. In this association, cause and effect are unclear; some would say that the capacity for industrial innovation had pushed these enterprises abroad, while others would insist that the causal flow had run the other way. In either case, one thing is clear: the close association between multinational enterprises and the introduction of these landmark products has figured centrally in the tensions between multinational enterprises and governments.

When developing and introducing major new products of this kind to the market, multinational enterprises have had to make a series of locational decisions—where to do the development work, where to manufacture the first runs of the new product, and where to market the product—which have been of consuming interest to governments. The basic disposition of multinational enterprises in all these decisions has been clear-cut: to use the home market, if at all possible, for all these operations. Numerous qualifications and exceptions exist, but the underlying tendency survives.

The propensity of multinational enterprises to use their home markets to develop and introduce new products stems from a series of powerful forces. It has been

confirmed again and again in empirical studies of various
sorts that successful innovations tend to be those that
respond to the market conditions surrounding the innovation.[4] The original idea may be developed almost
anywhere, but successful innovation depends strongly on
the compelling character of the demand. When France
was cut off from Spanish alkalis in the Napoleonic wars,
the Leblanc process for synthetic alkalis was developed;
when Germany was deprived of Chilean nitrates in World
War I, the response was the Haber process for nitrogen
fixation; and the United States responded to the Japanese
occupation of Southeast Asia in World War II by developing a synthetic-rubber industry.[5] Henry Ford found ways
of mass-producing a low-priced automobile, responding
to the fact that the United States was a country of great
distances and numerous middle-class families. Japan was
the leader in developing and marketing miniature television and radio sets, responding to the Japanese consumer's parsimonious use of living space.

That innovations spring out of the market conditions
in which they are introduced is demonstrated more
rigorously by a study analyzing a large group of innovations introduced in the United States, the United Kingdom, continental Europe, and Japan during the thirty
years following World War II. Some of the results are presented in Table 5. They illustrate that the innovations in
each of these four areas tended to be responsive to the
distinctive conditions of the area: the U.S. innovations
were more frequently directed toward saving labor and
satisfying high-income wants, while innovations in the
other areas were aimed more frequently at saving materials.

Once again the distinction between major innovations and run-of-the-mill projects has to be emphasized.
Innovative efforts of an incremental sort usually entail
little risk and usually achieve roughly what they were intended to do.[6] But spectacular advances generally require

Table 5 Innovations initially introduced in the United States, United Kingdom, continental Europe, and Japan, 1945–1974, classified by perceived purpose [a]

Type and purpose of innovations	United States		United Kingdom		Continental Europe		Japan	
	Number	Percentage	Number	Percentage	Number	Percentage	Number	Percentage
PROCESS INNOVATIONS								
Material-saving	58	18.8	122	47.8	95	53.7	12	48.1
Labor-saving	189	61.1	66	25.9	32	18.1	4	16.0
Capital-saving	58	18.8	61	23.9	43	24.3	7	28.0
Multiple-factor-saving	4	1.3	6	2.4	7	3.9	2	8.0
Total	309	100.0	255	100.0	177	100.0	25	100.0
PRODUCT INNOVATIONS								
Material-saving	117	22.6	127	40.3	100	50.3	20	29.0
Labor-saving	142	27.5	13	4.1	9	4.5	2	2.9
Novel-function	106	20.5	50	15.9	33	16.6	12	17.4
Other	152	29.4	125	39.7	57	28.6	35	50.7
Total	517	100.0	315	100.0	199	100.0	69	100.0

Source: Harvard Multinational Enterprise Project.
a. For detailed definitions of concepts, see W. H. Davidson, "Patterns of Factor-Saving Innovation in the Industrialized World," *European Economic Review*. 8, no. 3 (October 1976).

basic strategy decisions on the part of the innovating firm. The enterprise often cannot be sure whether the product under contemplation is technically feasible, what its production costs will come to, and what the demand will be at any given price. For the organization to take on a major commitment in those circumstances, motivations must be strong.

The signals must not only be compelling; they must also have an impact on those members of the organization in a position to respond.[7] According to numerous studies, the solid support of headquarters is usually indispensable.[8] Bright ideas about new products are not necessarily doomed if they have originated in subsidiaries of multinational enterprises located in foreign countries, but such ideas must run a remote gauntlet set up by a headquarters staff. Because the headquarters staff is insulated by physical and cultural distance from the outlying foreign markets of the firm, signals out of those markets tend to provide less stimulus and generate less response. Besides, when the home market is also the main market of the multinational firm, as is commonly the case, the signals from that market carry more impact than signals from abroad.

Having heard the signals and sensed the opportunities, multinational enterprises tend to place the innovational process itself close to headquarters. Major innovations, according to numerous studies, usually entail a long process of cutting and pasting, trial and error, test and adjustment. They demand the skills of engineers, laboratory technicians, and salesmen, all bent on developing an end product at a price that prospective users are prepared to pay. With major innovations, the process is likely to be drawn out and expensive, punctuated by critical stop-or-go decisions and by unanticipated overruns.[9]

With large risks and rewards riding on the outcome, the decision-making process is usually involuted and complex. Because the difference between a plausible judgment and an implausible one is not always immediately obvious, a repeated process of search and verification is required. The nature of the search demands a constant shuttle between those in the firm that are working on the design of the new product and those in the firm that will be expected to produce and market it. That sort of process is helped greatly when the principals responsible for swapping information and speculating on its significance enjoy easy face-to-face contact and see themselves as sharing a set of common goals and values.

To be sure, the extent to which multinational enterprises tend to keep their innovational activities close to headquarters can be exaggerated. Multinational enterprises commonly do maintain some research and development facilities in countries other than the home territory. In fact, European-owned subsidiaries in the United States have been known to develop independent programs of innovation, in response to the special conditions and compelling size of the U.S. market. As early as the 1950s, for instance, Shell's weed-killer programs were established in California, while some of Unilever's higher-priced consumer products were also developed in a U.S. subsidiary. Later on, Hoffmann-La Roche developed Valium and Librium in the United States, with the needs of the high-strung U.S. market centrally in mind.

U.S.-based multinational enterprises have similarly conducted a certain amount of innovative work through their subsidiaries in foreign countries. According to a careful survey covering the years 1971 and 1972, U.S.-based firms spent over one billion dollars annually in their foreign subsidiaries, mostly in Europe, on activities they classified as research and development.[10] But the nature of the foreign research activities has typically been determined by how distinctive and how critical the foreign markets have been from the viewpoint of the innovating enterprise. In the absence of some compelling force from the other direction, multinational enterprises of all nationalities have tended to keep their high-risk development activities close to headquarters.[11]

The predominant pattern, therefore, has been one in which multinational enterprises have developed their new products at home and begun production at home. At that stage, the tendency has been to serve any foreign markets by exports. The tendency, to be sure, has not been quite so automatic in recent years as it was a decade or two ago; Eastman Kodak, for instance, set up its first production unit for one of its new line of instant cameras in Germany, not the United States.[12] And even when the initial production unit is generally located at home, it is unlikely to hold its distinctive position forever. Eventually, if the product is not undergoing much modification and if the foreign demand for the product is growing, the innovating enterprise usually considers establishing a production site abroad. That decision generally turns on the usual factors of cost and risk that govern the locational decisions of enterprises: whether tariff and other import barriers are forbidding or likely to become so, and whether the cost of labor and other inputs in the foreign production process seems low. Responding to factors such as these, multinational enterprises have commonly determined at some point to establish overseas production facilities for products originally produced exclusively at home. A study tracing the current production locations of 158 new products introduced by multinational enterprises in the United States in the period 1945–1968 has found that by 1975 about two-thirds of the new products were being manufactured abroad by subsidiaries of the innovating enterprises.[13]

The eventual decision to set up producing facilities abroad is far from inevitable, however. In some fields, the rate of obsolescence of innovative products has been so rapid that the innovators have never found themselves required to consider overseas production. In aircraft, for instance, the production of the DC-6 had ended within

eleven years of its beginning; the DC-7 was produced for
five years and the DC-8 for thirteen.[14] In chemicals, according to conventional wisdom, the turnover rate for
products is also rapid. Even studies of less dynamic industries, such as the textile industry, find similar patterns
of product obsolescence which have allowed the innovating firms to avoid the question of whether to produce a
maturing product in markets outside the home base.[15]

Because governments place so high a value on having
new products developed and produced in their home territory, the multinational enterprise has been unable to
avoid creating some tension over its decisions on the location of such activities. But other considerations have figured in the tension as well. To pursue these, it helps to
distinguish the operations of the multinational enterprises in the industrialized countries from those in the
developing world.

From the viewpoint of multinational enterprises
based in the United States, the years immediately after
World War II were a golden period. The dominance of the
U.S. economy had been asserting itself for a long time
prior to the war, as evidenced by an impressive record of
Nobel prizewinners in science and of successful innovations in industry.[16] After World War II, European and
Japanese industries were out of the technological race for
the time being; their main opportunities lay in filling the
accumulated demands of their economies for staple commodities, using the products and processes that came
most easily to hand. The Soviet challenge in 1957 in the
form of Sputnik and the U.S. response with a successful
lunar-landing program seemed only to underline the capabilities of the American economy. Nonetheless, doubts
about the durability of the U.S. technological lead persis-
ted.[17] By the early 1970s a stream of studies from U.S.
scholars purported to demonstrate U.S. slippage.

What is clear beyond serious question is that for a

fixed group of products, all of which would have been
classified in the 1950s or early 1960s as "technology-inten-
sive," U.S. production and U.S. exports have been declining in relation to those of Europe and Japan.[18] But these
trends have mainly reflected the fact that by the 1960s factories in Europe were at last producing some of the refrig-
erators, television sets, plastics, drugs, and machine tools
that industry in the United States had been producing for
some time. In this respect the European and Japanese
economies were only repeating the patterns of bygone decades, when U.S. factories had first secured, then shared,
then surrendered their early lead in a succession of consumer goods and industrial products.

For anyone with a sense of history these catching-up
capabilities of Europe and Japan had never been in
serious doubt. The automobile industry had long ago illustrated that the U.S. economy could not maintain a lead
over its rivals indefinitely. Even before World War II European automobile companies were showing strong signs
that they had absorbed Henry Ford's technologies and
were prepared to apply them to a product more appropriate to the income levels and road conditions of Europe. By
the end of the 1930s Fiat was producing its little Topo-
lino—its Mickey Mouse. In the 1950s and 1960s, the
catching-up process resurfaced, epitomized by Volkswagen's diminutive Beetle. Achievements of a similar
sort were recorded in many other lines, notably in
stripped-down and miniaturized household appliances.

From time to time, Europeans also produced wholly
novel products, such as Geigy's DDT, Sandoz' psycho-
pharmaceuticals, and Michelin's radial tire. But, more
commonly, European innovations took the form of new
machinery or new methods designed to reduce the production costs of some standardized product. Advances in
the steel, aluminum, and chemical industries proved
especially important.[19]

The propensity for the Europeans and the Japanese to

close the gap between them and the United States was strengthened by the rapid growth of their national markets, no longer diminutive relative to those in the United States. Besides, as the costs of labor, materials, and capital moved closer in the various parts of the industrialized world, the stimuli that these markets provided for innovations also grew more alike. European and Japanese businessmen, therefore, no longer had to retrace economic terrain that U.S. entrepreneurs already had traversed; at times they were out ahead.

Nevertheless, some of the conditions that gave U.S.-based multinational enterprises their earlier advantages in launching new products have continued to hold during the 1970s. The United States remains the largest mass market of high-income consumers in the world; its margin of primacy has shrunk, but the gap that remains is still very large. As for industrial products, U.S. leadership has continued in most branches of the computer industry and industrial electronics, in most lines of synthetic materials, in electric-generating equipment, and—with some important exceptions—in large-scale machinery over a very wide range of industries.[20] In more exotic activities with longer lead times and larger scale, U.S. firms also seem ahead: for instance, in the industrial use of the laser, in deep-sea minerals exploration, and in the use of extraterrestrial space for industrial purposes.[21]

The advantages imparted by the gargantuan size of the U.S. market, in fact, seemed more important in the first half of the 1970s than they had been in the 1940s. According to various fragmentary indications, the costs and risks involved in the completion of major industrial projects have been rising sharply over the decades. It is hard to find an index that reliably reflects the extent of the increase. But numerous illustrations suggest that the increase has been very large, several times larger, in fact, than the increase in the size of the world's leading industrial firms. The cost of the development of the DC-3 in the middle 1930s, for instance, was about $1 million, while the cost of the Boeing 747 in the latter 1960s was about $1,000 million.[22] The cost of development of ENIACC, the computer of the early 1940s, was about $500,000, whereas IBM's 360 series was developed at a cost of about $5 billion.[23] Even the development costs of innovative drugs have gone up with sufficient rapidity to create new barriers to entry.[24]

The U.S. lead in some of these products is to be traced not only to the enormous size of the U.S. market in general but more particularly to the opportunities created by large-scale government programs. Of course the introduction of the government as an important factor in the stimulation of innovation is nothing new in history. What has distinguished the U.S. government's efforts from those of other countries, however, has been their extraordinary size.[25] The French government's needs for military aircraft, for example, are on the order of one-fifth or one-tenth those of U.S. government. Britain's development of the STOL Harrier plane has been slowed by the same problem of market size.[26]

Apart from affording a large potential market to U.S. innovators, the U.S. government has also provided generous subsidies. A little more than half of U.S. industry's total expenditures on innovation has come from government sources. In relative terms, European governments have been about as willing to subsidize the developmental efforts of their industries as the Americans, but the absolute size of the U.S. economy has provided a certain advantage.[27]

If Europe's scientists, industry, and financial resources could be viewed as a single aggregate, of course, they would easily match those of the Americans or the Russians. But the European states have found it impossible to adopt a unitary European approach in the fields of high technology. Despite the formal existence of the European Economic Community, few European states—and

certainly not France or Britain—have been willing to sub-
merge their separate national identities or curb their independent national options in the pursuit of technological leadership. In general, national governments have
been lukewarm or downright hostile to mergers of high-
technology industries across international lines.[28]

Occasionally, a national government in Europe has
succeeded in encouraging a group of national firms in the
computer and aerospace industries to pool their efforts in
a response to the Americans.[29] In nuclear reactors, the
German firms of AEG and Siemens have merged their independent efforts in a single joint subsidiary, KWU, an
entity that appears capable of matching its American
rivals in the light-water reactor field.[30] But big innovational projects such as those in airframes, aircraft engines,
extraterrestrial rocket launchers, nuclear fuel-enrichment
facilities, nuclear reactors, and computers commonly have
posed financial risks too large for any national industry or
national government in Europe to tolerate on its own.

In spite of the general reluctance to find pan-
European solutions to their technological problems, European organizations have created transnational consortia
from time to time. When units in the consortia have been
public enterprises, however, they have been unable altogether to throw off the political inhibitions that have
stood in the way of a unitary European approach. And
private consortia among European enterprises have done
only a little better.

To be sure, in the few cases in which national identity has been erased and unity of command achieved, European enterprises have survived and prospered. Unilever, Royal Dutch/Shell, and Agfa-Gevaert, after long
hesitations stretching over two or three decades, have
emerged successfully as unitary organizations. Characteristically, however, European enterprises have tried to
achieve the advantages of unity and scale without being
willing to accept the form. The classic illustration is that of

Unidata, Europe's collective reply to the challenge of IBM. The partner firms, German Siemens, Dutch Philips, and French CII, have all insisted upon maintaining their own independent personality, strategy, and interests. As an instrument of effective challenge, therefore, Unidata has been brutally handicapped.[31]

The continuing propensity for national separateness among the Europeans has from time to time given U.S. firms opportunities to maintain a strong position in Europe. When European firms have felt threatened in fields of high technology—whether their rivals were other Europeans or U.S. firms—one response has been to turn to a U.S. partner for support. This response explains the willingness of the French to tolerate U.S. Honeywell as a partner in their national computer industry,[32] to let Westinghouse share in Framatome, France's chosen instrument for survival in the nuclear-reactor business, and to let France's leading aircraft producers continue their nonstop flirtations with Boeing and McDonnell Douglas.[33]

From the viewpoint of the Americans, it might be more desirable to try to dominate the high-technology markets in Europe through a network of subsidiaries. But the determination of France, Britain, and Germany to have their own national industries suggests that the Americans might not succeed in that objective. If they are unable to establish successful subsidiaries, the Americans clearly want some organic tie to any new European producer that might develop, as well as some opportunity in the meantime to penetrate the government-controlled markets of Europe.[34] From the viewpoint of all the parties, however, this arrangement is distinctly second-best, leaving the underlying problems of power and prestige largely unresolved.

When spokesmen for developing countries express their reactions to the growth of multinational enterprises, the worries that relate to technology in one way or another permeate the analysis. Of course, the technological concerns of these countries differ from those that preoccupy the Americans, the Europeans, and the Japanese, and they vary from one country to the next. Some developing countries are concerned with mastering a set of technologies that are well established and familiar in the more advanced world, such as the production of standard chemicals, machine tools, or electric motors. In the most backward countries of Africa and Asia, the ordinary requirements for the production of beer, bread, boots, and boxes, as well as the insistent need for added agricultural output, continue to provide the major technological challenges.

Despite these variations in capabilities and interests, the developing countries do share certain common concerns. For example, most of the product innovations relevant to modern societies are developed first of all for the conditions of highly industrialized economies. Automobiles and tractors are designed on the assumption that their worn-out parts will be replaced instead of repaired, a preference that reflects the relatively high costs of repairmen and low costs of capital in the advanced countries. New drugs are developed on the assumption that they will be administered under the supervision of doctors. Baby foods are formulated for a typical middle-class kitchen rather than for cooking facilities in an urban slum.

In this respect, the multinational enterprises whose home base is furthest removed from the conditions of the developing countries are seen as the greatest offenders. Thus the products and processes of U.S.-based firms have been somewhat further removed from the needs of the developing countries than those emanating from Europe or Japan; in the 1950s and 1960s, for instance, European automobile companies had a strong advantage over the Americans in Latin American markets.[35] By the same token, products and processes developed in Mexico, Brazil, or India are likely to prove closer to the developing countries' needs than those coming from Europe and Japan.

Nevertheless, because multinational enterprises have been one important conduit for the introduction of new products into the markets of developing countries, the refinements and differentiations that multinational enterprises have developed in their main markets have usually been available to the developing countries as well. Local subsidiaries, drawing on their multinational network, can readily produce a sports car for the teenage market or a throwaway baby bottle, provided they are allowed by the host country to do so and provided cost is not a restraint. In almost every developing country, affluent enclaves exist, prepared to buy such products almost regardless of price. High government officials, local businessmen, and others living at an elevated level inside the country often provide the market. The result is that multinational enterprises, without much explicit planning in that direction, often become the conduit for satisfying the wants of a special segment of the population. Moreover, because the volume of sales in such markets is usually small and the markets themselves are strongly protected from imports, the prices of the new products are commonly much higher than those prevailing in the richer countries.

From the viewpoint of developing countries the problem has been one not only of inappropriate products but also of excessive variations in product. In the extreme form of product variation, only the illusion of difference has been created. The distinction between reality and illusion is not always sharp. The stream of variations in cosmetics, food preparations, and cigarettes, accompanied by the repetitious drumbeat of advertising, comes close to pure illusion. The trivial manipulation of molecules on the part of the drug firms, accompanied by waves of new marketing efforts, is a more ambiguous case. In any event, multinational enterprises of all national origins—as well as the local firms with which they compete—are found playing the competitive advertising game according to the patterns developed in more affluent markets.[36]

Multinational enterprises have had a major hand in the development not only of new products but also of new production technologies.[37] Accordingly, the world's innovative efforts in production techniques, as in the design of new products, have been responsive mainly to the problems of the advanced industrial societies. Innovators in production techniques commonly have assumed the existence of a large and growing market in which economies can be achieved through increased production scale, and they have assumed that labor costs are relatively high and rising and that capital costs are accordingly low in relative terms.[38]

A few interesting exceptions to these general propositions have complicated the picture a little. The Netherlands-based Philips organization has devoted some resources to the special technological problems of developing areas; both General Motors and Ford have pushed their Basic Transportation Vehicle for Asian markets, hoping one day to have built up enough volume to bring down the price for mass sales;[39] Coca-Cola has made efforts to market in developing areas a nutritional drink that feeds as well as refreshes. But by and large, multinational enterprises have conducted efforts of this sort at a pace and on a scale that betokens good works rather than commercial campaigns.

Because of their tie to the advanced industrialized countries, multinational enterprises have come to be identified with capital-intensive techniques. Such enterprises are found clustered in the more capital-intensive industries, at least as calibrated by the industry mix of the developing countries: in chemicals or automobiles more commonly than in furniture or textiles.[40] Moreover, where the subsidiaries of multinational enterprises have operated alongside national enterprises in the same industry, the subsidiaries have tended to produce on a larger scale. Since an increase in the size of an industrial facility almost invariably goes hand in hand with an increase in its capital intensity, the differences in size have strengthened the association in the public mind between capital-intensive methods and multinational enterprises.[41]

Much more in dispute is another asserted link between multinational enterprises and the use of capital. It is contended that, when producing the same products on the same scale, multinational enterprises tend to choose production techniques more capital-intensive than those chosen by national firms. Such a pattern would not be surprising, since multinational enterprises may be paying less for their long-term capital. But the evidence in support of the conclusion is not very consistent. Some studies support the conclusion, some are inconclusive, and some point to exactly the opposite pattern, suggesting that the subsidiaries of multinational enterprises are more adaptive than their local competitors.[42]

My own impression is that, once the product and the scale of operations are specified, the technologies chosen by multinational and national enterprises are not very different. The common elements are mainly the existing offerings of the international equipment manufacturers, coupled with the degree of availability of skilled supervisory and maintenance labor in the particular country and the degree of manageability of unskilled labor. The patterns may be altered a little by other factors, but these other factors appear to be much less important.

The existing studies cast a little light on other aspects of the technological choices of multinational enterprises in developing countries, tending to fortify the impression that the technological choices of the multinational enterprises do not differ greatly from the choices of national enterprises. Studies indicate, for instance, that in some circumstances multinational enterprises vary the amounts of labor in the production process according to the conditions of the country in which they operate. The propensity to adapt is selective, however; it is strongest where the competitive pressures on the firm to reduce its costs are strong, and it is least apparent when the firm is attempting to sell its product on the basis of its claims to quality.[43] Accordingly, a multinational enterprise that has established a unit in a less developed country to manufacture components at the cheapest possible price can be expected to conduct its cost calculations with careful attention to the technical alternatives; but a multinational enterprise producing, say, pharmaceuticals in a developing country for sale under an international trade name is likely to be reluctant to test any hitherto-untried labor-using techniques.

Although comparatively little effort has gone into innovating for the special conditions of the developing countries' markets, however, in one sense the needs of these countries are sometimes served only too well. Many of the new technologies, although developed in response to the needs of the rich countries, have proved in dollars-and-cents terms to be the most efficient for the poor countries as well. Technologies that are saving of labor, for instance, prove also to be saving of capital.[44] In such cases anyone in the poor countries choosing a technology on the basis of simple cost considerations has to choose the capital-intensive technology. Unless the capital so saved is then clearly routed to other job-creating uses, the choice of the investor could easily be interpreted as adding to the country's unemployment problems.

Since the middle 1960s small signs have begun to indicate that the neglect of the technological needs of developing countries may be coming to an end. As an instance of the change, annual research and development expenditures in the private sector of India rose about 600 percent between the mid-1960s and the early 1970s, reaching the impressive total of 200 million rupees.[45] Some branches of Mexican industry and Brazilian industry have been displaying technological inventiveness and vitality not visible a decade or two ago. Here and there, too, we can see the beginning of a network of technological exchange among industries in the developing countries, a network that bypasses the advanced industrialized countries. Mexico's largest private steel company, for instance, has sold its home-grown direct-reduction process to Brazil, Iran, Iraq, Indonesia, and Zambia; Peru and Argentina have acquired a Mexican technique for making newsprint from sugarcane bagasse; and a Mexican process for extracting metals from crude oil has been sold to state-owned companies in Colombia and Jamaica.[46]

So far, the successes recorded in this area have not depended very much on the official efforts of national governments. Indeed, many of these efforts have been either ineffectual or counterproductive. Occasionally, institutions of a more ambiguous sort have created new products and processes. The International Rice Research Institute—created in the first instance by the efforts of the Ford Foundation and the Rockefeller Foundation, two well-known names in the world of multinational enterprises—is credited with the development of an impressive string of low-cost farm machines for manufacture and use in tropical rice-producing countries.[47] Various other institutes devoted to the development of what has come to be called "appropriate technology" have been established in Canada, Britain, Pakistan, and other countries and claim numerous small advances of this sort. An Indian firm of consultants, apparently operating with governmental encouragement and support, claims major advances in the scaling-down of plants for crystal-sugar processing.[48]

Efforts of this sort, especially when launched by institutions close to local markets, are likely to add to the stream of technological developments over the next few decades. From time to time, they will generate products or processes more suitable for exploitation by local entrepreneurs than by multinational corporations. In these cases, multinational enterprises will have to share or surrender a market in which they previously were dominant.

That development, however, is mainly for the future. Meanwhile, the developing countries see themselves mainly as the passive recipients of technologies generated abroad. And that self-perception finds focus in hostility toward one of the more visible institutions in the technological transmission belt, the foreign-owned multinational enterprise.

4 | Enterprise Strategies: The Drive for Stability

THE TENSIONS between multinational enterprises and national governments stem at times from the activities of the enterprises in generating change. But just as often the tensions arise from the efforts of the enterprises to acquire some measure of stability in the business environment.

The history of modern industry suggests that when an enterprise has managed to steal a lead in any product line, whether by innovation or otherwise, it had better anticipate a challenge sooner or later from other enterprises nipping at its heels. Maintaining stability in such circumstances demands some complex strategies on the part of the established leaders. One possible strategy is to fall back on the strengths associated with large scale and geographical spread.

Many large multinational enterprises have developed and maintained their strength and position without paying much attention to industrial innovation. In recent decades, for instance, the major petroleum companies have rarely spent as much as one percent of their sales revenues on research and development. The same can be said of the leading automobile companies: although incremental improvements continue under the spur of environmental controls and increased fuel costs, the only major advance in the industry for several decades has been the improvement of the automatic transmission.

Industrial innovation, therefore, has not been the source of strength of the leaders in certain industries; other factors have led to their success. As a rule, these factors have been associated with a large scale of operations. In the case of aluminum smelters, the advantages of scale are based on engineering efficiencies. In the marketing of transportation equipment and machinery, the advantages of scale are more subtle, having to do with the credibility of service guarantees, the availability of distributors and repair facilities, and other factors by which buyers decide among competing brands.[1] In any case, wherever advantages of scale have existed, they have acted as barriers to the entry of new competitors.

If money were all that were needed to overcome entry barriers based on scale, the barriers might not prove very formidable. The capital markets of the United States, Europe, and Japan have after all proved capable of prodigious feats of capital mobilization when the opportunity for profit was visible. But building an adequate organization presents a different kind of problem. Here, if any scale advantages are eventually achieved, they come about through specialization and interaction among a group of individuals.[2] Accordingly, a tried-and-tested executive cannot easily be recruited by a new organization unless he expects that other executives of high caliber will also be recruited. The same can be said of a network of distributors or of suppliers, whenever they are required to make some fixed commitment in order to serve the enterprise. As a result, the entry barriers for any organization starting from scratch can prove extraordinarily forbidding.

In some industries, a newcomer that has not yet developed a dispersed geographical network operates under an especially heavy handicap. Firms that rely upon many markets can count on differences in the various markets to contribute to the stability of their earnings. With greater stability, they can sometimes ride out a slump in some market that would be fatal to local competitors. Geographical diversity has also proved important for firms that process their own raw materials. Firms that depend heavily on any one source are especially vulnerable to national calamities and political embargoes, a lesson driven home with great force during the upheavals in the raw-material markets of the early 1970s.

Nevertheless, although size and diversification have strengthened the leaders in many product lines and have insulated them from the threat of new entrants, those strengths have also been associated with a special set of vulnerabilities. If the firm's cost advantage comes from the size of its plant, then a relatively high proportion of its total production costs is likely to be fixed, irrespective of the level of production. And if the firm's cost advantage comes from its organization, then key men have to be retained even when production and sales fall off. Accordingly, enterprises that have managed to seize the leadership in any product line by developing and exploiting the advantages of scale, whether in the plant or in the organization, are vulnerable in extra measure to any variations in their sales. The recognition of that vulnerability has shaped the basic strategies of many firms in these industries and has pushed them strongly toward the creation of a multinational network.

If we look back three-quarters of a century on the industrial giants of that early era, the forerunners of the strategies that eventually produced the multinationalizing trend are apparent. One familiar phenomenon of that time was the propensity of large national firms sporadically to dump their excess production in distant markets.[3] As long as the firm had no anticipation of a long-term commitment to those distant markets and was simply using them as a vent for its surpluses, it had no stake in the long-term stability of those markets and no reason to cultivate the goodwill or forbearance of rival producers located there.

It was not very long, however, before national leaders in widely separated markets began to recognize the dangers that they posed for one another. Before the nineteenth century had closed, leaders in various European countries were already developing agreements to limit their penetration of one another's markets.[4] After World War I, when the governments of Europe and North America introduced higher tariff and quota restrictions, the separation of national markets became even more obvious. To clinch that separation and plug such loopholes as might have been overlooked, one industry after another produced elaborate market-sharing arrangements. The leaders also seized the occasion to parcel out the markets of other countries where no domestic adversary as yet existed. The usual pattern reserved Latin America for the U.S. leaders, the British Commonwealth for the British leaders, and the remaining areas for the leading Dutch, Belgian, French, German, Italian, Swiss, and Swedish companies.

Occasionally there were variations. In 1928 the seven leaders of the international oil industry confronted a situation in which the geographical patterns of distribution were already well scrambled all over the world. Accordingly, they settled on an "as-is" formula, that is, an undertaking to preserve their respective shares in each national market. In chemicals, other patterns were followed: Du Pont and ICI, sensing the difficulty of preserving a division of third-country markets in an industry whose products changed so rapidly, agreed to operate in Canada and South America through a network of jointly owned subsidiaries. I.G. Farben and Standard Oil, looking for an even sharper division, agreed to stay out of each other's main product lines.

In any event, in the period before World War II the multinationalizing trend was muted. Growth managed to continue in industries in which the leaders of one country or another sensed that they retained a critical technological advantage; the unchallenged leadership of U.S. firms in the mass-produced automobile market, for instance, gave U.S. firms no incentive to curb their expansive tendencies. But in other industries, such as electrical equipment, the expansive trend was arrested or reversed.

When World War II ended, the factors that had kept the U.S. and European leaders mutually forbearing in standardized products temporarily lost their force. For a decade or two, one of the principal drives of the U.S. producers of standardized products was to develop and enlarge their stake in foreign markets.

Two elements served to encourage the American firms to shake off their earlier restraints. One was the operation of the U.S. antitrust laws. From the early 1940s on, a stream of cases was vigorously prosecuted; in these, U.S. and foreign leaders in various industries were charged with violations of the U.S. antitrust laws.[5] The second element was the relative strength of U.S. industry in the period just after World War II. European buyers stood ready to snap up anything the Americans would export, up to the limit of national governments' capabilities for providing the foreign exchange, and buyers in Asia, Africa, and Latin America who previously had relied upon European exports were obliged to turn to the Americans. U.S. exports of everyday industrial products shot up; by 1950, U.S. exports of trucks, electrical machinery, iron and steel manufactures, and agricultural machinery had all multiplied at least four times above typical prewar levels.

The export bonanza, of course, could not last. These exports were, after all, standardized products whose technological requirements were well enough known or could readily be learned. It was only a matter of time before the Europeans and the Japanese were themselves in a position to satisfy local demand. Indeed, in a gesture of innocence that has few parallels in modern history, American businessmen went to some lengths during the late

1940s and early 1950s to instruct Europeans in the techniques and products they might have been overlooking. A succession of productivity teams composed of European businessmen and engineers was dispatched to the United States, and their reports uniformly reflected bemusement over the openhandedness with which U.S. firms dispensed information on their production techniques.[6]

On the other hand, by the time the Europeans and the Japanese were in a position to elbow the Americans out of the markets they had invaded, many U.S. firms had a solid stake in those markets. On the basis of exports from the United States, trade names had been established, dealer networks developed, and control capabilities set up at the U.S. headquarters. As the Europeans tooled up to do battle for their markets, U.S. firms took stock of their peril. At that stage the question of production costs and delivery costs took on considerable importance, an importance much greater than in products that were technologically unique. To make up their minds about setting up foreign producing facilities, the U.S. firms had to weigh the volume of sales in their various foreign markets, the economies of production scale, the cost of local inputs, the freight bill, and the tariff. Commonly, the calculations suggested the desirability of setting up a plant in Europe or in some third-country market where the Europeans or the Japanese were threatening. The result was a sharp expansion in the product lines manufactured by the overseas subsidiaries of U.S. firms in standardized products, a result mirrored in Table 6.

Even though many leading U.S. firms were prepared aggressively to fill the void that the weaknesses of the Europeans and the Japanese had temporarily created, those that were producing standardized products on a large scale could hardly have lost sight of their special vulnerability to variations in demand, which may explain the growing tendency toward vertical integration in some industries during the 1950s and thereafter.

Table 6 Number of standardized product lines manufactured by the foreign subsidiaries of 376 multinational enterprises, based on a classification system of 53 product lines [a]

Foreign subsidiaries	Number of product lines [b]		
	1955	1965	1975 [c]
SUBSIDIARIES OF 180 U.S.-BASED ENTERPRISES			
In all locations	294	674	1633
In Canada	62	115	263
In Europe, including U.K.	82	246	647
In Latin America	69	120	211
Elsewhere	81	193	512
SUBSIDIARIES OF 135 EUROPE- AND U.K.-BASED ENTERPRISES			
In all locations	120	374	803
In North America	16	61	120
Elsewhere in Europe, including U.K.	62	159	329
In Latin America	11	39	72
Elsewhere	31	115	282
SUBSIDIARIES OF 61 JAPAN-BASED ENTERPRISES			
In all locations	1	84	237
In North America and Europe	0	37	103
Elsewhere	1	47	134

Source: Harvard Multinational Enterprise Project.

a. The classification is based on U.S. industry data as of the early 1970s. "Standardized product lines" are those associated with relatively low research and development inputs.

b. Each entry represents manufacturing activity by one multinational enterprise in one country in one of the 53 product lines.

c. Data for U.S.-based enterprises are provisional, as of 1975; others are final, as of 1970.

The idea that vertical integration could reduce the risk of variation in sales was, of course, nothing new. Standard Oil had been brought around to the need for such integration before World War I. By owning its own customers, the company could reduce the risk that its customers would switch to price-cutting competitors in times of surplus, and by owning its own sources of raw materials, the company could reduce the risk that suppliers might demand large premiums in time of shortage. Once any large firm began to reduce its vulnerability in this respect, the threat to competitors that did not follow suit became palpable. Accordingly, a move by any one large firm in the direction of vertical integration encouraged similar action by others.[7] Alcan's efforts to match the downstream integration of ALCOA and Pechiney, for instance, found it rounding up aluminum fabricators in Europe and elsewhere.[8]

Stability can be improved by other means as well. Rival firms that are trying to bolster their stability by vertical integration can serve that objective even better if they set up partnerships with one another. Where partnerships are undertaken to secure a source of raw materials, they add to the prospects of stability among the firms in the industry in several different ways: they pull the cost structures of the potential rivals more closely together, reducing the possibility of effective price competition; they create a mechanism for joint decisions on production levels; they allow each firm to diversify its commitments geographically to a greater extent than if the firm made the same amount of investment entirely on its own; and, finally, by placing potential rivals in the same foreign countries, they expose the rivals to a similar set of political risks and reduce the possibility of windfalls for any one of them.

In their efforts to retain some degree of stability in the markets for standardized products, multinational enterprises have commonly found themselves pursuing still another strategy. When any one of them decides to set up a producing subsidiary in a given market, others are disposed to look more favorably on creating a similar subsidiary in the same market. That tendency, observed by scholars some decades ago, was at first belittled as a slightly irrational bandwagon effect, as if the participants were a flock of children following a Pied Piper. Later on, however, the follow-the-leader pattern came to be recognized as a rational form of risk-minimizing behavior on the part of the leaders in an oligopoly, and it became the subject of systematic study.[9]

The connection between follow-the-leader behavior and the search for stability needs a word or two of elaboration. Remember that the leaders in industries that produce standardized products are concerned about the heavy fixed costs they are obliged to bear; these costs stem partly from the production process, but they may also arise from the need to maintain an organization and a distribution system. A dominant risk, as the leaders see it, is that others in the same product may build up their sales, reduce their unit costs, and overrun their competition. A vice-president of Ford reflects that preoccupation in terms of a slippery financial slide: "If we don't spend the money, our products will not be competitive. We will not get 25 percent. We'll get 20 percent. And if you fall back and take two or three years to recover, soon it will be 20 percent, then 18 percent. Then you can't spend money fast enough to catch up again." [10]

In situations of that sort, in which the threatening firms are known to one another and are limited in number, a policy of imitation is often seen as contributing to stability. If the initiating firm's move constitutes a genuine threat, then the others can blunt the force of the threat by imitation. The return on investment takes place through the avoidance of a threatened loss and the reduction of risk. If all the new subsidiaries prove unprofitable, the cost is shared by all in the industry and equilibrium is undisturbed. Indeed, if the wave of imitation actually raises the average costs of all the competing firms, that added cost can often be passed on to buyers. Imitation is therefore a risk-avoiding strategy.

In the decisions of U.S. firms to set up producing

subsidiaries in new foreign locations, follow-the-leader behavior has been widespread. Similar, albeit lesser, interactive behavior has been detected among Japanese firms and among German firms.[11] As one might expect, the pattern has been more in evidence in product lines dominated by a small group of leaders than in lines whose leadership was more dispersed, and it has been more in evidence in standardized products than in those associated with high innovative effort and rapid product change.[12] The bunching in the timing of entry of foreign firms in a given market can, of course, be explained on other grounds, such as an increase in market demand to which all the firms respond in unison. Various analyses, indicate, however, that the follow-the-leader phenomenon is the more likely explanation.

In any event, from the viewpoint of prospective host countries, the implications of the follow-the-leader tendency are important. The entry of one foreign-owned subsidiary producing a standardized product brings others in its train, all bent on reestablishing a state of equilibrium with their rivals in world markets. Perhaps more than any other single factor, the follow-the-leader tendency accounts for the extraordinary proliferation of foreign-owned automobile producers, consumer-electronics producers, tire companies, and so on in comparatively small and isolated markets in Latin America and Asia.

Other variations in the strategy of hedging-by-imitation have also appeared among competing multinational enterprises, giving an added impetus to their multinationalizing tendencies. Indeed, as the European-based and Japanese-based multinational enterprises expanded their presence in the United States following the patterns shown in Table 6, one possibility that began to gain credence was that the multinationalizing trend might be due in part to the desire of the Europeans and the Japanese to reduce the risks created by the earlier American expansion.

In some cases the apparent motive of European and Japanese firms was to have a foot in the American market in order to be stimulated by the opportunities and hardened by the difficulties of that market; the experience, it was widely thought, would improve the chances of the European or Japanese firm for competing with the U.S.-based firms throughout the world.[13] In other instances, the tendency of the Europeans and the Japanese to set up subsidiaries in the United States has been thought to have another purpose, namely, to reintroduce stability in global markets by establishing a balance of mutual threats among rivals.[14] Faced with the competition of U.S.-owned subsidiaries in their main markets, European and Japanese firms have had to weigh the possibility that the Americans might enlarge their foothold by selling at prices that do not fully reflect their global costs, such as administration and development costs. By setting up subsidiaries in the United States, the Europeans and the Japanese have placed themselves in a position to play the same game on U.S. territory.

Speculation over the exact motivations of the Europeans and the Japanese in belatedly following the multinationalizing trend during the 1960s and 1970s is bound to be somewhat inconclusive. Because the imponderables in decisions on multinational expansion are so critical and because learning-by-doing is often the only way in which the investing firm can secure needed information, firms have tended to make their decisions by a prolonged process in which the dominant motivations have been both complex and obscure.[15] The timing of the decision by some Europeans and Japanese to enter the U.S. market in the 1970s rather than earlier, for instance, was no doubt affected by the decline in the relative value of the U.S. dollar at the time. But I am inclined to regard such factors

as of only secondary importance, affecting short-run timing more than the long-term level of commitments. One
cannot fail to note the striking degree of identity between
the products of the U.S.-owned subsidiaries established
in European countries and the products of the European
firms established in the United States. Both in Europe and
in the United States and both before and since the decline
in the value of the dollar, foreign-owned subsidiaries
have been found mainly in chemicals, machinery and instruments, electronics, and food products.[16] This pattern
is more easily explained by oligopolistic strategies than
by the power of the exchange rate. The possibility that
many European firms were responding in part to a need
to reestablish some measure of global equilibrium
through strategies of imitation and countervailing threat
is therefore not to be excluded.[17]

Enterprises that decide to set up an overseas subsidiary have a choice: either they can set up a foreign enterprise from scratch, or they can acquire a going business
in a foreign country. A rational choice between the two
routes depends in part on the capabilities and needs of
the multinational enterprise. When such enterprises feel
that their own organizational capabilities are limited and
that speed is important, the strong tendency is to favor
acquisition.

Of course, multinational enterprises have always
used acquisitions to some extent as a means of expanding
abroad. Even before World War II, 37 percent of the
foreign manufacturing subsidiaries of the world's leading
multinational enterprises were brought into their networks through acquisition. For the period from 1946 to
1958, however, the figure rose to 44 percent and, for the
decade following, to 55 percent.[18] It is even possible that
the rate of acquisition might have been higher still if local
businesses of the type being bought by foreigners were
always available. Often, however, the foreigners are

engaged in a line of business that has no counterpart in the local economy. That, no doubt, is why acquisitions have been less common in the developing countries than in the advanced industrial countries, as Table 7 indicates. For similar reasons, multinational enterprises that are mainly in industries that use big capital-intensive plants have made relatively little use of the acquisition route; an aluminum refiner, after all, would not often have the opportunity to acquire an existing refinery, even assuming it were interested in doing so.

These differences aside, however, there are numerous indications in the data that firms have used the acquisition approach on the assumption that it was an efficient way to make up for their own lack of knowledge and experience.[19] For example, firms with long experience abroad tend to use the acquisition route rather less than firms with more limited experience, and firms with a narrow product line rather less than those with a broad list of products. In much the same vein, when firms do business overseas in product lines that simply replicate those at home, their propensity to pursue these relatively familiar lines through acquired subsidiaries is relatively low.

The tendency of comparatively inexperienced firms to use acquisitions has been especially strong when these firms were bent on matching the overseas moves of rivals. Acquisitions have therefore been particularly prominent in the course of a wave of follow-the-leader investments and especially important in industries that make extensive use of advertising.

Putting the pieces together, we can reconstruct a typical sequence that leads to heavy use of the acquisition method of expansion. First, a foreign-owned enterprise sets itself up in the local market with a new subsidiary, possibly in a product line that is conspicuous for its stress on marketing, such as cosmetics or drugs or packaged food. Other foreign-owned enterprises, fearful that the

Table 7 Foreign manufacturing subsidiaries of 391 multinational enterprises, classified by whether newly formed or acquired as going concerns [a]

Location and classification	Subsidiaries of 180 U.S.-based enterprises		Subsidiaries of 135 Europe- and U.K.-based enterprises		Subsidiaries of 61 Japan-based enterprises		Subsidiaries of all 391 enterprises in sample [b]	
	Number	Percentage	Number	Percentage	Number	Percentage	Number	Percentage
IN INDUSTRIALIZED COUNTRIES								
Total subsidiaries	3603	100.0	3207	100.0	46	100.0	6856	100.0
Acquired as going concerns	1974	54.8	1705	53.1	8	17.4	3687	53.8
Newly formed	1385	38.4	862	26.9	38	82.6	2285	33.3
Other and unknown	244	6.8	640	20.0	0	0	884	12.9
IN DEVELOPING COUNTRIES								
Total subsidiaries	2124	100.0	1454	100.0	516	100.0	4094	100.0
Acquired as going concerns	757	35.6	465	32.0	72	14.0	1294	31.6
Newly formed	1224	57.6	715	49.2	433	83.9	2372	57.9
Other and unknown	143	6.7	274	18.8	11	2.1	428	10.5

Source: Harvard Multinational Enterprise Project.
a. Data for U.S.-based enterprises are provisional, as of 1975; others are final, as of 1970.
b. Includes 15 multinational enterprises based elsewhere than in the United States, Europe and the United Kingdom, or Japan.

leader may preempt the market, try to speed up their own entry by acquiring a local enterprise. Meanwhile, local producers, worried by the entry of the first foreign giant, are fearful that the foreigner may be able to bring some special strength to bear in the local market, such as a large advertising budget, a superior technology of production and distribution, or favored access to some scarce raw material. As a result, local businessmen grow increasingly receptive to the acquisitive proposals of the foreigners who follow in the leader's tracks.

The sharp increase in the importance of this pattern of spread over the past decade or so stems partly from the fact that many countries were being introduced for the first time to the mass merchandising already well established in U.S. markets.[20] Although the U.S. mass merchandisers were often quite confident of their ability to carry their trade names, their products, and their distribution techniques across international borders, an occasional resounding disaster served to remind them that the pitfalls of merchandising in unknown national territories are numerous and can be costly. Accordingly, many multinational enterprises have acquired local distributors to serve as a core in the launching of their local sales efforts. And in doing so, they have added to the feeling on the part of the local authorities that the economy was being gobbled up by foreign interests.

In spite of the strenuous and unremitting efforts of leading multinational firms in many lines to develop some measure of stability and security among themselves, there is very little evidence that they have succeeded. On the contrary, in most lines the evidence suggests that the prospects for stability in the market are somewhat less secure than they were, say, a decade or two ago. The shock waves created by the multinational expansion of American leaders in the standardized product lines during the 1950s and 1960s are still being felt.

Other U.S. firms have felt impelled to follow the U.S. leaders; firms in other countries have felt obliged to respond in various ways; reaction and counterreaction have fed on each other as improvements in transportation and communication have increased the ease with which enterprises have been able to respond.

Some of the effects of this process, to be sure, have been to reduce the number of firms in Europe rather than to increase them. As these moves developed during the 1950s and 1960s, the number of mergers among European firms accelerated sharply. According to one study covering 1955 to 1969, nearly 4 percent of the manufacturing enterprises listed on British stock exchanges were absorbed each year in the merger movement, and in Germany the annual absorption rate for a similar group of companies came to nearly 3 percent.[21] Behind the mergers lay a widespread conviction in Europe that the advantages of scale were increasing rapidly in most industries.[22] Each appearance of a new subsidiary of a giant U.S. firm, ready to do battle for European markets, added to the pressure for merger. The result was that the national markets in Europe, taken one at a time, seemed to display an increasingly concentrated structure.[23] And the sense of increasing concentration in many of these markets has preoccupied many government officials, labor leaders, and scholars.

Notwithstanding the indisputable trend toward concentration seen since the 1950s in most of the national markets of Europe, however, the national leaders' control of their respective markets has probably grown weaker, not stronger. Remember how an increase in concentration is measured in this context. The distribution of production in the national market generally determines the size of the concentration index. With the growth of international trade and with the proliferation of multinational enterprises, however, the conventional measures of industrial concentration have become increasingly inade-

quate, primarily because such measures have not captured the buyers' perception of an increasing number of
substitutable sources for the products in which the buyers
are interested.

Over a broad range of standardized products in
Europe, buyers now confront a wider choice of alternative
sources, not a narrower choice, than they did a decade or
two earlier. In automobiles and trucks, durable consumer
products, prepared foods, industrial machinery, and fa-
bricated metals, the widening of choice is indisputable.
The increased choice is due to two factors. One is the
growth, product by product and market by market, of the
number of subsidiaries of major foreign firms offering
their wares to local buyers, a trend illustrated by the data
presented in Table 8. The second factor is an increase in
the volume and diversity of intra-European trade. During
the 1960s member countries of the European Economic
Community substantially increased their exports to one
another in both relative and absolute terms and characteristically shipped the same type of product in both directions across their borders.[24] Between 1958 and 1970, for
instance, France's imports of automobiles from other EEC
countries rose from 1 percent to 16 percent of the national
market; for Germany the increase was from 7 percent to 25
percent; for Italy, from 2 to 28 percent.[25]

A wider choice of alternative sources, however, does
not necessarily generate an increase in competitive conditions. National barriers inside the European market still
carry a certain weight, even in standardized products.
One reason is that government agencies typically give
some sort of preference to suppliers of their own nationality.[26] Moreover, the occasional reappearance of illegal cartels within the European market in recent years suggests
that the propensity among businessmen for carving up
territories among themselves is not wholly dead; in the
decade and a half in which the anticartel European Economic Community has been in existence, charges of il-

Table 8 Number of multinational enterprises in selected product lines producing in Germany, France, and the United Kingdom, 1950, 1960, and 1970 [a]

Product line (with SIC category)	Number of enterprises								
	Germany			France			U.K.		
	1950	1960	1970	1950	1960	1970	1950	1960	1970
STANDARDIZED									
Yarn and thread mills (228)	4	10	24	3	7	22	4	10	19
Pulp mills (261)	2	4	13	2	3	12	2	4	13
Miscellaneous converted paper products (264)	3	10	32	3	9	31	4	12	35
Blast furnaces and basic steel products (331)	2	11	36	2	9	33	6	13	33
Iron and steel foundries (332)	1	7	28	1	6	28	1	8	25
Primary nonferrous metals (333)	5	10	26	6	10	24	9	18	28
Miscellaneous primary metal products (339)	3	8	32	4	6	29	3	9	35
Metal cans and shipping containers (341)	1	6	17	1	5	15	4	8	20
Fabricated structural metal products (344)	2	13	35	2	8	28	5	12	37
Miscellaneous fabricated metal products (349)	5	15	62	8	13	55	10	20	66
Other standardized lines (30 lines)	33	78	255	37	75	247	51	116	280
Total for 40 standardized lines	61	172	560	69	151	524	99	230	591
ADVERTISING INTENSIVE									
Beverages (208)	2	8	24	3	11	29	10	14	31
Cigarettes (211)	1	3	3	0	1	3	3	4	4
Drugs (283)	6	9	38	10	29	39	23	37	43
Soap, cleaners and toilet goods (284)	10	20	40	10	22	43	22	28	48
6 other advertising intensive lines	5	13	45	3	13	36	18	28	57
Total for 10 advertising-intensive lines	24	53	150	26	76	150	76	111	183

Source: Harvard Multinational Enterprise Project.

a. This table is based on the same sample of 391 enterprises covered in previous tables. The number of multinational enterprises in a product line in a country is the number of parent firms producing the product line which are based in the designated country, plus the number of local manufacturing subsidiaries of foreign-based multinational enterprises producing the product line.

legal territorial divisions have been brought by the EEC
or national authorities against producers of rayon, steel
pipe, sugar, chemicals, and various other important products.[27] Finally, there is no blinking the fact that the prices
of some standardized products differ very considerably
from one European country to the next, more than can
readily be ascribed to differences in transportation or in
distribution costs. Nonetheless, European suppliers have
interpenetrated one another's national domains on a wide
front.

Over the past decade or two, large enterprises have
been penetrating one another's markets not only in the
rich, industrialized countries but in many of the developing countries as well. As a consequence of that expansion,
foreign-owned subsidiaries have been enlarging their
positions in the industrial sectors of the developing countries, both in absolute and in relative terms. That trend
can be seen in Mexico, where foreign-owned subsidiaries
raised their share of manufacturing output from 20 percent in 1962 to 28 percent in 1970.[28] Similar increases have
occurred in Brazil [29] and Argentina.[30]

The developing countries have been acutely conscious that the aggregate position of multinational enterprises in their economy is growing. They have paid
less attention to the fact that, as a result, multinational enterprises have had to share their early dominance in a developing country with other multinational enterprises. As
Table 9 indicates, that trend has been fairly pronounced.
Meanwhile, business communities in most developing
countries have been growing rapidly in size and capability—not as rapidly as the multinational enterprises in
their midst, but rapidly enough to create new sources of
potential threat for individual enterprises in standardized
lines.

Some of the implications of the growth of local business communities are illustrated by the changing position
of Japan's multinational enterprises in Asia and East

Table 9 Number of manufacturing subsidiaries of multinational enterprises in selected product lines in four developing countries, 1960 and 1970[a]

Product line (with SIC category)	Number of subsidiaries							
	Brazil		Mexico		Colombia		India	
	1960	1970	1960	1970	1960	1970	1960	1970
Grainmill products (204)	4	5	4	8	4	5	1	1
Yarn and thread mills (228)	6	6	1	1	3	5	2	2
Industrial inorganic chemicals (281)	10	19	20	27	4	7	2	12
Plastics materials and synthetics (282)	7	15	12	19	2	8	4	16
Drugs (283)	15	23	17	28	5	14	13	22
Soap, cleaners, and toilet goods (284)	7	13	11	14	4	5	3	4
Agricultural chemicals (287)	2	10	4	7	1	8	1	7
Miscellaneous chemical products (289)	9	14	5	7	2	4	2	5
Blast furnaces and basic steel products (331)	4	8	1	2	1	1	2	4
Metal cans and shipping containers (341)	2	2	1	2	1	2	1	1
Miscellaneous fabricated metal products (349)	5	7	3	11	1	1	3	4
Special industrial machinery (355)	3	7	2	3	1	1	1	8
General industrial machinery (356)	3	7	3	11	1	1	1	4
Office and computing machines (357)	5	5	5	6	1	2	1	2
Electric distributing equipment (361)	4	8	3	6	1	2	1	8
Miscellaneous electrical equipment and supplies (369)	5	9	3	7	2	2	1	4
Other [b]	114	182	100	176	26	38	43	94
Total [b]	205	340	195	335	60	106	82	198

Source: Harvard Multinational Enterprise Project.

a. This table is based on the same sample of 391 enterprises covered in previous tables.

b. Excludes subsidiaries in those product lines in which no subsidiaries were present in 1960.

Africa. A decade ago, the local business communities of countries such as Thailand and Kenya had just entered the beer-bread-boots-and-boxes stage of industrialization—the parochial, import-substituting stage, in which goals and capabilities are limited to serving a local market and then only in the simple necessities. A decade ago, therefore, the subsidiaries of Japanese firms could be tolerated in these economies, even if they were producing relatively simple products and using relatively simple technologies to produce them. At that stage Japanese trading companies were creating intimate three-way partnerships with their home suppliers and with local distributors, which owned and operated numerous subsidiaries of this sort.[31]

Within a decade, however, the technological mysteries of Japanese subsidiaries were no longer so occult. The skills needed to run the existing plants had been mastered. And in some lines, such as textile plants and food-processing facilities, newer plants could be bought. Although the newer plants were likely to require a larger outlay of capital, they also were likely to be more efficient, even in areas in which capital was dear and labor was cheap.[32] Accordingly, Japanese subsidiaries throughout South and Southeast Asia began to feel pressures to give up their existing lines of business to local businessmen and began to roll over into other lines, thereby sharing an experience that the Americans and the Europeans had undergone in Latin America and Mediterranean Africa.[33]

Despite the Japanese example, however, it is not clear that the increase in the number of multinational and national firms in the markets of many developing countries has always produced salubrious consequences for consumers. In most developing countries, the factors restricting competition have continued to be visible and powerful. The number of sellers has remained small; the restrictions on imports have remained strong; and the traditions of official and private price-fixing practices have continued to prevail. Moreover, the local enterprises

have commonly adopted some tools of competition that
are of dubious benefit to the consumer, such as elaborate
local advertising campaigns. Where domination by
foreign leaders has existed, the proliferation of effective
enterprises seems to be introducing a new threat to the
old equilibrium.

Looking beyond the separate national markets of
Europe and the developing countries, it is beginning to
be evident that multinational enterprises are having increasing difficulty in identifying the sources of new competitive threats. With copper firms moving into aluminum, aluminum firms into copper, oil firms into
chemicals, and vice versa, almost every major product
line has witnessed the entry of some powerful newcomers. And with the ubiquitous spread of these large
multinational enterprises, the threat of their competition
in any national market no longer needs to express itself
tangibly through facilities actually in being in that market. In any market, Michelin is seen as a threat by Uni-
royal, Volkswagen as a threat by Ford, ICI as a threat by
Dow. The degree of threat bears very little relation to the
production that any of these firms maintains in any particular market. If imports are possible, a plant may not be
needed. If imports are barred, a large experienced multinational enterprise may have no difficulty in setting up a
local plant on short notice.

In some standardized products, therefore, it is not altogether unrealistic to measure the trends in concentration by looking at the global market structure, rather than
at national markets one at a time. Assume that the competitive presence of each leader in any national market is
best measured by the leader's global output, not by its
output in that national market. Then the output of each
multinational enterprise in any given product line can be
taken as a single unit irrespective of where its production
takes place. Measured in this way, many industries show
unmistakable declines in concentration since World War
II.[34]

The extent of the decline can be seen from the data presented in Figure 1, which present the trends in the so-called Herfindahl index for eight commodities. Eight

Figure 1 Herfindahl index of concentration of world production in eight commodities, 1950–1975 [a]

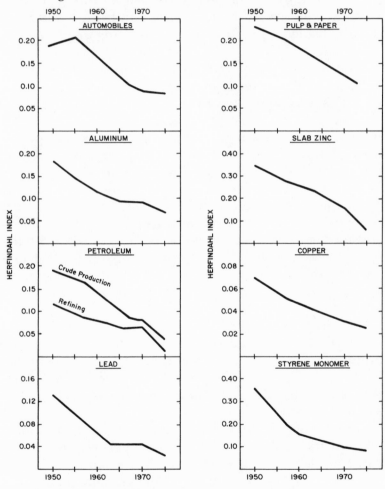

Source: Harvard Multinational Enterprise Project.

a. Production in communist countries and other countries with state monopolies is omitted.

commodities can hardly be said to portray a universal tendency, but they represent all the relevant cases that a diligent search could produce. These eight commodities include every standardized product for which a record of global production by individual firms could be obtained for the whole of the postwar period. What is impressive is the strong universal tendency toward declining concentration, as measured by the various indices. Clearly, industrial leadership in this sense was being dispersed at a rapid rate.

Of course, global figures of this sort, like those at the national level, can readily create a misleading impression of trends in competition. Even with a rapid dispersion of the leading firms, the capacity of the leaders to control the market and to restrain competition can still exist. A painstaking study of the world tractor industry indicates that, even with the appearance of new entrants, the leaders have managed to retain their share of the market and to resist the pressure on prices by skillfully using product differentiation and distribution structures as their defensive mechanisms.[35] In the international oil market, on the other hand, the diffusion of the leadership has led to a genuine decline in the power of the leaders. In this respect, the case of oil may prove typical of a wider group of products.

In the popular mind, the international oil industry is one that has managed to guard its secrets well. In the minds of scholars, on the other hand, it is an industry that has been thoroughly researched, one whose general structure and methods of operation are quite well understood.[36]

As I interpret the various studies of the international oil industry's behavior in the postwar period, a few propositions stand out. In 1950, seven leaders of the industry accounted for 90 percent of the oil then moving in international trade and were in a position to determine the behavior of that market, but by the mid-1970s their power of

determination had been vastly reduced. In the complex
twenty-year process that produced that result, a score or
more of additional oil companies broke their way into the
international market, reducing the majors' collective
share of that market to less than 60 percent. The entry of
the additional companies, as nearly as can be judged, was
an indispensable condition for weakening the control of
the seven original leaders.

The case of the oil industry, it is sometimes assumed,
is a case *sui generis,* rendered unique by various economic
and technical characteristics of the oil market and by the
accidents of history. That contention is hard to reject. But
all industries, including the oil industry, are unique in
some sense. In the competitive behavior of the oil industry since 1950, the similarities with other industries
stand out much more than the differences.

The first of these striking similarities is found in the
motives that led a number of U.S. oil companies in the
early 1950s to begin looking for oil outside the United
States. Up to that time only five U.S. companies—the so-
called majors—controlled any considerable amounts of
crude oil outside the Western Hemisphere; most oil companies were content to limit their business activities to
the United States. But anxiety obliged some of them to
begin looking abroad, anxiety stemming from the fact
that some of the oil companies already established on a
multinational basis had begun bringing some oil into the
United States from the Middle East. Faced with the competitive threat of a cheaper source of oil, some of the so-
called independents responded in the standard way; their
anxiety led them to take the plunge into distant foreign
environments.[37]

The entry of independent oil companies into the
Neutral Zone of Kuwait–Saudi Arabia in 1949, Iran in
1954, Libya in the later 1950s, Nigeria in the early 1960s,
and so on contributed slightly to the weakening of oil
prices during the period. Here and there, the newcomers

acquired more crude oil than they could easily dispose of. With a lesser stake in foreign markets than their multinational competitors and with a need to gain a foothold in such markets, they had less to lose by resorting to price-cutting.

The more enduring impact of the independents' entry was in their negotiations over the terms of their entry with governments of the countries where oil was to be found. In oil, as in some other extractive industries, the governments of exporting countries try to fix the tax rate at the level they think the traffic will bear. When the leading firms in these industries lose their ability to set the terms of doing business, their loss of power does not necessarily show up in lower prices; it can just as readily make itself apparent in higher taxes. In this case, that is what happened. The efforts of the independents to develop oil deposits in the Middle East and Africa palpably diluted the control of the majors. If the majors were prepared to pay 55 percent of their profits as taxes to the host country, the independents offered 57 percent, and if the majors were willing to give up 20 percent of the ownership of their producing facilities to the host countries, the independents proposed a higher figure. The upshot was a gradual decline in the ability of the majors to set the terms.

The entry of the independents, however, was only one of several factors that contributed to the decline in the negotiating position of the majors. In innumerable ways the social and intellectual remoteness of the Middle East was ending, as the young people of that area were sent off for education in the West and as the communication links grew stronger. As a result, long before the Arab-Israeli hostilities had become a factor in the situation and before the oil-exporting countries were exhibiting any capacity for joint action, a new generation of well-trained and knowledgeable specialists was appearing on the oil countries' side of the negotiating table. These men had less difficulty than their fathers might have had in recognizing that they confronted a less cohesive group of oil companies. They could also see that even after the independent companies had managed to secure a source of cheap oil abroad they still represented the weak link in the oil industry's defenses. The special vulnerability of the independents was visible in the various rounds of negotiation from the early 1960s until the crisis of 1973. And it derived from the fact that, unlike the established major oil companies, some of the independents had come to rely principally on only one source of oil in the area. Deprived of their main source, such companies would face major uncertainties in supplying their downstream refining and distributing facilities in Europe and the United States.

The unending process of negotiation and renegotiation instituted by the oil-exporting countries gradually was reflected in the profit figures of the oil companies. From 1954 on, the share of profits retained by the oil companies in the production of Middle East crude oil declined, moving to under 40 percent by the late 1960s. In the same period the profits recorded by the majors fell from about 80 cents per barrel to about 30 cents.

Up to that stage in the postwar development of the oil industry, not much distinguished it from many other industries dominated by multinational enterprises. Then came a series of events that seemed to turn oil into a special case. In the early 1970s the growth in the demand for Middle East oil experienced a special fillip. Part of the increase was due to the coincidence of a sharp increase in industrial activity simultaneously in Europe, Japan, and the United States. Part of the increase also was due to a sudden decline in the efficiency with which gasoline was burned in U.S. automobiles, a result of the introduction of antipollution controls. As the pinch became apparent in 1972 and 1973, some of the oil companies that felt threatened by inadequate crude oil supplies stepped up their efforts to enter the Middle East and Africa. At the same time, some big industrial users of oil, such as public utilities and chemical companies, made unprecedented efforts to buy their needed supplies directly from the agencies of the oil-exporting countries. For the moment, the bargaining strength of the oil-exporting countries was at peak levels, and, at almost that very moment, in October 1973 the Arab-Israeli war erupted, creating the cement that would permit the oil-exporting countries for the time being to concert their policies in the international oil market. That capacity for concerted action expressed itself through OPEC, the Organization of Petroleum Exporting Countries.

The quadrupling of the world's oil prices in the winter of 1973 had a profound impact on businessmen, scholars, and politicians appraising the future of multinational enterprises. Had the power of these institutions been overrated? Was the era of the multinational enterprise, after all, to be short-lived?

With the perspective of several years and with the added light provided by various studies of the crisis, it seems increasingly clear that the structure and behavior of the international oil industry have not been changed beyond recognition and that the important changes associated with the crisis were already evident before the crisis began.

The first point clarified by the crisis and illuminated by hindsight is that vertical integration and geographical dispersion still offer powerful technical advantages to any firm operating in the international oil market. During the height of the crisis in the winter of 1973, these characteristics enabled the multinational oil companies in effect to absorb the embargoes imposed by the Arab exporters on selected countries, by providing non-Arab oil to those destinations and spreading the shortages more or less evenly across all the major markets. These capabilities blunted the impact of the Arab embargo; they also added to the profits and survivability of the oil companies themselves.

The second point of importance is that the capacity of the industry's leading enterprises to manage the distribution of oil in foreign markets remained a necessary—though perhaps not a sufficient—element in protecting the profit margins of the oil companies and the countries. Without OPEC those margins might well have shrunk. But by the latter 1970s neither OPEC nor the national agencies of the oil-exporting countries had yet developed the intricate organizations, the habits of operation, and the expectations of mutual forbearance that the oil companies had built up over decades of operations. Without these the enormous range, variety, and geographic dispersion of the international crude oil market could reasonably be expected to produce a series of small price adjustments that eventually would break the price structure for crude oil.

The final point is that the greatest source of instability for the future appears to be the same as in the past: a relative decline in the barriers to entry into the international oil market. Although the requirements for survival in the industry push firms persistently into a multinational structure, the power of each individual firm has been declining as the number and diversity of such multinational firms increase. From the viewpoint of the firms, the goal of long-run stability continues to be threatened.

5 | Enterprise Strategies: The Struggle against Entropy

ENTROPY, to paraphrase Webster, is the process by which bits of matter lose their inner energy and grow indistinguishable from the inert particles that surround them. In any product line that faces the prospect of the entry of new firms, the established leaders tend to see themselves as threatened by entropy. If the leaders have enjoyed an especially high price or a special degree of stability because buyers think their products are unique, the entry of new firms is seen as threatening the premium or weakening the stability that the leaders enjoy. If the product commands a premium because the leaders have learned to avoid price-cutting as a means of competition, the efforts of new sellers to get into the market may also pose a threat to stability.

Because the need to fight off entropy permeates so much of the strategy of leading firms, no sharp line can be drawn between strategies that emphasize growth and stability and those designed to ward off the process of decline. A firm that invests heavily in the development of new products may be thinking of the inevitable loss of some of its existing ones. A firm that builds bigger and more capital-intensive facilities may be thinking of the possibility that newcomers will be able to reduce costs and undersell it. And a firm that engages in a frenzy of advertising in one of its product lines may see the product as

imperiled by entropic forces, pulling it down to the status
of an indistinguishable commodity.

From the viewpoint of the foreign-owned firm, one
means of coping with entropy may be as good as another,
provided it works. Yet from the viewpoint of governments, the means that foreign firms select to hold off the
effects of entropy are of considerable importance. While
the firms typically attempt to survive by introducing
product changes and product differentiation, governments are constantly on the alert for the possibility that
local interests may be able to squeeze the foreigner out.

New products are often introduced in the market
under the control of a single seller, and they commonly
acquire a few added producers in the years that follow.
Multinational enterprises often dominate the market
when the sellers are few in number. But when the number
of sellers multiplies, if it ever does, smaller firms come
into the market, many of them national rather than multinational in scope.

There are numerous uncertainties along the way, of
course. A product may never get beyond the oligopoly
stage before the demand for it disappears, superseded by
the demand for something new; this happened in the
1950s as computers began to displace electric calculators.[1]
In other cases, the entry of smaller firms has repeatedly
been thwarted by changes in the production process.
New capital-intensive methods of manufacture have been
developed, giving large firms a renewed grip on the product line. This has occurred in automobile manufacture
over the past few decades, almost—but not quite—post-
poning the day when national firms could effectively
compete.[2] In still other cases, a web of restriction has
stifled the entry of newcomers even though the problems
of technology and scale have been overcome. The international tractor market, for example, has been described in
such terms.

But many products do manage eventually to enter the stage at which the size of the firm and the extent of its multinational spread no longer count for much in the competitive race. At that stage, multinational enterprises have been known to withdraw from a product line altogether, leaving the field to smaller rivals.

The cycle from monopoly to oligopoly to workable competition occurs in many products, as has been richly documented in the literature of business strategies. One of the more elaborate demonstrations of such a cycle is found in an unusual study of petrochemicals.[3] In this case, for each of eighty-two petrochemicals, the industry pattern was reconstructed from the date of first introduction of the product until the late 1960s. The eighty-two products represented every major petrochemical with three or more producers in the U.S. at the time of the study. In all cases, the number of firms producing the item in the United States rose during the course of the product's life, from a near-monopoly at the beginning to some larger number of firms at maturity, generally on the order of ten or fifteen. More to the point, as static and dynamic economies of scale pushed down the costs of production, petrochemical firms reduced their prices. It would be hard to say if the pricing decisions were made on the initiative of the producers operating in their own interests or in spite of their desires. But ancillary data strongly point to the second possibility, suggesting that price competition became effective.

Although the turnover phenomenon patently exists, its relative importance is much less clear. To test its prevalence and importance, data on the output of individual producers must be in a form that permits individual products to be identified and traced. Unfortunately, studies that distinguish manufactured products by homogeneous categories, in terms that make sense to buyers and sellers, are extraordinarily rare. The usual study that traces the rise and decline of an industry is done in broad aggregates; chemicals are likely to be treated as one class, machinery as another, and so on. It is generally impossible to tell if the individual firms are surrendering their old product lines and rolling over into new lines within the broad aggregates. My guess is that something of the sort has been happening quite widely in national markets, both in the advanced industrialized countries and in the developing countries.

Figure 2 presents an idealized version of the cycle just described. Various individual cases exist which more or less fit the pattern. So far, these individual cases have not proved sufficiently important to arrest the growth in the relative position of multinational enterprises in most countries. Still, the objective of many countries has been to speed up the rate at which multinational enterprises surrender their old product lines to local firms. But the success of that strategy will depend on factors over which nation-states have little control, including future trends in

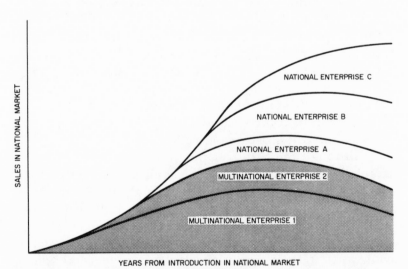

Figure 2   Schema of changing industry structure in a national market

the introduction of new products and processes and in the role of scale.

Another signal of the entropic creep in some indus-tries is the increasing tendency on the part of leading firms to set up so-called offshore producing facilities, that is, to produce components, intermediate materials, and even completed products in countries where labor costs and the tax structure are favorable to low-cost production.[4]

It is no accident that the practice of offshore sourcing has commonly been associated with industries in which price competition is relatively strong: textiles, clothing, toys, and dolls, for instance. In these industries, however, multinational enterprises have not been prominently involved. As a rule, the offshore sourcing has been done by national distributors through bulk-buying arrangements with independent or semi-independent contractors in the low-cost countries. In these industries, too, oligopoly behavior has not been very strong. Once again, we are reminded that multinational enterprises are not often found in those industries into which entry is comparatively easy.

Yet the practice of offshore sourcing has also appeared in a few product lines that *are* dominated by multinational enterprises, and in some of these cases the strategy has been precipitated by worries over the process of entropy. The outstanding case of this sort so far has been that of the consumer electronics industry, in which the offshore location of labor-intensive processes has been extensive. Production processes such as the manual testing of minicircuits, for example, have been assigned by multinational enterprises to subsidiaries located in Taiwan, Korea, Hong Kong, and Singapore.

Obviously, too much can be made of entropy as the driving force that leads multinational enterprises to reduce their costs by setting up production units in low-cost locations. Rational managers in a multinational enterprise would normally be expected to seize any opportunity to reduce their costs and increase their profits. In practice, however, an enterprise must always weigh the effects of its move upon the behavior of its rivals. When a move toward offshore sourcing would simply lead to a similar step by others, the innovator has to consider if anything is to be gained by making such a move. Another inhibiting factor is that the supply of high-level management in any large firm is usually regarded by the firm as one of its scarce, rationed resources, to be directed only to those tasks that promise the highest payoff.

As a rule, therefore, savings in production costs typically have a weak claim on the attention of high-level management. But when the firm feels strongly threatened by the price-cutting of other firms, the problem becomes important. In the electronics industry, for instance, U.S. firms have tended to exploit offshore sourcing possibilities most extensively for those product lines in which price competition is strongest and have done less sourcing for product lines in which sale price is a less critical consideration.[5]

The tendency for multinational enterprises to carry out some of their offshore sourcing through producing subsidiaries rather than through an arm's-length relation with contractors probably reflects their perceiving remnants of an oligopolistic advantage in these products. In the case of consumer electronics, the remaining advantage lies in the marketing phase, where trade names and distributor networks may still play some role even in highly price-sensitive products. Because that is the case, multinational enterprises continue to worry about maintaining effective quality control over their components and about ensuring promised delivery. As long as anxieties of this sort exist, they lead multinational enterprises to lean toward their own subsidiaries as sources of supply, in preference to independent contractors.

The consumer electronics industry illustrates once again, however, that there is no inevitability in the completion of the entropic process. By the early 1970s new advances in the technology of producing microcircuits succeeded in eliminating some of the most labor-intensive aspects of the operation. By that time, for instance, the testing of microcircuits could be done automatically, provided it was done on a massive scale. As a result, many U.S. firms began closing down some of their Asian facilities.[6]

The generalization that emerges is one that permeates almost all descriptions of the behavior of oligopolies in conditions of change. Nothing is certain, but some patterns are more likely than others. The entropic pattern, although far from inevitable, is commonly encountered in the life of products. To the extent that it occurs, it limits the hegemony of multinational enterprises. To the extent that it is accelerated, the power of multinational enterprises is further reduced.

The struggle to maintain stability and the struggle to survive in the face of entropy are not always easy to distinguish. The distinction between the two types of strategy is essentially this: in one case, the firm's efforts are centered mainly on staying with its existing activities; in the other, on shifting as painlessly as possible out of these activities into others.

As suggested earlier, problems are created for the leading firms in any product market as the number of multinational enterprises increases. As new multinational enterprises enter the field, the leaders struggle to maintain some sort of stability. In some products the field becomes so crowded with multinational enterprises that the possibility of maintaining stability and gaining an oligopolistic profit becomes slim. At that stage some of these enterprises will drop out of the race. For them the struggle for stability shifts to a struggle against entropy.

In the past the new multinational challengers taking

on the leaders in their established markets characteristically came from the United States or Europe. By the
late 1960s the challengers were beginning to include Japanese firms. And by the 1970s some comparatively large
firms headquartered in the developing countries were
being stimulated to set up subsidiaries in nearby foreign
markets. In Asia the presence of Indian and Taiwanese
firms was beginning to be noted. In Latin America and
the Caribbean the spread of Brazilian and Mexican firms
began stirring reactions.[7]

The products in which these large firms from developing countries tend to specialize do not have had quite
as strong an oligopolistic flavor as the products of multinational enterprises from the advanced countries. Like
the Japanese multinationals of the 1960s, Indian and Mexican firms have been found mainly in textiles, food preparations, and relatively simple consumer products. And according to preliminary indications the capacity of these
new multinational firms to find a niche in the developing
areas has rested on factors analogous to those of the Japanese.[8] Conditions in the home market have produced
both a scale of operation and a use of capital, labor, and
materials quite compatible with conditions in the markets
of nearby developing countries. The adaptations required
for efficient operation have accordingly been less than
those that the multinational enterprises of the United
States and Europe have confronted. For instance, according to a study of the proposals filed by several hundred
foreign firms to establish manufacturing susidiaries in
Thailand, the production facilities proposed by Indian
firms in that market were substantially less capital-intensive and somewhat more efficient in cost terms than those
proposed by European and American firms in similar
products.[9]

Yet another factor seems to be operating to
strengthen the competitive position of the multinational
enterprises from developing countries. In the case of In-

dian firms, manufacturing subsidiaries abroad have characteristically used both capital equipment and management personnel imported from their home country. The capital equipment, being little known in international markets, has not commanded the prices that, say, equivalent Swiss or British machinery would command, and that advantage has been enlarged by the Indian government's practice of extending a large subsidy, on the order of 20 or 30 percent, to such exports.[10] Moreover, Indian management personnel operating in foreign markets are paid at the Indian level of compensation, a level far lower than that of the managers of other foreign-owned plants and even lower than that of managers of locally owned plants. Accordingly the factor costs prevailing in India itself have helped to shape the competitive position of the subsidiaries of Indian firms abroad.

Although the foreign subsidiaries of multinational enterprises from developing countries have enjoyed some elements of advantage over competitors from the richer countries, their advantages over local competitors have seemed a little less apparent. Here again the earlier experience of the Japanese firms is instructive. The Japanese edge over local competition in South and Southeast Asia was mainly one of early positioning and early reaction. At the time when the local markets of Asia seemed capable of supporting production facilities in textiles or noodles or batteries or other comparatively uncomplicated products, Japanese firms were already supplying those markets by way of exports from Japan; by teaming up with their local distributors, Japanese firms were often in a position to establish those facilities before an unaffiliated local entrepreneur could assemble the capital, technology, and distribution facilities needed for the project.[11]

It is important to note, however, that this sort of advantage proved fragile and vulnerable.[12] In some cases the period in which the Japanese had an unchallenged lead in the market was quite brief. In other cases the local participants in Japanese joint ventures turned on their Japanese partners, demanding a larger voice in the joint operation. The pattern, in short, seems to have been one that has been common in the experience of the U.S. and European firms, but it was telescoped into a shorter period of time, consistent with the lesser strength and greater fragility of the foreigners' initial lead.

Once again, however, it must be underlined that although entropy may be a law in nature, it does not have the power and predictability of law in the behavior of human institutions. The introduction of multinational enterprises from the developing countries only adds another threat to the control of the original multinational leaders. The power of the leaders to generate offsetting strategies still remains.

(3)   The running-down process has been evident enough in individual products. And the capacity of large enterprises to survive by a strategy of continuous rollover, moving from one product to another, also has been apparent at times. Freeport Minerals has moved from sulfur to copper and other metals, Pfizer from penicillin to industrial chemicals and cosmetics, W. R. Grace from plantations and shipping to chemicals, ITT from the manufacture of telephones and the operation of telephone exchanges to almost anything under the sun. All these cases illustrate the capacity of some firms to shift their organizational attention and their financial resources from a product in which the individual firm's power is on the wane to a product in which the entropic process is less advanced.

Yet not infrequently in the history of multinational enterprise, firms have been incapable of mastering the rollover strategy. Many have felt obliged to withdraw from foreign markets. Others have given up the ghost altogether, through merger or through liquidation.

Because the process of withdrawal has so rarely been

accompanied by a flourish of trumpets, it is possible that this contrapuntal theme in the multinational spread of enterprise has not been given its proper emphasis. Yet as one reads Hobson's *Imperialism*, published in 1902, or Lenin's book of the same name, published in 1917, a striking aspect of both works is the archaic nature of their illustrations, the repeated reference to cases that no longer exist.

The dominant examples of multinational enterprises in these classic studies are foreign-owned plantation companies, electric-power companies, traction companies, textile plants, railroads, banks, and mines. Yet today foreign-owned companies in most of these activities are practically gone. If any multinational firm sought to produce power or to provide transportation in a foreign market, it would usually confront an array of local rivals capable of assembling the technical and financial ingredients for a more-or-less similar service. Trained abroad as a rule, the engineers and entrepreneurs needed to perform the relatively routine functions would provide the local alternative.[13] As for foreign-owned plantations, the trend has been similar. In some products, such as bananas and other tropical fruits, multinational enterprises have sometimes kept a hold on plantations abroad because of the advantages of large scale or because of tight control in the marketing process, but in nonperishable products, such as coffee, cocoa, sugar, and tea, the international marketing mechanism has become well enough organized that the special marketing facilities provided by multinational enterprises have lost some of their unique quality. Although the capacity of the foreigners to organize the local growing process may still be superior to the local alternatives in many countries, the difference has been shrinking over the years and is no longer sufficiently compelling to insulate the foreigner from the running-down process.

One of the more spectacular illustrations of the shrinkage syndrome can be seen in the changes in certain

U.S.-owned interests in Cuba during the regimes of
Fulgencio Batista, from 1933 to 1944 and from 1952 to
1959. In the 1950s, with putatively friendly regimes in
Havana, U.S. ownership in Cuba's industry grew quite
strongly. Over the quarter-century, however, U.S. ownership of Cuban sugar plantations dropped from about 65
percent of the nation's total to about 40 percent, and U.S.
banking exhibited a similar slippage.[14] In cases such as
these, the position of the multinational enterprise is un-
dermined by the readiness with which the technology on
which the enterprise based its initial strength can be
learned by others. Further, in the case of sugar the process
of learning and dissemination can be speeded by governmental institutions such as experimental stations and extension services.[15] Once again, the improvement in the
international network of communication and transportation has had a great deal to do with process, permit-
ting both an easier exchange of information and a central-
ization of some types of research.

Systematic data on the withdrawal of multinational
enterprises from areas in which they previously maintained producing facilities have been compiled for several
hundred large multinational enterprises headquartered in
the United States, Europe, and Japan. Although the figures are incomplete in various ways, they affirm the fact
that multinational enterprises have commonly given up
production facilities in areas in which they had previously been established.[16] Indeed, between 1968 and
1974 180 U.S.-based multinational enterprises sold or
liquidated 717 manufacturing subsidiaries located in
foreign countries. Coming out of a total population of
about 6,500 such subsidiaries, these withdrawals were
not insignificant. Of that group, to be sure, 268 were fairly
new ventures at the time of their disposal, having been in
their respective networks less than five years; these no
doubt represented cases in which the multinational enterprises had simply had second thoughts. But the re-

maining 449 subsidiaries appear to have been well-established in their networks at the time of liquidation, suggesting the existence of an entropic process in the multinational enterprise.

The era of the multinational manufacturing enterprise is well enough advanced by now to suggest that such enterprises will commonly be able to master the rollover strategy in most markets, moving from product to product or from function to function as the process of entropy eats away at their existing strengths. Casualties are likely in the future, as in the past, wherever multinational enterprises find themselves unable to master the rollover imperative, and these casualties will often signal the broadened opportunities created for national enterprises. Even as the individual subsidiaries of multinational enterprises are imperiled, however, the multinational form of enterprise continues to enjoy palpable benefits. The survival prospects of the multinational enterprise as an institution continue to appear very favorable. And governments cannot count on the possibility that multinational enterprises will simply fade away, thereby eliminating the seeming source of their tensions.

6 | The Strain on National Objectives: The Industrialized Countries

AS MULTINATIONAL enterprises have pursued their various strategies over the face of the globe, national governments and other national institutions have generally been obliged to concentrate more single-mindedly upon the home territory. As long as the governments and institutions have been those of the industrialized countries, the differences in perspective between these national entities and multinational enterprises have usually been manageable enough. Nevertheless, strain and tension have arisen from time to time, as the global perspectives of the multinational enterprises have seemed to place the objectives of the national institutions in jeopardy.

In any list of problems associated with the operations of multinational enterprises, though, national security does not rank very high. Although the subject of national security usually demands the most unambiguous declarations of loyalty and affiliation, the tensions that multinational enterprises have generated in this field have been fairly muted.

This happy state depends, however, on the durability of one existing condition. So far, most of the operations of multinational enterprises have been concentrated in North America, Europe, and Japan, areas linked by close military alliances. If Japan should begin following

an independent military course or if NATO should eventually lose its primacy in the strategic plans of the North
American and European states, the national security issue
could easily be elevated to a problem of the most acute
sort.

Military planners in any nation have to recognize
that, when allies fall out, all facilities located in any
country are wholly at the service of that country. In the
two world wars, the subsidiaries of Allied firms on enemy
territory conscientiously ground out their share of ar-
maments along with the rest of the enemy's industry, and
the facilities of German firms in the United States and
elsewhere also performed according to the needs of the
host country. As nationals of the state where they were
located, these enemy-owned subsidiaries could hardly do
otherwise.

Even in peacetime, allies differing with the United
States over a security issue have usually assumed that
U.S. pressures to bring the foreign subsidiaries of U.S.
firms into line would not be applied very hard or, if
applied, would not achieve very much. When in 1965 the
U.S.-owned subsidiary of Fruehauf in France tried to
respond to the commands of the U.S. government forbidding the shipment of truck trailers to the Soviet
Union, the French government found ways under French
law of compelling the subsidiary to make the shipments.[1]
When in the 1960s U.S.-owned subsidiaries in Canada
were advised to resist the Canadian government's invita-
tion to sell flour to Cuba and drugs to North Vietnam, the
Canadian government readily found other firms to handle
the business.[2] An even more pointed indication of the
impotence of the United States in using the country's
overseas subsidiaries as an instrument of U.S. security
policy was provided by the actions of Gulf Oil's subsidiary in the 1976 civil war in Angola. After the briefest
hesitation, Gulf Oil's subsidiary turned over several
hundred million dollars to the winning side, even though

the U.S. government had backed that side's enemies and had not yet recognized it as the victor.[3]

That subsidiaries in foreign countries may be out of the control of security planners has to be linked with one other sobering fact, worrisome to such planners. Many multinational enterprises are important producers of key military hardware.[4] The capacity of such enterprises to communicate complex ideas among their affiliates has increased the difficulty of sealing in technical ideas at the borders of the United States. Although there is no way of testing the point objectively, it is difficult to resist the conclusion that technologies that the military would prefer to remain a U.S. monopoly can now slip over the borders more readily. To be sure, U.S. firms generally try to set up elaborate leak-proof conduits inside their organizations for communicating streams of technological information. But often the mere knowledge that a given problem has been solved is quite sufficient for others to duplicate the solution, and that kind of knowledge is always difficult to conceal.

Does weakening the system of information-control impair the security of the United States? At the risk of appearing offhand with respect to an issue of considerable importance, my conclusion has long been that U.S. strategic controls have contributed little to U.S. security—indeed, at times they have adversely affected U.S. security.[5] Given that assumption, a weakening of controls is not necessarily bad. But that conclusion is not one that many U.S. policymakers in the defense establishment would endorse. Accordingly, the threat to the U.S. strategic control system contributes something to the tensions that U.S.-based multinational enterprises generate among U.S. policymakers.

The calculations of security planners in countries other than the United States have to reflect the somewhat different positions of those countries. French military planners, for instance, would like to possess an indepen-

dent national capability that could respond to the broad-
est possible range of contingencies. Accordingly, in aircraft, rocketry, nuclear energy, advanced computers,
and other exotic electronic applications, France would
like to have an industry invulnerable to American influence.

The reality, of course, is that no national industry by
itself is capable of top performance in the various technologies of warfare unless it has intimate access to the contributions of other national industries. That painful fact
least restrains the countries with large military programs
(for which read United States) and restrains practically everyone else much more. Accordingly, the technological
links that tie French industry to other countries, including
the United States, are numerous and vital. Westinghouse
and General Electric are linked to France's nuclear efforts,
IBM and Honeywell to its computer industry, the U.S.
aircraft-engine manufacturers to its aircraft industry, and
so on. The efforts of France to shake off the dependence of
its national industries on these links have been unavail-
ing, generating an acute sense of frustration among
French planners.

Governmental reactions have not been quite as
strong in Canada, Japan, Britain, or Germany. The Canadians are aware that for them aspirations *à la française*
are chimerical; as for Japan and Germany, neither is
ready as yet to step out from under the protective wing
of the United States; and Britain, as usual, is torn between its pull to the United States and the white Commonwealth, on the one hand, and pragmatic needs to
throw in with Europe on the other. Nevertheless, no
country is altogether free of the frustrations that the
French have been so ready to articulate.

Lacking a strategic alternative to the U.S. military
umbrella, the Europeans have accepted the necessity of
organizing their defense-related industries on lines not
wholly at variance with a collective Atlantic strategy. That

acceptance, however, has not ruled out the possibility of intense technological rivalry among members of the Atlantic alliance; with military considerations taking second place, questions of national prestige and hopes of commercial advantage still have stoked the competition among the Atlantic powers.

As was noted in Chapter 3, the field of defense-related technology has been one in which the governments of the various European states have been unwilling to opt for a European solution. Repeatedly, one European government after another has thrown cold water on a genuine pan-European approach, in which the identity of the separate nations would be submerged in a common effort.

In the middle 1960s, for example, a time when American industry held a strong lead over Europe in the construction of nuclear reactors, France discouraged the possibility of a European program for the development of a rival nuclear technology and insisted on going it alone with a national program.[6] Later on the Europeans were unable to agree on how to meet their need for fuel-enrichment facilities and split themselves into two consortia, URENCO and EURODIF.[7]

The efforts of the British and French governments to build up their respective national computer industries have been just as divisive. At first the prevailing British idea was to organize the rest of Europe under British leadership, in order to stave off American domination.[8] When the other Europeans resisted, the idea was dropped. French efforts to develop a computer industry have paid even less attention to the possibility of a common European effort.[9]

Nevertheless, sheer frustration has led the Europeans to turn back repeatedly to the idea of pooling European resources. Whenever that idea has been converted into action, however, the governments have found themselves not quite able to go the whole way. What has emerged, as

a rule, has been a hybrid, a consortium among states that
attempts to capture all the advantages of a joint response
while retaining the advantages of separate national identity.

In various shapes and forms, consortia of this sort
have come and gone in Europe over the past fifteen years
or so. Some have existed to execute only a single project,
such as the Concorde and the Jaguar in civil aircraft; [10]
some, a series of projects, such as the family of French-
German missiles. These consortia by now have been the
object of several careful studies.[11] And as I read the evidence, the consortia seem unlikely to provide an effective
response to the challenge of the United States in major
technological projects.

A few European consortia, it is true, have been clear
successes. According to most reports, CERN, Conseil
Européen pour la Recherche Nucléaire, has fulfilled most
expectations. That organization, however, has simply
provided a common resource—a set of expensive research
facilities—for the joint use of the various national scientific communities. Some highly successful tank and mis-
sile projects resulted from French-German collaboration,
as did the still-to-be-tested A-300 airbus, but none of
these projects has entailed major technological advances
or broken significant new ground on the industrial fron-
tier. None of them, therefore, has quite achieved the objective typically sought by France and Britain: to register
an outstanding success on the commanding heights of
modern technology, which would stimulate the technological capabilities of the nation and add to national prestige.

The consortium approach has been disappointing
mainly because it has failed to achieve the critical advantages that go with large size and unitary structure. In the
United States the political decisions defining goals and
providing financial resources have rested with only one

government, not with two or more. Besides, the U.S. government usually has dealt with a prime contractor that enjoyed continuity of existence and some internal unity of command. European consortia, on the other hand, have generally involved two or more governments and two or more groups of national contractors, coordinated and orchestrated through a temporary organization.

The differences can be seen first of all in the level of costs. As a rule, each country participating in a consortium has been allotted a share of the production, its share being nicely calibrated to the value of the country's financial contribution. In the allocation process, considerations of cost and efficiency have sometimes had to take second place. In all probability, however, the more important impact on costs has arisen from the fact that the organizations created for the purpose of carrying out these European projects characteristically have had neither a past nor a future. Therefore all the shakedown and learning costs of the organization—the costs of learning how to retrieve information, execute commands, and coordinate diverse activities—have usually been laid upon a single project.[12]

The consortium aspect of European projects has added not only to their costs but also to their inflexibility. With various groups of national contractors working on different parts of a complex jigsaw puzzle such as an extraterrestrial rocket, the usual problems of coordination have taken on added difficulties. When any government of the consortium has faced a political crisis, the consortium has been frozen on its existing course, unable to generate new instructions from its public masters. Even when political crises were not a problem, the participation of several governments has meant extra difficulties in dealing with the unplanned and unforeseen. Technicians have felt obliged to live with their existing mandates, even when circumstances have called for basic re-

consideration. This aspect of the consortium approach
may prove to be the Achilles' heel of these European projects.[13]

Despite the limitations of the consortium approach,
however, cooperative patterns of this sort may well grow.
But the effect of this trend will be to increase the importance of the international links among enterprises, as the
demands of integrated production, standardization, and
compatibility assert themselves. As long as the European
side of the integrative process continues to consist of a
series of separate nation-states, each struggling to retain
the shreds of control over its own national security, the
American end of the connection will be seen as dominat-
ing the exchange. While the U.S. military planners worry
about the diffusion of technology by way of the multinational enterprises, the Europeans will be concerned about
their continuing reliance on the technology of their U.S.
partners.

Much more strenuously and volubly articulated are
the points of contention between multinational enterprises and national labor interests. As a rule, labor
leaders in the industrialized countries see multinational
enterprises as threatening their interests.[14] Two different
kinds of threats are perceived. One has to do with labor
leaders' preferences for a strong and vital national government; the other, with their desire for a dominant and
unassailable negotiating position.

The principal labor organizations of Europe and the
United States cover a wide spectrum of ideologies, structures, and operating methods. They include unions
organized by industry and unions organized by craft, organizations identified with a strong ideology and those
identified with only bread-and-butter objectives, organizations linked intimately to political parties and organizations that resist such links. In spite of their differences,

however, labor organizations have some fundamental interests in common.

By and large, these organizations identify their interests as congruent with the growth of the modern welfare state, including the development of unemployment benefits, retirement benefits, housing assistance, and health-care systems. The greater their successes in building up these national programs, the greater their interest in protecting the vitality of national institutions. Even the communist unions, nominally dedicated to scrapping the modern welfare state, have insisted on a share of the credit for having broadened its welfare functions.

Many labor unions have an added reason for supporting the growing power of national governments. A strong state might improve labor's chances of participating in the management of the enterprises themselves. Of course, not all unions have that objective in mind. Labor organizations in the United States and Britain, for instance, for a long time shied away from sharing the managerial function. But the objective of sharing in management is common among European labor groups. Some have been attempting to get seats for labor in the managing bodies of big firms, some have been for nationalizing the big firms, and some for socializing the national economic system as a whole.

From the viewpoint of many labor groups, the growth of multinational enterprises has proved to be a threat to these objectives. Labor groups that are for nationalization as a policy can see that foreign-owned subsidiaries might be in a position to throw up special obstacles that national businessmen would be in no position to employ. Even when local labor groups simply seek a role in management, they have to reckon with the possibility that the subsidiaries of foreign-owned enterprises would be especially resistant, as many subsidiaries of U.S. firms in Germany have proved to be. Besides, labor

leaders have to weigh the possibility that managing one
unit in a global network, whether in the headquarters
firm or in a foreign-owned subsidiary, might prove to be
a frustrating shadow play. The activities of the other units
in the network—in research, in marketing, in profit-
taking—would ordinarily shape and restrain the choices
of any single unit. Accordingly, when aiming at achieving control, labor unions have an interest both in bolstering the power of national governments and in holding
down the growth of multinational enterprises.

Labor unions have seen objectives other than participating in management threatened in various ways by the
expanded role of multinational enterprises. The appearance of foreign-owned subsidiaries in a country has
seemed to add to total job opportunities there, but the
added jobs have sometimes proved a mixed blessing.
Such enterprises have often settled in backward, de-
pressed regions of a country, the very areas in which
organized labor is weakest. This has been particularly
true of foreign-owned subsidiaries in the United States,
which have frequently established themselves in the deep
South and Appalachia; it has less commonly been the case
in Europe, where labor organizations have a more ubiquitous control over the countryside.

Foreign-owned subsidiaries are sometimes disturbing in another sense. Although most have been quick to
fall in with national labor practices, whatever they are,
some have held out for practices of their own that are
deviations from the national norms. In Britain, for instance, some U.S.-owned subsidiaries have been responsible for developing agreements with their workers that
link increased compensation to increased productivity, a
concept that is anathema to some of Britain's labor
leaders.[15] In Belgium, the "human relations" practices of
some foreign-owned subsidiaries, presumably U.S.-
owned, have been said to be alienating the workers from
their union organizations.[16] From this point of view, the

more benign the labor policies of a multinational, the more dangerous they are to the interests of local labor movements.

Once the unit of a multinational enterprise settles into a country, labor's problems sometimes take a different turn. In the day-to-day negotiations between labor and management, the labor side must be constantly alert to the possibility that the multinational enterprise might turn away from a country in which the environment was persistently hostile. Sometimes representatives of a multinational enterprise have found it useful to remind the other side of that potential, hoping to weaken the negotiating will of the labor leaders they confront.[17] Not surprisingly, therefore, the president of the United Automobile Workers was found saying at one stage that he would not welcome European automobile companies that set up subsidiaries in the United States, even though the step might seem to increase the number of jobs in the U.S. automobile industry.[18]

Labor's efforts to deal with the growth of multinational enterprises have taken various forms. One response, for instance, has been to try to coordinate the bargaining of labor unions in different countries when they confront a common multinational employer. These efforts at coordination, however, have been plagued by some underlying weaknesses.[19] When labor unions of different nations confront a single employer, they are generally a diverse, polyglot group. The differences noted earlier—craft versus industrial, communist versus socialist, political versus bread-and-butter unions—have prevented the unions from creating a formidable countervailing force. Besides, the national unions of different countries commonly have interests that are flatly in conflict. At times, unions in different countries find themselves bidding against one another to have a multinational enterprise plan its next expansion for their territory. As a result, programs for coordinating the bargaining efforts of unions have done very little to alter the bargaining power between multinational enterprises and labor.

The need of labor unions to find some effective way of dealing with the multinational enterprise has led them to coordinate their policies toward the European Economic Community. Communist, socialist, and Christian trade unions have managed to set aside their ideological differences and arrive at common positions on such issues as rights of participation in management and protection in the case of mass dismissals.[20] But that development can be only as important as the Community's power to govern is important. Meanwhile, labor's basic interests continue to be focused at the national level, which contributes to the tension in labor's relations with the multinational enterprise.

Concern over labor's interests, however, has not been confined to the labor unions and their leaders. National planners, bent on increasing jobs within a country and improving the distribution of income, have found themselves asking whether it was a good idea to encourage the multinationalizing trend of their own enterprises and whether it was desirable to promote the entry of foreign-owned enterprises.

One thing has been reasonably clear. Units in the networks of multinational enterprises, whether parent units or subsidiaries, have as a rule been faster-growing and more export-oriented than other enterprises in the countries in which they are located. That finding has been demonstrated for enterprises in the United States, the United Kingdom, France, Japan, and Sweden.[21]

From the viewpoint of public policymakers, however, this demonstration is no more than an introduction to the main issue. Is the national economy better off than it would be if multinational networks did not exist? If, for instance, national policies had barred multinational enterprises and their subsidiaries from the chemicals, machinery, transportation equipment, electronics, and food-processing industries, would the industries have developed in the industrialized countries any more slowly, less profitably, or with less emphasis on exports? [22]

Although we need to compare reality with what might have been, it is not easy to satisfy the need. No studies, existing or likely, can help the objective analyst beyond the very first stage in mapping out the might-have-been. Whenever we try to identify the longer-run implications of a new line of policy designed to further inhibit or further encourage multinational enterprises, the projection rapidly moves onto soft terrain. As a result, the principal utility of the various objective studies in this field has been to test and perhaps discard the unsupported polemic, not to provide a sure guide to a better line of policy.

Wrestling with that limitation, policymakers in the rich industrialized countries have tried to puzzle out the employment implications of the existence of multinational enterprises. As a rule, employment studies have concentrated on one country at a time—Britain, France, or the United States. Sometimes, they have focused on the effects of foreign-owned subsidiaries moving into the local economy, sometimes on the reverse current, that is, the multinationalizing of home-based enterprises. In either case, the central question has been the same: Would employment levels be different if multinational enterprises did not exist?

Of the various areas of possible research on this question, the one most exhaustively covered has been U.S.-based multinational enterprises and their effects on the U.S. economy. A number of conscientious analysts have wrestled with the estimating problem. [23] In all these cases, in order to be able to get on with their estimates, the researchers have found themselves obliged to make some heroic simplifying assumptions about how the world actually works. One familiar assumption, grossly at variance with the facts, has been that the enterprises operate under the classical conditions of a competitive market. Unavoidably, the estimates based on this assumption have been abstract and remote from the real world.

Nevertheless, one common result emerges from these studies: whatever the direct and immediate effects of the multinational structure may be upon employment totals in the United States, the aggregates produced by such statistical exercises are small. The estimates range from a few hundred thousand jobs added to the U.S. economy to a few hundred thousand jobs lost; and the estimates at the extremes are on the whole less plausible than the estimates in the middle. On the present evidence, therefore, the question of aggregate employment effects in the United States is a secondary issue.[24]

More certain than the change in the total number of U.S. jobs is the change in the mix: the number of jobs available for the unskilled has been reduced, while the number available to the skilled has been increased. In social terms, that shift is hard to evaluate, for it may burden the present generation while offering new promise to the next.

Estimates of the effects of multinational enterprises on the U.S. economy, however, are not a reliable guide for the economies of Canada, Japan, or the countries of Europe. In some of these countries, the multinationalization of home enterprises is a more important trend than the influx of foreign-owned enterprises; in other countries, the opposite is the case.

The Canadians are distinctive in the extent to which U.S.-owned and European-owned subsidiaries already dominate their economy. With over 60 percent of Canada's industrial sector already in such foreign hands, it is futile to try to estimate the net employment effects of the existing situation as compared with some hypothetical alternative.

The nine members of the European Economic Com-

munity, meanwhile, are exposed to strong multinationalizing currents moving in both directions, inbound
and outbound. At the same time, the Community
members are affected by the process of economic union,
which is a bone in their collective throats. Because a customs union exists inside the area, no country is in a position to prevent the subsidiaries of an enterprise, wherever it may be located in the Community, from shipping
its goods into the country's national territory.[25] For the
moment the effects of the multinational enterprise on the
European states cannot be assessed independently of the
effects of the customs union as a whole.

The question of whether multinational enterprises
contribute on balance to employment has repeatedly
emerged in European discussions nonetheless. In recent
years Dutch interests have been incensed over AKZO's
plans to redistribute its production facilities more ef-
ficiently around Europe, some French interests have been
disturbed by Pechiney's growing foreign activities, and
some Germans have protested Volkswagen's plan to produce automobiles in the United States. Outside the European Community various European interests have been
alarmed by the possibility that their home firms, such as
Volvo and SKF in Sweden, might set up foreign production units that would deprive the home country of some
much-needed jobs.

As for Japan in the mid-1970s, the issue of employment in relation to the multinational enterprise has not
yet surfaced in any consequential way. The employees of
Japan-based firms have not yet felt threatened by the
number of firms setting up extensive overseas networks;
perhaps the usual lifetime employment practices of Japanese firms help to temper labor's concern.[26] Meanwhile,
foreign-owned subsidiaries have not yet become important employers of Japanese labor. However, although the
issue is in abeyance for the time being, it seems improba-
ble that it will remain so for very long.

Despite the uncertain indications provided by the

data, the operations of multinational enterprises may well have some very substantial effects on labor in the advanced industrial countries, which may be seen when national economies are compared with a hypothetical world in which only national enterprises operate. For one thing, the negotiating power of national labor groups has surely been affected; whether the effects are substantial may be a matter for debate, but not the direction of the change. For another, the productivity of the economies of the advanced countries has probably been increased. Here again, the extent of the change may be debated, but the direction is reasonably clear. The pie to be shared is probably somewhat larger, while labor's capacity to bargain for a share has probably been somewhat weakened. So the economic effects, as far as labor is concerned, are left in considerable doubt, even while tension continues, nurtured by the unsupported claims of the adversaries.

The concern that various countries have sporadically exhibited over the risk of losing jobs as a result of the operations of multinational enterprises has sometimes been supplemented by concern that they might be losing the savings of their nationals or losing scarce foreign exchange.

In the latter 1960s, it will be remembered, the concern over foreign exchange led the United States to impose various restrictions on capital outflows.[27] At about the same time, the British were reconsidering whether the direct investment activities of their firms were contributing to a foreign exchange drain. Although a number of careful studies on the subject were undertaken at the time, none shed much useful light on the question. On the whole, these efforts produced estimates that were uncertain in direction and limited in magnitude.[28] And in order to measure even some of the seemingly measurable effects, researchers were obliged to make some heroic assumptions, such as the assumption that the supply of cap-

ital was both a necessary and a sufficient condition determining output. Moreover, none of the estimates could
capture some of the critical long-run effects of the multinational enterprise, such as those arising from the broadened geographical horizons of their managers.

The various studies of the relationship of capital
movements to multinational enterprises have produced
one important thread of consensus, however. The affiliated units of multinational enterprises are especially
capable of accommodating themselves to any government's restrictive program, with minimum effect on their
basic strategies.[29] As European commentators have rue-
fully observed, the U.S. government's restrictions on the
export of capital in the 1960s had no significant effect on
the multinational spread of U.S. enterprises. What the enterprises did in response was what they had already been
doing in considerable measure even before the advent of
the U.S. restrictions: borrowing in capital markets outside the United States to meet some of the financial
requirements of their overseas projects.[30] European commentators professed to see in this response a clear case of
egregious insult added to painful injury; the savings of
Europeans, it was said, were being used to finance the
U.S. purchase of European industry.

Some American commentators also were troubled by
the capacity of U.S.-based multinational enterprises to
mobilize funds not their own, but their preoccupation
took a totally different turn. They observed that U.S.
banks from the Midwest and elsewhere were sporadically
shipping their funds to London for placement in the
Eurodollar market and that U.S. firms were borrowing extensively in that market to finance their offshore operations. Accordingly, their concern was that the savings of
Americans might be financing the operations of multinational enterprises abroad at the expense of U.S. capital
needs at home.[31]

Until the mid-1970s one country that seemed notably

impervious to worries over capital movements associated
with multinational enterprises was Japan. Its system of
controls, exercised through its Ministry for International
Trade and Industry (MITI) and the Bank of Japan, appeared quite sufficient to control both the foreign-owned
subsidiaries operating in Japan and the Japan-based multinational enterprises operating abroad. By the mid-
1970s, however, the first symptoms of concern began to
appear even here, especially with regard to the overseas
operations of Japan's own firms. As those operations have
grown and diversified, Japanese firms are gradually developing their own network of associations with foreign
businessmen and banks abroad. Willy-nilly, Japan's
economy also has begun to be sucked into an international system, although the degree of involvement still is
under control.

These illustrations serve to underline one central fact.
The capital markets of the rich industrialized countries
have become linked in innumerable ways. Accordingly,
controls imposed on one channel are more likely than ever
to divert capital flows to other channels. Besides, the linkages mean that any analysis associating any particular
pool of national savings with a particular pool of national
investment, as if one were accountable for the other, is increasingly artificial.

Apart from being concerned over the movement of
national capital and national savings, national groups also
have had qualms about the effects of the operations of
multinational enterprises on the national exchange rate.
Multinational enterprises in the ordinary course of operations dispose of vast quantities of money across the international exchanges, on the order of two billion dollars
daily. Most of that flow is concentrated in forty or fifty
multinational networks that draw their impressions and
their advice regarding the relative stability of different
currencies from common sources—half a dozen banks, an
even smaller number of financial journals, and an inces-

tuous round of lunches and conferences. Viewed in the abstract, the situation is set up for disaster; a common tilt in the group becomes a source of irresistible pressure on any currency.

Here a distinction has to be made between multinational enterprises in the banking business and other multinational enterprises. Tempted out of their middleman's role in the purchase and sale of foreign exchange, a few banks were known in years past to have taken fliers in the foreign exchange market, presumably adding thereby to the volatility of exchange rate movements.[32]

When officials have expressed their concern over the danger that non-bank multinational enterprises might also be engaged in currency speculation, the treasurers of such enterprises have commonly responded in a classic dialogue of the deaf. According to most treasurers, the only foreign exchange transactions they undertake are those required in the ordinary course of their business. Using that criterion, a treasurer ordinarily feels free to direct a foreign subsidiary in a threatened currency area to speed up its payments to the parent, lest the value of the remittances to the parent be reduced by a subsequent devaluation. On the other hand, a treasurer would feel uneasy about directing the sale of a threatened currency in amounts greater than the anticipated payments; in treasurers' terms, such sales would be thought of pejoratively as "speculation."

Anyone familiar with the problems of foreign exchange stability will recognize the treasurers' policy as the characteristic lead-and-lag phenomenon that often affects the stability of foreign exchange markets. Some tend to dismiss the lead-and-lag problem as one that cannot greatly upset the market. In their judgment, alert professional speculators and central bankers can be counted on to absorb any transitory disturbances brought about by such forces. On the other hand, those who put less store in the capacity of the market to muffle aberrant disturbances see the lead-and-lag phenomenon as a dangerous threat, capable of creating or enlarging unnecessary fluctuations in the exchange rate.

Moreover, there is widespread concern that the responsiveness of multinational enterprises to the lead-and-lag problem is greater than the responsiveness existing among independent buyers and sellers of different nationality or among lenders and borrowers dealing at arm's length. Multinational enterprises are big; being big, they can afford to set up facilities that routinely undertake transactions to reduce their foreign exchange risks. Besides, the propensity of the multinational enterprise to make such transactions may be increased because the enterprise need not involve another party in the execution; the decision of the enterprise to delay or accelerate a payment between affiliates can be made entirely in-house.

The practices that multinational enterprises actually follow in handling their foreign exchange transactions are just beginning to be explored. One study suggests that, at least in the crises over the German mark during the early 1970s, U.S.-owned subsidiaries in Germany may have added to the revaluation pressures building up at the time; at any rate, a considerable proportion of the 167 subsidiaries in the study managed by one means or another to build up their positions in the mark.[33] Two more comprehensive studies have attempted to determine the foreign exchange practices of multinational enterprises in a number of currencies, both strong and weak. Both of these studies were confined to U.S.-based enterprises, both covered a substantial sample of such enterprises, and both related to the early years of the 1970s.[34] One of the studies offers the finding that currency holdings in strong currencies were allowed to grow during periods of crisis. But neither study finds that multinational enterprises systematically reduced their exposure in currencies that appeared weak.

We are brought back once again to a familiar conclusion. Multinational enterprises have the potential for contributing substantially to the instability of currencies. So far as anyone can tell, the potential has remained just that and has not so far been realized. But that conclusion generates only a limited amount of comfort for those who fear that one day the dam may burst.

Until a very few years ago, the principal industrial countries that served as home base for multinational enterprises gave very little thought to the taxation of profits that these enterprises were earning abroad. To the extent that the tax problem arose in such countries, it was usually in the context of ensuring that "their" enterprises were not handicapped when doing battle with rival enterprises in foreign markets. Without much concern, therefore, firms doing business abroad could funnel their foreign earnings into foreign tax havens, thereby protecting them from the home tax collector. They could also bring their earnings home with the assurance that home taxes on such earnings would not be onerous.[35]

Although most industrialized countries have shared that general approach, the specific formulas they have used for taxing the foreign income of their home enterprises have varied considerably from one jurisdiction to the next. In the case of the United States, the basic principle has been that the U.S. government takes second place in the taxing queue. A U.S. parent is not obliged to pay U.S. taxes on the income of its foreign subsidiaries until that income is received in the form of dividends. When the U.S. parent figures its income-tax liability to the U.S. government arising out of income from its overseas units, it ordinarily deducts any income taxes that the overseas unit has paid to a foreign government, thereby reducing its U.S. tax liability by an equivalent amount. Other countries provide similar treatment—or in some cases even more generous treatment—by other formulas.

Of late, however, various home governments have begun taking a less benign view of the relatively liberal tax treatment accorded the offshore earnings of their enterprises. As is usual in such matters, the U.S. government has been in the lead in reexamining the implications of such liberal treatment.

One question has been whether, as a matter of equity, the U.S. government is getting an appropriate amount of taxes out of the foreign operations of its multinational enterprises. It has been noted, for instance, that in 1972, a typical year, U.S.-based enterprises paid only $1 billion to the U.S. government on their foreign income, yet in that year they generated $24 billion of taxable income abroad and paid $13 billion in taxes to foreign governments.[36]

U.S. concern over the paucity of tax payments by U.S. firms on their foreign income was in fact evident as early as 1962, when the U.S. Congress drastically curtailed the use of foreign tax havens by such firms. That early move was followed by the closer policing of transfer prices between the affiliates of multinational enterprises. The efforts of national authorities to fix transfer prices more equitably, however, have been inhibited by various factors. One is that any multinational enterprise obliged to allocate its profit among units located in different countries must make some important decisions that are wholly arbitrary. Take some important cost items in the enterprise. The units of any such enterprise commonly draw upon a central pool of information and experience; they commonly avail themselves of the network's collective credit rating; and they often exploit the system's pool of patents and trade names. How are the individual units to be charged for access to these common facilities?

The questions about the allocation of costs in a multinational system are matched by even more obscure questions about the allocation of benefits. The operations of any individual subsidiary in a multinational system commonly enhance the profits or reduce the risks of others in the system, yet often no way exists of reflecting that fact fairly in the income accounts of the individual units.

As long as no international rules exist on the allocation of costs and income, the tax decisions of any national authority accordingly must be arbitrary. Yet the consequences of unilateral action by any major country can be quite substantial. One analysis concludes, for instance, that the U.S. government could increase its annual tax revenues by several billion dollars simply by requiring U.S. parents to calculate their net profits from the operations of their subsidiaries according to certain reasonable principles.[37] Parent firms, for instance, might be required to assign to their foreign subsidiaries a proportionate share of central research and development costs as well as of central administrative costs.[38] If other governments refuse to recognize the validity of such assessments upon the subsidiaries, as some are likely to do, then the U.S.-based enterprise will be obliged to pay twice on the same income, a possibility that can raise the tax rate on the affected income close to the 100 percent level. If other governments relinquish their right to tax the profits, it will be an act of relinquishment under duress. Such acts have not been unknown in the economic relations of the industrialized countries. But the imposition of such measures—even the threat of the imposition of such measures—would represent another source of substantial tension among the industrialized countries.

Another issue raised by the taxation of foreign income, however, is based not on questions of equity but on questions of efficiency. The issue here is whether the various formulas for taxing foreign income have the effect of encouraging enterprises to invest more abroad and less at home than they should. Economists of the classical tradition have characteristically insisted that the tax structure of governments should be "neutral," that is to say, that the structure should be of such a kind as not to affect the investor's choice among competing opportunities for investment. When governments tax foreign income with a lighter hand than home income, according to the argument, the tax structure ceases to be neutral; it tips the investor's preferences toward foreign investment.

In the U.S. case, it has been noted, multinational enterprises engaged in manufacturing typically pay a smaller tax on their foreign income than on their home income, a difference that comes to several percentage points on the average.[39] This is the case because other industrialized countries generally tax business income at lower rates than those that apply in the United States. Accordingly, if a U.S. parent fails to bring back all the income that its subsidiaries have earned abroad, that income never takes the full brunt of the high U.S. tax rates. The result, so the argument goes, is that U.S.-based enterprises tend to overinvest abroad and underinvest at home.

While some economists have appealed to the neutrality principle to urge higher taxes on foreign income, labor interests in the United States have used less elaborate rationalizations for the same policy. Eager to discourage investment abroad, labor leaders have supported most measures that they think might serve the purpose.

The debate over taxes has yet another side. While some groups have argued that the U.S. tax structure has been driving U.S. investment abroad to the detriment of the domestic economy, others have insisted that a heavier U.S. tax on the foreign income of its enterprises would be hurtful to the economy at home.[40] They picture the overseas subsidiaries of U.S. enterprises as adjuncts to the U.S. economy, necessary for the acquisition of raw materials, the retention of markets, and the garnering of income on U.S. technology. As they see it, American firms must compete in foreign locations with the enterprises of other countries. To hobble U.S. enterprises with an especially heavy tax burden, according to the disputants on this side, would be to drive U.S. firms out of foreign areas and so would hurt the U.S. economy.

As is so common in debates over the multinational enterprise, the stridency on both sides in the tax dispute seems out of proportion to the practical importance of the issue. The contention that U.S. investment may be drawn abroad by a lower tax rate no doubt has a certain measure of validity. But there are numerous reasons for assuming that the influence of that factor is slight.[41] The long-term investor who must operate in a world of changing exchange rates and different national inflation rates is bound to weigh a few percentage points in an existing tax rate as an economic factor of only trivial significance. Besides, the motivations of multinational enterprises in setting up subsidiaries abroad, summarized in Chapters 3 and 4, are relatively impervious to small differences in current cost. To be sure, firms that have already determined to set up a subsidiary abroad for strategic reasons may prefer an overseas location with a lower tax rate. Moreover, firms with subsidiaries already operating abroad may go to some lengths to shelter the income of those subsidiaries from the U.S. tax authorities. But the basic decision on whether to establish a subsidiary abroad does not appear to be sensitive to the tax question. Nor does it seem likely, as the proponents on the other side of the debate have sometimes insisted, that many U.S. firms located abroad would pull back to the United States if the tax incidence on foreign income were raised by several percentage points. So threat and counterthreat seem considerably overdrawn.

Nonetheless, the mischief that can be produced in the future by the jungle of different national tax jurisdictions may prove to be considerable. The rapid increase in offshore earnings by the large enterprises of the world and the swift growth in the efficiency of national taxing authorities almost guarantee such a result. In some cases,

the tension will be manifested by disputes between national groups within the industrialized countries; in some
cases, by hauling and pulling between the authorities of
different countries. Without international action of some
sort, the problem seems intractable; with such action, it
seems only a little less difficult.

In formulating or executing most economic policies of
any consequence, planners in the advanced industrial
countries cannot ignore the multinational structure of industry. In issues of pricing, the existence of a multinational network often takes on central importance.

Multinational enterprises often have strong reasons
for setting themselves up in a vertically integrated structure, that is, as a chain of affiliates that stretches from the
processing of raw materials to the ultimate marketing of
finished products. Chains of this sort often cross international borders. As a result, a considerable proportion of
the merchandise imports and exports of the industrialized
countries—perhaps as much as one-third—actually consists of transfers among affiliated firms.

Although a transfer may be between two affiliated
firms that are part of a single multinational network, the
transaction must be carried out at a specific price. National customs agents and revenue officers insist upon a
price in order to measure tax liabilities; controllers inside
the network demand it in order to measure the efficiency
of the various affiliates and to maintain some sort of control over their operations. Nevertheless, when setting a
price in such circumstances, the multinational enterprise
is released from certain constraints that would ordinarily
inhibit an unintegrated business. Although the multinational system as a whole must make a profit in order to
survive, each of the affiliates in the system does not independently have to meet that test. Moreover, the price in
any given transaction between a pair of affiliates need not
be tested against competing offers in the open market.

Where a going market price exists for a product or service, that price often serves best in transactions between affiliates, but such a price does not always exist. Tailor-made components produced, say, by an IBM subsidiary for its foreign affiliates need not have a going market price. If such a price does exist, it may be a price created by the multinational enterprise itself, as in the case of replacement parts produced by General Motors for General Motors cars. Or it may be a price framed by just a few leaders located in different countries, with each leader tailoring its role to take account of the expected responses of the other leaders. So the multinational aspect of enterprises can have a considerable bearing on the setting of prices.

The plot thickens and the analysis grows more complex whenever countries go beyond the narrow question of interaffiliate pricing and try to understand how the operations of multinational enterprises affect their national markets in a more general way. That issue has arisen in forms bewilderingly diverse. One hypothesis, however, persistently recurs: when a number of different multinational enterprises find themselves in contact in the same foreign market, that contact can facilitate restrictions on competition that will affect markets both at home and in third countries. A preoccupation with this situation has surfaced both in Germany and in the United States.[42]

A number of good reasons support that concern. In many countries the national environment does not discourage collaboration, cooperation, or collusion. Even where a disposition exists to prevent anticompetitive practices, national authorities are disposed to tolerate cooperative arrangements among the producers of standardized products, such as oil, aluminum, and chemicals, which reduce seemingly unnecessary cross-hauling. In industries of this sort, leading firms commonly supply the needs of the customers of their putative competitors and expect the same service in return.[43] Beyond that, various nations are prepared to tolerate and even to encourage tighter patterns of cooperation among business firms. When enterprises cooperate in one market, that cooperation will reduce their incentive for warfare in other markets, because of the risk that the warfare will have spillover effects.

Another kind of assumption leads to the same conclusion. In some vertically integrated industries such as oil and copper, the most formidable barrier to entry often exists at a stage in the operations located outside of the home country. In oil, for instance, a newcomer needs to control large quantities of cheap foreign oil, and in copper, large deposits of rich foreign ore. When multinational enterprises control such sources abroad, competition can be reduced at home in various ways. If leading multinational firms develop offshore partnerships among themselves—such as ARAMCO in Saudi Arabia and Southern Peru Copper in Peru—the existence of the partnerships may dampen the quality of downstream competition in home markets by generating a common cost basis for the raw materials and a joint decision-making process regarding levels of production.[44] Moreover, national firms at home that simply want to refine, fabricate, and distribute products may have trouble getting their raw materials at prices and in quantities that will keep them in the competition.

As long as the multinational structure is tolerated and as long as key facilities of such enterprises are located abroad, national authorities may not be in a position to increase competition in their home markets. But if multinational enterprises were prohibited, so goes the argument, the activities that take place in home markets— refining and distribution in oil or fabricating in metal— might prove more competitive. That argument is what lies behind various legislative proposals to separate the

U.S.-based multinational oil companies from their foreign oil affiliates.[45]

The view that foreign ties among multinational enterprises may tend to subdue their competition in U.S. markets is exceedingly hard to test, but the available evidence does no violence to it. The difficulty with basing a national policy upon that view, however, is that it represents only the first step in any adequate analysis of the effects of multinational enterprises upon competition in U.S. markets. Recall some of the evidence, presented in Chapter 4, that the multinationalizing strategy of the U.S. leaders in many product lines had stimulated a follow-the-leader move by other U.S. firms in those lines. It was also suggested that the multinational surge of U.S. firms was inducing firms based in Europe and Japan to respond by setting up subsidiaries in the U.S. market, in an effort to reduce the threat posed by the U.S. firms' expansion. It is partly as a result of these processes—and partly for other reasons as well—that the number of effective sellers in numerous product lines seems to have increased substantially since the end of World War II. Accordingly, the proliferation of multinational enterprises in any national market confronts the policymaker with disparate tendencies, some suggesting the possibility of increased competition, some suggesting the opposite.

While the United States can be expected to test the effects of multinational enterprises by the yardstick of competition, other governments are likely to use different criteria. The European Economic Community's interest in fostering competition has been mainly to ensure that private arrangements among producers in Europe do not stifle the achievement of a European Common Market.[46] The national policies of Germany have come a little closer to the U.S. position, sometimes exhibiting the special fervor of a latter-day convert. But Germany has been known at times to reverse its field when German industry seemed handicapped in confronting foreign giants.[47] The United Kingdom has been less doctrinaire than either the United States or Germany, consciously distinguishing those cases in which it thought more competition would improve social performance from those cases in which it thought it would not. In the first situation, Britain has sought to enforce competition, and in the second, to encourage merger. France, too, has made this same distinction, at least in theory; in practice, it has generally followed the Cartesian tradition of opting for merger.[48] Japan has pursued yet another variant, tolerating a certain amount of competition inside its national market but restraining competition in its international trade.[49]

With the spread of multinational enterprises among the nations of North America and Europe, we might suppose that the disparate approaches of the various countries would produce some major confrontations in national policy. If a U.S. court were to order the dismemberment of a U.S. firm on the pattern of the Standard Oil dissolution of 1911, for instance, such a step could break up some subsidiary abroad into unrelated units; and if a French ministry were to order the merger of two unrelated U.S.-owned subsidiaries on French soil, this act could create its own unprecedented complications.

So far, the conflicts that have occurred have not been nearly so fundamental. In a number of antitrust proceedings, British and Dutch courts have sternly directed their firms not to comply with some official U.S. requests for information. In several other instances, U.S. authorities have irritated foreign governments either by refusing to allow foreign firms to buy a going U.S. business or by refusing to allow U.S. firms to buy a going foreign business.[50] But none of these disputes so far has been elevated to the level of high politics.

Still, in a world in which oligopolies are rapidly becoming global in their scope, national policies and preferences with regard to market structure are bound to find themselves increasingly at loggerheads. This will lead either to conflict or to impotence—or, conceivably, to both. So far, with multinational enterprises, the differences among nations can be said to have led to impotence. The United States has subordinated its aspirations for competition, the Europeans have scaled down their earlier hopes of increased efficiency through merger, and the Japanese have felt a pervasive sense of vulnerability in an increasingly open world.[51]

Apart from feeling uneasy about the structure of their industry and their markets, the governments of the industrialized countries have found themselves obliged to address numerous other problems surrounding the management of multinational enterprises. One of these, vividly illustrated by the oil crisis of 1973, has been the protection of supplies of materials vital to the economy.

Looking back at the period from the middle 1950s to the early 1970s, we are struck by how little thought the governments of the advanced countries gave to the issue of protecting vital supplies. From time to time, it is true, the U.S. government worried a little about its growing reliance on the importation of critical materials, but it rarely considered the implications of the nation's relying upon multinational networks to perform the task of importation. An occasional sally by Italy or France against the U.S.-based oil companies operating in Europe was all that disturbed the comparative serenity of the period.[52]

When the oil crisis of the 1970s emerged full-blown, the limited capacity of governments to deal with the provisioning of vital materials became immediately evident. No government possessed the kind of data an operating agency would need for overseeing the day-to-day conduct of the international oil industry. The problem was not so much a lack of facts as it was the sheer complexity of the business. That complexity made informed discussion and

reliable interpretation of the oil situation especially difficult, except among a few experts.[53]

As it turned out, that particular emergency was well
handled. If official neglect were ever benign in outcome,
this was surely the outstanding case. Proceeding without
conscious strategy or plan, governments allowed each international oil company to grapple with its own supply
problems. If the companies operated pursuant to any
principle, it was the principle of avoiding intolerable
strains in the marketplace, dubbed by some observers the
principle of "equal suffering." The result, according to
various studies subsequently undertaken, was that the
transitory pinch in supplies of late 1973 and early 1974
was distributed in a remarkably uniform way among the
major national markets of the world.

Once the acute phase of the oil crisis had subsided,
the alignment of forces in the international oil market still
contained many of the elements that had existed before
the crisis. Despite the nominal loss of ownership of their
oil supplies, the leading international companies still
manage the movement of more than half of the oil in international markets and still retain their basic partnership
in Iran, Saudi Arabia, Kuwait, and other major producing
areas. In short, they still occupy the dual position of principal adversary and principal partner of the oil-exporting
countries and still represent a key factor for the time being
in maintaining stability in the international oil market.

Moreover, as far as the oil-importing countries are
concerned, the prospects for the future role of the oil companies are not greatly changed. An International Energy
Agency has been created which could play an important
role in any new crisis, but its intention quite clearly is to
lean heavily on the machinery that lies under the companies' control.[54] In any new emergency, it appears, the international companies will continue to manage the international oil market, exercising their power with due
deference to various international bodies such as OPEC

and IEA. But bodies such as these, at least as they are presently conceived by their members, are incapable of taking over the essential management functions of the companies. And herein lies a latent problem that fills many national groups with a sense of great unease.

The case of oil is illustrative of a more general proposition that has begun to trouble the national governments of various industrialized countries. Whenever national governments use multinational enterprises as an executive arm carrying out national policies, they must recognize that the enterprises on which they rely have interests that extend beyond the borders of any single country.

In some cases, to be sure, that fact is helpful from the public viewpoint. Consider, for example, the various programs in the industrialized states aimed at building up the backward areas of the national economies. Britain, France, and Italy have all had schemes to persuade enterprises—any enterprises, national or multinational—to settle in such areas. In Canada and the United States, the provinces and the states have pushed programs of a similar sort.

The propensity of foreign-owned firms to respond to regional development schemes could be seen repeatedly in various European states during the 1950s and 1960s, as U.S.-owned subsidiaries set themselves up in Scotland, the Italian Mezzogiorno, and the backward corners of France and the Low Countries.[55] A somewhat similar tendency for some foreign-owned enterprises to move easily into backward areas could also be glimpsed occasionally in the United States and Canada, as Volkswagen, BASF, Michelin, and other firms responded to the blandishments of subsidized credit and capital facilities offered by local development agencies. For various technical reasons, it has proved difficult to measure exactly how much the "foreignness" characteristic of these enterprises has contributed to their willingness to select the more remote corners of their host countries and how much is explained

by other factors, such as the mix of industries represented, but there is no doubt that foreignness has played
some role in such decisions.

Once a foreign-owned facility has established itself
in a country, however, the geographical mobility that
exists inside the network of multinational enterprises
begins to play its disconcerting role. National authorities
can never feel quite sure how long they can expect the
foreign-owned subsidiary to stay put.

The capacity of multinational enterprises to set up facilities in other countries has been somewhat disconcerting for all industrialized countries, but it has hit Europe
with special force. In increasing numbers, European firms
pushed by the need for survival and growth have been
setting up subsidiaries in other markets, including the
United States. As Europe's subsidiaries have grown, the
managerial attention of Europe's national firms has been
diverted from the home market. Subsidiaries in the
United States have been especially distracting; the vast
size of the U.S. market has sometimes given those subsidiaries a weight that allows them to challenge the control of the parent at home.[56] Although national firms have
rarely abandoned their home base in favor of another, a
tone of distraction has sometimes crept into their responses when they have been invited by their home
ministries to concentrate on some national project. And
that inescapable consequence, when seen through the
eyes of national observers, has invited dark, accusatory
reactions, filled with implications of disloyalty and un-
trustworthiness.[57]

By various bypaths, therefore, we are brought back
again to a generalization made repeatedly in these pages.
The capacity of any government to command a particular
firm to undertake a specified task in support of a public
policy, such as settling in a backward region or holding
down a key price, has been reduced; large firms now have

a capacity that they never had before for choice between competing nations. At the same time, the number of multinational enterprises operating in any major sector of industry in the industrialized countries has tended to increase over the years. Accordingly, more enterprises exist to which a government can turn for the discharge of some national task. In some situations, the proliferation in the number of enterprises can prove to be the controlling factor and can increase the powers of government; in other situations, the increased mobility of enterprises can be the controlling factor and can weaken the powers of government. We cannot be sure of the net effect without specifying the nature of the problem and the style of governance of the country concerned. Meanwhile, however, governments in the rich industrialized countries seem more conscious of the weakening aspects of the new situation. This consciousness has increased their sense of tension as they confront the multinationalizing trend.

Yet none of these concerns and tensions quite captures the real uneasiness of our times. The 1970s, as scholars never tire of emphasizing, are a period in which the consequences of industrialization are being seriously questioned. As numerous polls demonstrate, North Americans and Europeans show a remarkably low measure of commitment to the leading institutions of industrial societies: government, business, political parties, and the traditional church organizations. Although U.S. society, as its political leaders sonorously proclaim, still clings to the title of "acknowledged leader of the free world," its stock has gone down with all the rest. And the Soviet Union, trying to hold on to its leadership role in the socialist world, has not fared any better.

The causes of the pervasive mood of alienation are variously identified as the Vietnam war, pollution, crowding, social inequities, and all the disconcerting aspects of modern life. Whatever the causes, the extent of that alienation has been higher in recent years than at any

time since World War II.[58] It pervades not only the United
States but also the big and little countries of Europe.
Because the questioning is partly generational in its ori-
gins, it also seems to have some hold in the communist
countries, manifested in such aberrant phenomena as
Russian hooliganism and China's Red Guard riots.

The multinational enterprise cannot escape the consequences of the pervasive unease in the industrialized
world. It is visible, powerful, and influential. It is thought
of mainly as a product of the American culture. So it
stands on the barricades with the other questioned sym-
bols of contemporary industrial society.

7 | The Strain on National Objectives: The Developing Countries

DEFINING the national objectives of the developing countries entails a double challenge.

First, the so-called developing countries are an extraordinarily heterogeneous lot, whose differences are more evident than their similarities. Some, like Libya, are very rich; some, like India, Mexico, and Brazil, are well along in the process of industrialization; some, like Algeria, have a highly developed public sector; some, like Thailand and Colombia, have a rich national tradition and national history; but many in the group have neither income nor industry nor public sector nor national history. Accordingly, what binds the group of a hundred or so countries together is what they are not. They are not highly industrialized, and they are not members of the Organization for Economic Cooperation and Development, the rich man's club among international organizations.

Identifying the national goals of so diverse a group is complicated by another factor. Diversity is the dominant characteristic not only among these countries as a group but also within each of them. Although Libya may be rich, many of its people live in a culture and at a standard of living not greatly different from those that prevailed a thousand years ago; although Mexico is well along toward industrialization, the income per head in its poorest state is about one-tenth the income per head in its richest.

The goals of these countries are difficult to define for still another reason. In most countries of the group, the institutions that formulate and articulate national objectives are under the control of a small, atypical sector of the population. That, of course, is a chronic situation in all countries, rich or poor, developed or otherwise, but it is encountered in particularly acute form in the developing countries. In the socialist economies, such as those of Guinea, Mozambique, and Cuba, the function of defining and formulating national goals is assumed by a small political cadre. In the regimes of more ambiguous political structure, as in Pakistan, India, Korea, and the Philippines, independent expression has no effective way of making itself heard; the only articulation of national objectives is the official version. Elsewhere, where freedom of expression does exist in a formal sense, economic factors typically limit its exercise to a comparative handful— a few opposition politicians, some journalists, and some intellectuals.

Despite all these problems of definition, certain common factors and common convictions do exist among the poor countries and condition their views of the multinational enterprise.

Most of the hundred or so countries of the developing world think of themselves as new nations. Most of the countries on the African continent are literally new. For many others, the sense of newness reflects mainly a feeling that they may be for the first time in a position to shape their own future.

From a cultural and historical viewpoint, of course, many developing countries are ancient nations and are deeply conscious of that fact. But their ancient achievements were dimmed during the nineteenth century by the hegemony of Europe and the United States over Africa, Asia, and Latin America, and many of these countries see themselves as having emerged again only within the past decade or two.

The changes in perspective of the government leaders of the developing countries have been apparent in many ways. In foreign affairs, the restraints imposed by the gunboat diplomacy of the Americans and the Europeans had already begun to lose their force in the 1960s, and by the early 1970s, as the events of the oil crisis vividly demonstrated, those restraints no longer counted for much. Accordingly, the rulers of the developing countries are now playing the diplomatic game with intensity and commitment. Organizations such as the Group of Seventy-seven, OPEC, and a myriad of African, Asian, and Latin American regional groups have pitted themselves against the United States or the OECD or the international copper companies or some other power. At the same time, following the textbook strategies of Europe and America, the poor countries have seized on the possibilities of playing one industrialized countries against another, especially the United States against the USSR. Here and there, a few have sensed opportunities to change their role from sardine to shark by establishing new hegemonies over other countries in the developing world, as India has done over Sikkim, Nepal, and Bhutan, and Algeria over the western Sahara. They have, in short, been elevated to full membership in the unceasing rivalry among nations.

The business classes in the developing countries have also felt the impact of the increase in national options.[1] As the new countries have weakened their links with the enterprise economies of North America and Europe, some of them have begun to think of developing alternative economic systems based on the principles of the command economies of the Soviet Union and China or of the Socialist economies of Yugoslavia and Algeria. In some cases, therefore, local businessmen have confronted the threat of being displaced by public enterprise. On the

other hand, new opportunities also are being opened up
for local businessmen, not unlike the increased opportunities available to government leaders. Governments
have been ready to close their borders to foreign imports:
in the first stage, to simple consumer products such as
batteries and biscuits; in later stages, to more complex
products such as chemicals and metals. And many local
businessmen on the Asian subcontinent and in Latin
America have profited from the new wave of opportunities.

The existence of multinational enterprises has had
diverse effects on the opportunities of local businessmen.
In some cases, multinational enterprises have been quick
to set up their subsidiaries inside the protected markets,
thereby squelching the chances of local entrepreneurs.
But the presence of foreign-owned enterprises has also
generated some added benefits for local businessmen: opportunities to act as contractors, suppliers, and distributors; opportunities to extract a junior partnership, sometimes on bargain terms; opportunities eventually to take
over a foreign-owned enterprise, sometimes by enlisting
the help of the national government and sometimes on
the basis of the local businesses' own growing capabilities.

Accordingly, in many of the new countries, the local
business class has rapidly come to reflect growing con-
fidence and competence.[2] Even in countries in which the
relative position of the foreign-owned enterprises is expanding and acquisitions of local enterprises are com-
monplace, as in Mexico and Brazil, the local business class
displays a new ebullience and drive.[3]

Other elements of the national leadership in the new
countries seem to be moving in the same direction. In the
arts, in literature, in music, and in journalism, it had been
London, Paris, Rome, and New York that historically set
the ground rules and provided the arena for international
competition. But that dominance, too, has begun to break

down. Even in the 1920s, Mexico displayed signs of the new relation, as Rivera and his followers developed a distinctive art form. In the succeeding decades, a torrent of poetry, literature, and art has come pouring out of Latin America, Africa, and Asia, exhibiting qualities suggesting the beginnings of a cultural independence.

Accordingly, even when vast ideological differences have existed among the various leadership groups within any developing country, those groups have held a common view on one important point: their increased sense of national identity and national choice is precious and is to be nurtured and protected.

Even as the leaders of the developing countries have gained a sense of identity and independence, they still have had to reckon with the constraints of their nations' various ties with the outside world: international trade; international licensing; economic agreements with command economies, such as that of the Soviet Union, whose capacity for central control has made them especially powerful in economic negotiations; and the operations of the world's multinational enterprises.

Multinational enterprises differ from other international links in one critical respect: their involvement in the internal economy. Unlike trade or licensing or government-to-government trade agreements, the operations of such enterprises are a part of the local economy itself.

The distinctive position of the multinational enterprises has been further set apart in some developing countries by an added fact. The leaders of the countries have characteristically reacted from a set of ideologies and values that reject the multinational enterprise as an institution. Multinational enterprises or something like them have had a prominent place in the various theories of imperialism ever since Hobson's pioneer work on the subject three-quarters of a century ago. The intellectual link has been repeatedly renewed and strengthened in the works of others, notably Lenin, Frank, Kolko, and

Galtung.[4] These theories as a rule link the multinational enterprise intimately with the government of the country in which the parent is located, and they see the policies of enterprise and government as inextricably related. According to such theories, the government needs the economic power of the enterprise to help extend its political reach, and the enterprise needs the government to protect it from other hegemonic governments, as well as to help maintain orderly conditions when stability is threatened.[5] Inevitably, the issues at stake in these theories are much larger than the question of the survival of multinational enterprises; they include questions about the ownership of productive assets, the choice of representative government, and the protection of human rights.

The multinational enterprise has proved an especially provocative factor in the ideological debate, however. Foreign investors have demonstrated an unsurprising preference for a stable and friendly economic environment. In a number of developing countries that preference has meant that multinational enterprises have expanded their activities sharply immediately after a rightist government has taken power or have reduced their activities immediately after a leftist regime has taken control.[6] A second point, less well documented but hardly in doubt, is that inside the developing countries the supporters of foreign-owned enterprises have come mainly from the antisocialist end of the national political spectrum.

The hostility of many leaders in the developing countries toward multinational enterprises, however, has often been based on factors that have familiar counterparts in more industrialized countries. Industrialization has been accompanied by a sharp increase in the visible rich, all the more striking because of the concurrent existence of urban and rural poverty.[7] Other concomitants are apparent: unremitting huckstering of trivial wares by billboard, radio, and television; insouciant pollution of air and water by some industrial producers, a few of whom belligerently insist on their inherent right to so continue; and the endemic use of influence, bribes, and extortion by public figures and private sellers.

Corruption, pollution, and shoddy production are much in evidence in all sorts of industrializing societies, both socialist and capitalist. Nevertheless, public opinion in many developing countries is bound to link the seamier side of the industrialization process with the operations of multinational enterprises. The multinationals are much larger enterprises on the whole than those that are only national in scope, with bigger, more visible, and more capital-intensive plants, as well as bigger advertising campaigns. In the host countries, they have borne the special burden of being foreigners, and in the United States, if not elsewhere, the additional burden of being big. Accordingly, wherever they appear, they are seen as epitomizing the disconcerting ills that seem constantly to dilute the gains from industrialization.[8]

Further, in the minds of leaders in developing countries, whatever their political coloration, the power of the multinational enterprises has been associated with the power of the countries in which the enterprises have been headquartered. As the rich countries lost some of their power to coerce or persuade during the 1950s and 1960s, the multinational enterprises in developing countries became more vulnerable, easier to attack without fear of retaliation. No multinational enterprise was wholly immune from the new aggressiveness, but U.S. firms did bear a somewhat heavier burden. This unwanted distinction no doubt reflected a widespread feeling in the developing countries that during the 1950s and 1960s the Americans were fallen from a higher state of grace to much greater depths than most other countries.

Multinational enterprises, therefore, have served as unwitting and unwilling lightning rods for a number of quite different forces in the developing countries. Their presence has drawn the hostility of those eager to develop a strong national identity free of outside influence, those repelled by the costs of industrialization, those at war with capitalism as a system, and those distrustful of the politics of the rich industrialized states, especially the United States. Such feeling has been strongest among those to whom these issues are most important—the leaders of various national groups, for instance, more than those in the lower reaches of national life.[9] At the upper levels, this shared feeling has created a common cause in which government and business leaders in the developing countries can join with philosophers and revolutionaries.

For those who know history, none of this is very new. In the 1850s a German observer was already complaining, "The treasures in our country's soil thus serve to increase the capitalist dominance of foreigners, nourishing the foreign capitalist through the fruits of German labor . . ."[10] In 1904 the foreign minister of Rumania was saying, "Guard yourself against the Standard Oil Trust and all those that are in league with her." By 1910 the new industrialists of czarist Russia were already hard at work to clip the wings of the European-owned enterprises in their country.[11]

What is new, however, is the drastic change in the degree of exposure of the developing countries both to the opportunities and to the threats of the outside world. A country determined to shape its own future no longer has much opportunity for choosing a splendid isolation, except at a cost most countries would reject. All the forces of contact have grown more powerful than they were a few decades ago: examples are the power of multinational enterprises to thrust their way into a developing country on the basis of a unique technology or mastery of scale or capacity for research; and the power of some developing countries to slough off a multinational enterprise by reaching out to an alternative source of capital or technology or customers.

So far in the changing equilibrium between those two increasing sources of power, the multinational enterprises have enlarged their position in the developing countries, a growth that has added to the sense of tension. But other manifestations of interdependence have also grown. Developing countries have dramatically increased their foreign licensing, their foreign borrowing, and their attachments to overseas distribution networks. Some of these new arrangements have not been as deeply entangling as the old; for instance, some licenses can be acquired with a one-time lump-sum payment. Some surely have not entailed acute feelings of handicap and inferiority. But the need to negotiate for a steady stream of money and technology and for widened access to a foreign market has been inescapable.

The apparent inability of the developing countries to avoid a state of dependence on the markets of the industrialized world was driven home with particular force in 1975, as the markets of the industrialized countries went into a slump. By that time, many developing countries had managed to build up a substantial volume of exports in manufactured goods to these markets. Some, such as Brazil, depended heavily upon foreign-owned subsidiaries to handle their exports; [12] some, such as India, relied upon seemingly independent national firms. As usual, the exposure of the country to outside forces could be more easily pinpointed and personified when multinational enterprises were involved; so Volkswagen could be singled out for special criticism when an export order originally intended for execution by its Brazilian subsidiary was eventually assigned to its German plants. [13] Ultimately, however, the distinction did not seem to matter very much. The impact of the slump on the manufactured-goods exports of developing countries seemed unrelated to whether the countries relied upon multinational enterprises or avoided such reliance. Brazil seemed to ride out the storm in spectacular style, for instance, while Mexico did poorly. And India did well, while Pakistan suffered.[14]

The explicit articles of indictment that the new countries have drawn up against the multinational enterprise cannot, in my opinion, be understood without these pervasive and universal factors in mind. Some of the problems that burden developing countries seem to have little to do with the multinational characteristics of foreign-owned subsidiaries; some seem trivial if taken at face value; others rest on unsupported assumptions; still others are flatly at variance with a formidable body of contrary facts. But the forces that have led to the indictment are far from trivial, for they stem from the basic ambitions of the leaders in the developing countries and from the deep-seated concerns of many others over the future of those countries. The more explicit points of contention that the poor countries voice in their debates over the multinational enterprise, therefore, often represent nothing more than semantic handholds, tactical sallies in a struggle that arises from much more fundamental sources.

Nearly all nations accept the proposition that the developing countries, at the present stage of history, are entitled to some measure of preferential treatment and assistance in international economic affairs. Some would base the entitlement on past history, an indemnification of sorts for the exploitive policies of the colonial countries in the past two or three centuries. Some would justify the treatment in pragmatic terms; they are concerned that the developing countries may "turn communist" or take other measures hurtful to the industrialized countries. Some simply hope to reduce the gap in income between rich and poor states.

Inevitably, however, the leaders of the developing countries are determined to establish that they are entitled to these small benefits and much more not as a matter of charity but as a matter of right. In the debate that ensues, the multinational enterprises find themselves cast in a central role as the instruments of past injustices and present inequalities.

One charge in the characteristic indictment is that many multinational enterprises established themselves in the economies of the developing countries on terms that reflected the unequal bargaining positions of the parties at the time of entry.

On casual analysis multinational enterprises seem to have set themselves up for business in developing countries under enormously varied circumstances. United Fruit backed into the banana business in Central America during the last years of the nineteenth century because its original venture, building a railroad into the interior, was badly in need of a source of freight.[15] Firestone set up its vast rubber plantations in the empty Liberian hinterland as a way of breaking the control of the international rubber cartel.[16] In many other cases, the investment decisions of multinational enterprises in developing countries have often approached conditioned reflexes, instinctive reactions calculated to fend off some threat or to match the initiative of a rival firm.

As a rule, however, the early multinational enterprises knew a little more about their risks and opportunities in the developing countries than did the government officials they confronted. When setting up plantations or mines producing materials to be marketed in the industrialized countries, for instance, the multinational enterprises were responding to the conditions of a distant market with which the host countries had had scarcely any contact.

By the 1920s, however, it was already apparent that

the knowledge gap was shrinking fast. The level of discussions between Mexican government officials and
foreign oil companies during the 1920s suggests a high
degree of sophistication on the Mexican side.[17] The same
impression can be gleaned from the negotiations between
Iraq and the international oil companies in the 1930s over
complex provisions of their concession contracts, as well
as from the negotiations with Venezuela in the 1940s over
the repartitioning of crude-oil profits and the negotiations
with Libya in the 1950s over the grant of new concessions.[18]

As I read the historical evidence and reflect on the
meaning of the negotiations I have seen at first hand during the past twenty years, the question of relative knowledge seems to have been a subordinate factor in determining outcome. The objective positions of the parties
have been much more important. And when those positions have changed, the probability that the terms would
be brought into line with the change has been fairly
high.[19] From time to time, one could detect signs of neg-
ligence on the part of government officials, including an
unwillingness to use the available services of experts and
an indifference to the implications of the available information. From time to time, too, the smell of extortion or of
bribery has hung heavily over one arrangement or another in the developing countries. But these factors go
only a little way toward explaining the terms of arrangements between multinational enterprises and developing
countries.

At the outset of any new project in a developing
country, both the government and the foreign-owned enterprise are likely to see the undertaking as a relatively
risky affair entailing a large gamble and an uncertain outcome. In many cases that perception is quite in accord
with reality, especially for mammoth projects in the raw-
materials field. For instance, the Toquepala copper mine
in Peru did not come into production until $12 million

had been spent on feasibility studies over a ten-year period, to be followed by $237 million in capital investment. The Bougainville copper project entailed five years of study, followed by a $350 million capital commitment.[20] And INCO's new nickel facilities in Indonesia promise to cost over $800 million.

When undertakings such as these are abandoned or fail, that is the end of the matter; the consequences are absorbed by the stockholders of the parent company and by the taxing authorities in the parent's home jurisdiction. When the initial risks are overcome, however, and the capital is put in place, the attitudes of both parties— business and government—undergo a basic change. The capital has been sunk; the initial risks have been overcome. The project now offers much more promise to the enterprise; the terms now seem much less reasonable to the government. The struggle is on to shift the terms toward the new point of negotiating equilibrium.

This pattern—sometimes dubbed the pattern of the obsolescing bargain—also applies to some extent to less risky and less spectacular undertakings by foreign-owned enterprises in developing countries, such as those involving manufacturing and service operations. Where technology has been the strong entry suit of the multinational enterprise, the eventual diffusion of the technology to other firms has generally reduced the technological preeminence of the original holder; where supplies of capital have been its strong point, the sinking of the capital has generally weakened the firm's position.

The struggle of the adversaries to adjust their existing bargain to their new negotiating positions has usually been accompanied by appeals on both sides to higher principle. On the side of the enterprises, the appeal has typically been to the sanctity of contract. On the side of the governments, the contention, in one variant or another, has been that the original arrangements were unfair, being the product of inequality, duress, or fraud.

Perhaps the most durable and most nearly universal of the claims regarding inequality has been the well-known contention of the developing countries that the prices of raw materials tend to decline over the course of time in their relation to the prices of manufactured products. A ton of copper, according to the argument, will buy fewer tractors in 1976 than in 1956. This assumption, brilliantly developed as a general hypothesis by Raúl Prebisch a quarter of a century ago, is based partly on the view that the industrialized countries effectively restrict competition in the sale of their products, whereas the developing countries are unable to match those restrictions.

In the passionate interchanges over this issue, facts have as usual counted for very little. Numerous attempts have been made to determine if Prebisch's early assumptions about the declining terms of trade for raw materials have any basis in hard fact. All told, the studies seemed to show an indeterminate relationship between the price of raw materials and the price of manufactured goods.[21] Indeed, on the available data, it appears slightly easier to sustain the opposite proposition, namely, that the prices of manufactured goods have been declining in relative terms.[22] The imperviousness of the debate to facts such as these, however, in no way impugns the sincerity with which developing countries address the question of fairness. All that it demonstrates is that the discontent of the developing countries is much more deep-seated and more general than any of the specific arguments—that the arguments themselves are mere surrogates for other causes.

The terms-of-trade argument is linked to the multinational enterprise issue by the dominance of such enterprises in the export of certain raw materials such as oil, copper, bauxite, and bananas. In these products the exporting enterprises generally have had some degree of control over the prices at which the raw materials were sold. That control, as a rule, was possible because the exporting firms were selling some of their output to affiliates in their own multinational networks.

In actual practice, multinational enterprises have sometimes used their control to hold export prices down, sometimes to keep them high. Whether their interests are better served by a high export price or by a low export price has varied from one product to the next depending on such factors as the organization of the industry and the nature of the production and distribution process. In crude oil the multinational companies have preferred to export from the developing countries at a high price, not a low one.[23] In copper ore, the U.S.-based multinationals and the European-based multinationals have had rather different preferences. For complex reasons, the Americans have leaned toward a price lower than the open-market price, whereas the Europeans have been willing to export at prices that reflect more of the market's volatile swings.[24] In bauxite, for which no open market exists, the market price has had practical importance only insofar as it has determined the tax liability of the aluminum companies to the countries in which the bauxite is mined. Here, the practice—as far as is known—is to peg the price to its principal manufacture, pig aluminum, a practice that seems to stem from the preferences of both the firms and the countries concerned.

But the debate over the fairness of policies of multinational enterprises has not been confined to the price issue. With the price of the raw material given and the profits from extraction set, the debate has centered on the division of the profits between the enterprises and the host countries. Here, too, the debate has assumed an abstract quality and seems almost impervious to the facts. Once again, I would be inclined to reject the easy explanation that the debaters are disingenuous and to suspect instead that they implicitly realize that this portion of the debate also stands for a larger set of issues.

On the facts, the multinational enterprises that export raw materials from the poor countries have characteristically been the leading members of an oligopoly, dedicated to the proposition that the prices of their final products should be high and stable. In oil, that outcome has translated itself quite directly into higher profits at the raw-material stage than a competitive market would be expected to produce. In aluminum, the outcome has not been clear, and the question is one of intense dispute. In copper, the pattern has been complex, and no easy generalization will serve.[25] In any event, between the 1940s and the 1970s the poor countries managed by one means or another to enlarge their share of the profits: in oil, by spectacular amounts; in other products, to a more limited degree. The outcome was not the result of a tide of fraternal goodwill on the part of the multinational enterprises but of a weakening in their bargaining position. In general the increased number of entrants in the raw-material industries, coupled with the improvement in international communications, helped to tilt the negotiating balance. Nonetheless, the multinational enterprises and the developing countries remained united on one cardinal point. Both recognized that their interests lay in high and stable prices, even if the division of the rewards was gradually shifting in favor of the developing countries.[26]

The debate over the division of profits has involved not only the sale of raw materials by the units of multinational enterprises but also the transactions of manufacturing subsidiaries in the developing countries. Various studies confirm that the transfer-pricing practices of multinational enterprises in the manufacturing industries follow a complex pattern.[27] The effect in the end is sometimes to lay a special cost burden on local subsidiaries, sometimes to relieve them of a burden.[28] For some years, nevertheless, one study has dominated the discussion of transfer pricing in developing countries. This study is an unusual investigation of the pricing of pharmaceuticals sold during 1968 and 1969 to the Colombian subsidiaries and licensees of multinational enterprises.[29] Various studies for other countries and other periods had already established the point that the pricing of the drug companies, when measured by the standards of other industries, seemed to generate unusually high profit margins,[30] but the Colombian study produced results that fell outside the range of prior expectations.

The reasons for the unusual Colombian results emerged slowly. At the time, Colombia had placed a ceiling on the remission of profits by foreign companies, a practice that had not yet grown common among developing countries. Moreover, the ceiling was couched in terms that fell with particularly heavy weight on the drug companies. Stated in terms of a return on local investment, the ceiling made no allowances for the drug companies' investment in product development and trade names. Colombia also set price ceilings on the local resale of drugs, using a formula that took into account the imported cost of the product. In these special circumstances, the multinational drug companies had unusually strong incentives to set high prices on products sold to their Colombian affiliates and licensees, and, according to the data, that is what they did. Using these figures as a basis for extrapolation, Constantine Vaitsos and others produced various exotic estimates of the costs of overpricing to the Latin American economy.

Although the extraordinary pricing of the drug companies took place in unusual circumstances, the companies themselves had no reason to clarify the reasons for their practices. Being hung for a sheep instead of a lamb would not have improved their position. Attacks on the Vaitsos study, therefore, centered on its relatively uninhibited techniques of extrapolation and did little to clarify the basic reasons why the results might be atypical.[31]

With representative data so limited, the persistence of the claim of unfair and exploitative profits is easy to understand. Many subsidiaries of multinational enterprises operate in small markets that are protected from imports. Accordingly, they levy prices that are generally much higher than those at home and in some cases produce goods aimed at an affluent market in a poor society. Nevertheless, the surface indications of the profit rates of these subsidiaries have been blandly disarming. For U.S.-owned subsidiaries engaged in manufacturing in the developing countries, annual profits after the payment of taxes to the host government have amounted to a little less than 15 percent of book investment. With royalties and fees thrown in as if they were profits to the parent, the ratio might be thought of as a little over 16 percent; with a generous allowance for other sources of profit to the parent, such as profits from the sale of intermediate products to the enterprise, it might be thought of as 20 percent.[32]

Figures purporting to show the profit margins of the subsidiaries of multinational enterprises are not always to be taken very seriously. When a manufacturing subsidiary is deeply embedded in the global network of a multinational enterprise, any separate accounting for the subsidiary is permeated by arbitrary assumptions. The earning power of a subsidiary of International Harvester or Philips Electric in any market, for instance, depends heavily on the nature of the multinational network to which the subsidiary belongs, including its store of information, trademarks, trade names, patents, and capital facilities all over the world. In any calculations of a return on investment to any subsidiary, both the system's profits and the system's investments must be partitioned among the various subsidiaries. Accordingly, both the numerator and the denominator of the return-on-investment ratio are results of arbitrary—unavoidably arbitrary—assignments of income and capital.

Over the course of the years a considerable amount has been learned about these allocative practices, afford-

ing insight into the meaning of the figures finally produced.[33] In the early life of a manufacturing subsidiary in
a developing country, for instance, the parent firm appears
to exercise a certain restraint when levying payments for
access to the system's global store of information, operating systems, trademarks, trade names, patents, and
credit. The motivation for that early restraint can only be
inferred, but it seems to be due to a recognition at headquarters that the early years of a subsidiary's life are likely
to be burdened by the special costs of the learning process. Reluctant to saddle a local manager with the psychological impact of apparent failure, headquarters staffs
have been known to use one distortion in accounting as a
means of offsetting another; they have undercharged for
the services of the multinational system in order to reduce
the impact of the learning-cost charges. But that forbearance has been apparent only in the early years; when subsidiaries have come of age, parents have been much more
exacting in their financial demands on them.[34] From the
viewpoint of host countries, therefore, the parent-sub-
sidiary relation has generated a wide range of outcomes.

From the concepts of fairness let us turn to those of
profit and loss. Various attempts have been made to calculate in hard, quantitative terms just what the developing countries have been getting out of the operations of
the multinational enterprises. That question has had analysts looking once again at the profit-and-loss figures with
a technical question in mind: How can the figures be ad-
justed to reflect the "true" profits of the subsidiaries?

Despite the inherently arbitrary nature of that calcu-
lation, numerous disinterested efforts to find an answer
have been made. Beginning with the assumption that the
published rates of return are prima facie implausible,
some analysts have looked for items inappropriately allo-
cated between the subsidiaries and their parents. One
common assumption has been that the license fees and

administrative charges that parents often levy on their
subsidiaries are actually profits to the parent in another
form, that is, income garnered by the parent without any
added cost; accordingly, these have been added back into
the parents' profits.[35] Another characteristic assumption,
mentioned earlier, has been that parents overcharge their
subsidiaries for products sold to them or that parents pay
too little for products bought from the subsidiaries.
That assumption has been a little harder to quantify as
a rule, but has commonly been thought to justify a generous further boost in the declared profit rates of the subsidiaries.

As has already been suggested, these assumptions
have been quite in accord with the facts in some cases.
The studies of the transfer pricing of pharmaceuticals in
Colombia, whatever their technical limitations may be,
still point strongly in that direction. Further, that multinational enterprises commonly maintain sales subsidiaries in tax-haven countries adds still another thread
to the argument.[36]

On the other hand it is not clear that the understa-
tements of the profits of subsidiaries in developing countries are any stronger than the overstatements of profits.
Indeed, U.S. tax authorities are apparently convinced that
U.S. parents have been failing to charge their foreign subsidiaries for various services that in the open market
would ordinarily entitle them to substantial revenue, including the access of the subsidiary to research results,
patent rights, and trademark rights. It is hard to say,
therefore, what kind of adjustment is needed to bring the
published figures closer to some sort of unbiased reality.
The conventional adjustments to which I referred earlier,
which generally raise the declared profits of the subsidiaries to roughly twice their reported level, are simply
guesses based on the principle that all the uncertainties in
the data should be resolved in favor of raising the estimated profits of the subsidiaries.

Estimating the profits of the subsidiaries, however, represents only one step on the way to answering a larger question: How would the developing countries have fared if the subsidiaries had not been established? As a rule, serious analysts try to answer that question by developing one single figure that will stand for all the economic costs and benefits associated with the multinational enterprise, such as a social rate of return or a benefit-cost ratio or an implicit exchange rate.[37]

In practice these approaches have a certain utility, but a utility that is distressingly limited. Approaches of this sort are at their best when a credible international price can be placed on the goods and services bought and sold by the enterprise. But contrary to a widely held impression, the bulk of the transactions of foreign-owned manufacturing subsidiaries in developing countries—about 80 percent—consists of local transactions effected inside the economy of the country, consisting of payrolls, local taxes, and purchases of local supplies.[38] Unfortunately, any figure that purports to stand for the social value of local labor or local tax revenue or local goods not traded in international commerce is at best no more than a guess.

Besides, the social costs and social benefits that most deeply concern the developing countries generally do not lend themselves to easy pricing. Indeed, when developing countries consider whether to permit the establishment of foreign-owned subsidiaries in their markets, they are often at a loss to know what to classify as costs and what as benefits.

Almost every important element of choice presents a classic dilemma. If the subsidiary of a multinational enterprise introduces new products and processes, it may injure the local economy's development by molding it in a foreign image,[39] but if the subsidiary undertakes to produce the same products and use the same processes as a local firm, then it may not contribute anything to the local

economy.⁴⁰ If the subsidiary undertakes to bring in its
own technicians, it may stifle the opportunities of local
workers, but if the subsidiary fails to bring in foreign
technicians, it may deny the local economy the expertise
needed. If the subsidiary proposes to draw on foreign
capital in large quantities, the easy supply of funds may
crush the local business community, but if it uses local
capital in large quantities, it may preempt funds otherwise available to the local economy. If the subsidiary pays
more than the prevailing wage, it may draw off the cream
of the labor supply, but if it insists on paying no more
than the prevailing wage, it may be appropriating all the
benefits of an increased productivity.⁴¹

Pushing these disconcerting problems aside and concentrating on manageable measures of cost and benefit,
we soon discover that the net benefits associated with the
manufacturing subsidiaries of multinational enterprises
are neither consistently greater nor consistently less than
the net benefits associated with the obvious alternative,
that of "unbundling" the project and seeking the needed
technology and capital from independent sources. Although very little research has been done squarely on the
point, that conclusion has already been adumbrated by
various studies.⁴²

A few sample calculations will illustrate why the
choice between the alternatives, when measured by yard-
sticks of simple economic cost and benefit, does not fall
obviously in one direction or the other. If a developing
country is prepared to search for and find an appropriate
source of technology for a local manufacturing operation,
it must be prepared to pay licensing fees on the order of 3
or 4 percent of gross sales.⁴³ If it can find a source of capital, the annual costs would presumably come to 15 or 20
percent of the capital.⁴⁴ Putting these two costs together
in a "typical" local firm, we can envisage annual payments for foreign technology and capital at the rate of
about 20 percent of capital.⁴⁵ Compare that figure with

representative figures for the aggregate profits and fees of foreign-owned manufacturing subsidiaries in developing countries, a figure estimated earlier as on the order of 20 percent.[46] The close concordance between the two averages warns the conscientious analyst that, on the basis of economic costs alone, he cannot establish a universal preference between multinational enterprises and the unbundling alternative and he will be obliged to look at the facts in each individual case.

Only the exceptional developing country has so far been prepared to accept the costs of terminating its economic ties with the outside world and living on its own material and technical resources. Burma and Cambodia might qualify for this category, but not many others. More common are developing countries that have curtailed their economic relationships with capitalistic countries and transferred them to other socialist countries; Cuba, for example, has shaken off its dependence on the United States and has developed in its place a dependence on the USSR. Most developing countries have taken more eclectic approaches, however. Inside their economies, state-owned enterprises have operated alongside private enterprises. And abroad, contacts have been sought with both socialist and capitalist economies. Most developing countries, therefore, still entertain a wide range of options in choosing both the means and the ends of their programs.

The drive on the part of developing countries to control the course of their own development expresses itself in many ways. One of these is the insistent desire to find products and processes more appropriate to their needs than those offered by the industrialized countries.

The efforts of various private and semipublic organizations to develop products and technologies more appropriate for the conditions of the developing countries have had some success. The official policies and programs of

governments in the developing countries, however, have
not contributed much to that objective. Here and there,
governments in developing countries have set up laboratories whose task is to produce innovations that respond
to the countries', special needs, but such laboratories appear to have been relatively unproductive. As in the industrialized countries, notably France and Britain, these
government-supported laboratories have usually been
captured by the nation's leading scientists. Few scientists
have been prepared to devote themselves to the mundane
routines of cutting and pasting, trial and error, testing
and retesting which are usually so critical to success in industrial innovation. Besides, success in such activities is
not crowned by the laureate's wreath. Referring to Latin
American countries, one sympathetic observer notes,
"The scientific communities in the underdeveloped countries are outposts of advanced-country science, with very
limited links with the economic and social realities which
surround them." [47]

Official policies in the developing countries also have
been unhelpful in other ways. Governments have commonly reduced the job opportunities in their economies
by insisting on the latest and the best in capital equipment and have regarded it as an affront when anything
else was supplied by the foreign investor.[48] Many developing countries have subsidized the use of capital in one
way or another, by giving generous tax treatment to the
capital users, by depressing the interest rate on borrowed
funds, or by other devices.[49] Their promotion of such
policies has usually been well-intentioned. Crash programs to increase agricultural production or industrial investment, for instance, have frequently produced such
policies. The final results, however, have been disconcerting. In a study of the tractor markets in twenty-one developing countries, twenty governments were found sub-
sidizing the buyers in some form.[50]

It is tempting to blame the disappointing perfor-

mance of official policies on a sheer lack of resources for
the job. But that hypothesis was literally exploded when
India and China demonstrated themselves capable of assembling the manpower and resources needed to produce
a nuclear device. The problem, it appears, is partly one of
priorities, not one of resources alone.

Developing countries have not done much better in
dealing with another important problem. Many of the
products being developed and promoted by enterprises
today are of doubtful social value wherever they are sold,
and when they are sold to the poor in developing countries, their adverse social effect can be exacerbated. The
per capita consumption of soft drinks in Mexico is one of
the highest in the world, a fact deeply disturbing in social
terms. Yet the governments of most developing countries
have done very little to curb such sales. Here and there, it
is true, we can see some efforts at control. Government
authorities in developing countries have sometimes
turned down proposals of multinational enterprises to
have their subsidiaries produce some trivial variant of an
existing product. In a few instances, authorities also have
compelled foreign-owned subsidiaries producing rival
variants of some needed product, such as automobiles, to
agree on a common design.[51] But by and large the response of governments to the problem continues to be
limited. And in that muted response we can sense not the
political power of the multinational enterprises but the
unwillingness of the governments to take actions that
might prove unpopular with their people.

In the creation and application of appropriate products and appropriate technologies, the developing countries might reasonably have hoped for some guidance
from the socialist economies. The most interesting laboratory for this purpose is, of course, the People's Republic
of China.[52] Here some of the restraints under which many
developing countries are obliged to operate do not exist.
Although the country is poor, it does not suffer from the

limitations of a small internal market. Moreover, unlike most other developing countries, it can draw on a nucleus of highly trained and competent scientists to solve problems that demand a scientific approach.

Chinese policies have produced two distinctly different approaches to industrial innovation. Relatively small plants, beginning with relatively archaic technologies, have been encouraged to serve local markets as best they could. Their performance, according to various sober and systematic appraisals, has been mixed. Measured according to various narrow criteria of economic efficiency, output has not been high. Measured by any criteria, grievous errors and downright failures have occurred from time to time. All told, the plants have made only a modest contribution in key products such as nitrogen, cement, pig iron, and simple electronic items. Yet the Chinese have managed to use local resources that otherwise might have been idle, and they have engaged the ingenuity of local workers that otherwise would have been dormant. Moreover, a unique ideological quality has added to the performance, which has encouraged communication between producers and users as well as between different producing plants. The long-run objective, it is evident, is to raise the scale and modernity of such plants, as the training of workers and the efficiency of the internal transport network justify the change.

Meanwhile, side by side with the development of these decentralized facilities, China has continued to exhibit some of the manifestations of a highly centralized economy. Once or twice the nation has been engulfed by a wave of new instructions from the center, leading to the bizarre era of backyard blast furnaces and to the period of Red Guard involvement in the factories. At other times China's size and centralized character have allowed it to mount large-scale programs in fields of advanced technology, including nuclear reactors, turbine engines, and electronic controls. Here the Chinese have emulated the

Soviet Union and Japan, buying prototypes or whole plants according to their needs, while trying to master a technology developed in another culture.

The Chinese approach to technology, as it turns out, is not embodied in either unique products or unique processes; it is mainly an effort to make do with existing resources and to stimulate the participation of workers in upgrading those resources. From time to time a product or process manufactured in China has proved to be appropriate in other economies as well; at other times not. But these outcomes have been a matter of chance. The Chinese themselves exhibit no sensitivity to the fact that any such transfer may require some adaptation to local conditions. Early reports of the operations of the Tanzam railroad, for instance, suggest that this Chinese-built project is likely to prove inefficient and unreliable in the conditions of East Africa. Similarly, the internal Chinese approach cannot be easily transferred to another developing country without at the same time transferring Chinese values, organization, and scale. As far as most developing countries are concerned, therefore, the Chinese case does not offer a real alternative.

Apart from questions of developing appropriate technologies, however, the experience of China and other socialist countries is of interest to the developing world because of its need to avoid wasting resources on useless consumer products. In this case, the lessons to be drawn from socialist experience are still unclear. The Chinese live at sufficiently low levels of income that their experience has only a limited applicability elsewhere. Presumably, if the emphasis on decentralization continues, local areas in China will be allowed to indulge local preferences, even if these include paper dragons, firecrackers, and medicines of uncertain therapeutic value. On the other hand, if limits are imposed from the ideological center, a refreshingly decentralized aspect of Chinese life may be imperiled and the problem of remote elites imposing their values on a defenseless populace will reappear. In any event, conclusions on this subject are premature.

As for the Soviet Union, its performance so far offers very few hints for the developing countries. Soviet consumers appear to be following inexorably in the footsteps of the West, from bicycles to automobiles, from radio to television, from natural fibers to man-made fibers. Although socialist states on the Soviet model have partly avoided the costs of excessive variety, they have been unable to solve a closely related problem, namely, that their state-owned facilities chronically produce shoddy goods and persistently disregard consumer preferences. The socialist model, therefore, has not offered a clear alternative to the developing countries.

Accordingly, in their efforts to cope with the problems of appropriate technologies and appropriate consumer products, many developing countries have turned to more mundane possibilities such as the reform of existing institutions that seem to contribute to the present unsatisfying patterns. National patent and trademark laws have been an obvious area for study. In most developing countries, these laws were originally adopted without much thought about the needs of the country, generally under the direction and tutelage of national specialists steeped in the mystique of industrial property law. Until recently the result was a set of laws that aped the patterns prevailing in the industrialized countries. The principal beneficiaries of the patent and trademark grants of these countries have been foreigners and their enterprises; for instance, about 85 percent of the patents issued by the developing countries have gone to foreigners.[53]

Patents and trademarks, it has to be remembered, are monopolies created by the state; hence, the conditions on which they are issued are something for each state to determine for itself. Among the industrialized countries, the various states have produced different laws and different procedures, responding to the states' perceptions of their interests. A few international conventions have existed on the subject, notably the Berne Convention for the Protection of Industrial Property. But contrary to the general impression the constraints imposed by such conventions by and large have been of minor significance. The conventions have left enough leeway, for example, that countries can refuse to issue patents on certain types of products such as drugs, can fix the life of a patent as they choose, can subject an application to search or not, can define the terms that represent "abuse" of a patent, and can limit the rights of the abusing patent-holder. The developing countries, therefore, are not seriously restrained from following a wide range of policies to hold down the windfall profits of foreigners and to prevent the use of patents or trademarks that contribute to product proliferation.[54]

Multinational enterprises are among the most obvious beneficiaries of strong patent and trademark laws. But most multinational enterprises are realistic enough to know that in the conditions of modern society patent rights offer only uncertain protection anywhere [55] and practically no protection at all in developing countries. In spite of their patent and trademark laws, governments in countries that decide to prevent foreign-owned enterprises from exercising their monopoly advantages can carry out their decision in various ways. Among other things, they can follow the U.S. example and use antitrust statutes for the purpose. They can also use tax provisions or price-fixing powers to curb local monopolies. The debate in developing countries over the reform of patent and trademark laws, therefore, like so much of the debate over multinational enterprises, has been more symbol than substance. The inherent power of the state to control monopoly practices has always existed; the substantive question is whether the developing countries have the will and energy wisely to apply that power.

In quite another line of policy, however, developing countries have been pressing hard. This is the policy of requiring foreign-owned subsidiaries in their jurisdiction to acquire local partners.[56] That policy, now firmly established in most developing countries, is widely regarded as the cornerstone of any successful campaign to contain the multinational enterprise.

The formal justification for policies that require foreigners to have local partners usually rests on two points: first, that local ownership will cut down the future outflow of resources from the country and, second, that it will increase the local economy's control over the operations of the foreign-owned facility. Despite the near-unanimity with which developing countries accept these assumptions, it takes only a little reflection to recognize that both assumptions are highly vulnerable.

Consider first the assumption that an increase in local ownership cuts down the future flow of payments to foreigners. The vulnerability of that assumption is illustrated by tracing what happens when local buyers acquire a share of an existing foreign-owned facility. If local buyers pay a price fully commensurate with the stream of earnings they are to receive, all that they will have done is to export scarce capital to a foreign seller, capital that might otherwise be used within the country. Stated differently, the local savings that are used to buy out the foreigner or to prevent the foreigner from setting up a new venture are no longer available for other purposes. And unless we can trace the effects of that diversion upon the economy, we have no basis for determining whether the local economy has been helped and whether future outflows from the local economy will be reduced.

Realistically, of course, a foreign firm that is doing very well in the local economy may be prepared to offer some of its equity to local buyers at a bargain price simply to reduce official pressure. In that case, the outflow of profits may conceivably be reduced. But risks are also in-curred by the developing country that follows the policy of promoting joint ventures. Once the local affiliate has shifted from the status of wholly owned subsidiary to that of joint venture, according to various studies, the parent of the multinational network will for obvious reasons begin looking hard at some of its ongoing relations with the local enterprise. Questions that are bound to be reexamined are the schedule of charges and prices levied by the foreign parent and the allocation of markets among the various producing units affiliated with the multinational enterprise. The outcome of the reexamination will depend upon the relative bargaining power of the local joint venturers. On the limited evidence available so far, we cannot be sure what the outcome will be, but more often than not, according to the spotty data, joint ventures end up with somewhat less favorable terms than do wholly owned subsidiaries.[57]

Even when local buyers do manage to buy an equity interest in a foreign-owned facility at bargain prices, as sometimes happens, the outcome still carries some distressing implications for the local economy. Often the bargain price has been extracted under implicit threat by the government, which in effect has used its coercive power to throw a plum to a few selected local buyers.[58] Once the local shareholders have secured their plum, it is an open question whether they will show much interest in promoting policies that improve the social performance of the foreign-owned subsidiary. Almost the only area in which the interests of local stockholders and those of local government are likely to coincide is the desire to divert some of the global profits of the multinational enterprise from the rest of the network to the local subsidiary. The capacity of local stockholders to do much on that score, as noted earlier, is uncertain. That possibility aside, it is difficult to find areas in which local stockholders add much to the social performance of foreign-owned subsidiaries. Local stockholders are unlikely to insist that the enterprise restrain itself in the exercise of its local market power. Neither do local stockholders exhibit much interest in adapting products and processes to local conditions or in elevating the pay of local labor or in increasing the size of local research programs in greater tax probity. On the contrary, insofar as local stockholders do exert their influence effectively, they are likely to direct it at their own government in support of the foreign-owned subsidiary in which they have an equity interest. In these cases, the influence may or may not improve the performance of the enterprise, when measured in terms of social yield.

Of course, some of these concerns have less force when the local joint venturer is a government-owned enterprise rather than a private stockholder. But even in these cases, we must be cautious about the implications of a joint venture. Not a great deal is known about the performance of government-owned enterprises, and most of what is known—such as the lurid descriptions of Pertamina's operations in Indonesia during the early 1970s—is anecdotal rather than systematic. In any event, in the case of many developing countries there is no strong reason to assume that government-owned enterprises, when teamed up with foreign partners, have any more concern about social criteria than do privately owned enterprises. On the scanty record, we are entitled to a certain amount of skepticism that the public-private joint venture represents a constructive response to the needs of the developing countries.[59]

In addition to pushing for the partial divestiture of foreign-owned subsidiaries in favor of local stockholders, governments in most developing countries try to press the foreign owners on other fronts. Some have laid down fairly difficult conditions at the very outset and have accepted the risk that the conditions might frighten off some potential investors; India has fallen into that category. Other governments, such as that of Brazil, have been much less restrictive at the time of entry of a foreign-owned subsidiary.

Even where seemingly severe restrictions on the entry of multinational enterprises exist, however, developing countries cautiously or overtly compete with one another for the attention of multinational enterprises and, in the process, offer a menu of special incentives for those firms that meet the entry tests.[60] The incentives have been important in certain kinds of cases, notably, where several different countries have been competing to attract the same subsidiary. Unfortunately, however, incentives have commonly been offered even in instances in which multinational enterprises already had their own strong motivations for setting up local subsidiaries, such as the motivation to follow the leader. In these cases, the incentives have had only a marginal impact on the decision of multinational enterprises to set up a subsidiary.

As for the subsidiaries of multinational enterprises already established in the developing countries, the common policy of the countries has been to tighten the terms that existed at the time of entry as far as the situation will permit. Subsidiaries that had been permitted to import industrial materials and equipment have in the course of time been compelled to turn to local sources, and subsidiaries that had been set up originally to serve the local market have been pressured to export a share of their product. Tax provisions and pricing rules have been tightened, training provisions have been imposed, and various other changes in the rules of the game have appeared.

As long as a foreign-owned goose can still lay golden eggs, however, the policy of most developing countries has been to squeeze the goose, not to destroy it or to have it fly away. Accordingly, multinational enterprises that perform a unique function, such as providing access to some difficult technology or some otherwise inaccessible foreign market, have generally been less vulnerable to

government pressures, while subsidiaries whose withdrawal is thought to entail very little national loss have
been more vulnerable. This byplay has produced the obsolescing bargain described earlier, along with the tensions and protests that have accompanied the groping
toward a new equilibrium. It is a process that promises to
continue.

The least ambiguous of the various lines of policy
toward foreign-owned subsidiaries, of course, is the policy of unbundling—that is, the policy of encouraging local
enterprises to find independent sources of capital and
technology and to develop independent access to foreign
markets. As the earlier discussion suggested, a policy of
unbundling could well prove to be economic from the
viewpoint of a developing country. Japan's success with
such a policy throughout the early stages of its development—indeed, until the 1960s—has stood as a challeng-
ing example of what can be done.

The case of Japan, however, emphasizes one central
fact. A successful unbundling strategy entails a very large
public commitment. For decades during the early stages
of its development, the Japanese government financed the
overseas sojourn of large numbers of Japanese for sus-
tained periods of learning, as well as supporting a chain
of overseas outposts from which foreign markets and
foreign technology could be observed at first hand. In addition, many foreign technicians were brought to Japan,
and many were encouraged to remain for long periods.

Almost every developing country has made one gesture or another in these directions. Many countries have
developed overseas listening posts, acquired foreign
technology, and improved their educational systems. But
in general these programs have been conceived and financed on a scale much less adequate than the analogous
Japanese commitment. Of course, the Japanese case covered an earlier era and may have entailed a much larger
effort in order to overcome the communication barriers

and other hindrances of that era. Nonetheless, I am inclined to see the current efforts of most developing countries as altogether inadequate for implementing a broad policy of unbundling; much greater national efforts will be needed before that policy can be widely applied. Yet if individual countries find themselves unable to carry their unbundling policies as far as they would like, that will contribute to the sense of frustration and inadequacy that many of them have felt over the past few decades.

8 | Transnational Processes and National Goals

THE INTERPLAY between multinational enterprises and nation-states can be observed and interpreted from numerous angles of vision. One that proves especially useful lets us see the multinational enterprise as an institution responsive to both sides of its double identity: it must comport itself as a national of the country that sanctioned its creation, and it must respond to its organic link with units in other countries. Because of its double identity, a foreign subsidiary in a network must be prepared to shoulder one of the usual burdens of any resident *ausländer*, namely, the burden of demonstrating that it is not the agent of some foreign interest, public or private. At the same time the parent in its home territory must be prepared for periodic waves of others' doubt regarding its commitments to the interests of the homeland.

Efforts to generalize about the actual behavior of multinational enterprises have generally been handicapped by the voluminous, unstructured, and confusing nature of the evidence. Partly as a result, relatively simple ideas such as the Leninist theory of imperialism have had enormous appeal. Yet any close-up view of the relations between the multinational-enterprise networks and the countries in which they operate suggests that theories of this sort are excessively simple.

For example, the disinterested observer is likely to

conclude that United Fruit has drawn considerable support at times from the presence of the U.S. Marines in the
banana republics of Central America,[1] but the observer
would also have to note that the Department of Justice has
sporadically attempted to break up the United Fruit monopoly in Central America.[2] Also difficult to explain in
simple imperialist terms is the U.S. government's policy
during the early 1950s toward its oil companies in the
Middle East: why, for instance, was the U.S. government
aggressively trying to break down the oil companies' pricing system in the Middle East [3] at the same time that the
CIA was helping to overthrow Mossadegh in Iran? [4] U.S.
policies toward its foreign investors in Cuba in the 1940s
and 1950s are also hard to fit into the tight shoe offered by
the imperialist model.[5] Nor will such a simple conceptual
structure explain why the U.S. government during the
Marshall Plan years resisted the development of restrictive business practices between U.S. and European enterprises and persistently urged European governments
to collaborate in that effort.[6] A close-up view of British experience and the experience of European states, as well as
of some of the recent policies of Canada, suggests that the
standard capitalist-imperialist model is not any more ap-
plicable in those contexts.[7]

Although simple concepts such as the capitalist-imperialist model are not very helpful, it is still possible to
make some useful generalizations about the complex
relationships between multinational enterprises and nation-states. What we are observing can be thought of as
the interaction between two powerful systems. The two
systems respond to different principles and operate in
different dimensions. They are not rival systems; the multinational enterprise cannot conceivably be expected to
perform the central role of the sovereign state, while the
sovereign state would be grossly handicapped in trying to
perform the multinational functions of the enterprise. Yet
as the two systems operate today they interact in ways

that at times are incompatible and even threatening to both.

One source of mutual threat is that the network of the multinational enterprise can become a conduit through which the power of one sovereign state is projected into the territory of another. In the abstract, various possibilities of this sort exist.

Because the units that make up any multinational enterprise are linked, national authorities are aware that their own ability to command the unit lying within their jurisdiction may give them a way of tapping into the network as a whole. That obvious point has always been the source of considerable tension. To understand why, we have only to think of a deliberately provocative example such as the use of the multinational enterprise as a cover apparatus for national intelligence agencies working in foreign countries. The U.S. case, as usual, is much better aired than any other.[8] But any national intelligence group that thinks such an association useful has presumably tried to create it.

The undercover example, however, is probably much less important in its substantive implications than the more overt uses that governments have made of multinational enterprises in recent years as conduits for their objectives in foreign countries. At various times, for instance, nearly every industrialized country has encouraged its enterprises to embark on ventures abroad in order to guarantee sources of raw materials for the home market.[9] Other objectives also have been involved. France, for example, has had the aim of exposing the French parent, through its foreign-owned subsidiaries, to the technological and marketing stimuli provided in other national environments such as that of the United States.[10] In this case as in others, the official policies of the home government led to the extension of a multinational network into the jurisdictions of other sovereign states.

The best-advertised cases in which the policy of one

government has reverberated through multinational networks into the economy of another involve the U.S. handling of a series of antitrust suits in the 1950s [11] and the
so-called trading-with-the-enemy cases of about the same
period. In these cases, the U.S. government's grip on the
parent enterprises provided the basis for the government's action, but the ultimate targets of the U.S. action
were overseas subsidiaries. Given the U.S. style of governance, with its public pronouncements, hearings, and appeals, the efforts of the U.S. government to reach these
foreign subsidiaries could not be disregarded by governments abroad; thus, a series of *causes célèbres* was created.

In practice, of course, almost all countries in which
multinational enterprises are headquartered maintain
policies and programs that affect the behavior of subsidiaries located in other countries. The U.S. program to
improve its balance of payments during the latter 1960s
included various provisions intended to reduce the flow
of capital from U.S. parents to their overseas subsidiaries
and to stimulate the flow of dividends from subsidiaries
to parents. In much less transparent form the French, Japanese, and British governments have maintained licensing programs that have the effect of restraining or guiding
the movement of capital between affiliates in multinational networks. The British government's rescue of the
failing subsidiary of the Chrysler Corporation in 1976 was
an egregious example of an official program that affected
other subsidiaries; in this case, Chrysler shifted its
planned production from continental subsidiaries to Britain as part of the plan. [12]
Conflicts of this sort, we hardly need to be reminded,
are usually debated amông nations on the basis of the
highest available principle. When other nations have ob-
jected to U.S. action in the field of antitrust or export controls, for instance, the principle generally invoked has
been the unacceptability of extraterritorial application of

U.S. law. In the case of multinational enterprises, however, the concept of extraterritorial application has proved
difficult to define and apply. Nations have often demanded action quite at variance with the tidy concept of a
world sliced up into watertight national jurisdictions. For
instance, governments have demanded data from U.S.
authorities in order to prosecute U.S. businessmen for
secret payments made abroad, even when the payments
were not in violation of U.S. law.[13] Governments have
demanded also that the foreign parents of subsidiaries in
their jurisdiction reveal the details of business operations
undertaken in other parts of the multinational network.[14]
And from time to time, as if to underline the confusion
and uncertainty over the principle being invoked, governments that have demanded data from abroad have
rebuffed similar demands made upon them by others.[15]

While home governments have commonly reached
through the parent firms in their jurisdiction to influence
subsidiaries abroad, host governments have not overlooked the possibility of exerting their influence in the
other direction, namely, through the subsidiary upon the
parent. Host countries have used their powers over subsidiaries to galvanize parents in a number of ways. One of
the more striking instances of this sort is the Canadian
government's use of the leading U.S. automobile companies during the 1960s in securing U.S. congressional consent for free trade in automobiles between the two countries. Once the Canadian government had developed an
appropriate package of promises and threats aimed at the
Canadian subsidiaries of U.S. companies, it was in a
position to enlist the U.S. parents in persuading the Congress.[16]

The national authorities that control the subsidiaries
of multinational enterprises influence the home territory
of those enterprises in numerous other ways. Some countries have granted tax concessions to foreign investors to
persuade them to set up facilities in their jurisdiction.

Others have taken special pains to levy taxes on corporate dividends by formulas that would hit the foreign investor harder than the home investor; still others have simply placed ceilings on the foreigner's remission of profits.[17] In Mexico and India, among many other countries, foreign-owned subsidiaries have been required to step up the export of products headed for other affiliates in the network, such as automobile components and electronics components. As a rule, measures of this sort have had a direct impact somewhere else in the system.

From one point of view, the object of such measures has been exemplary: to increase output and jobs and to improve the balance of payments of the country initiating the program. From another viewpoint, the object has been predatory: to gain these benefits by incidentally depriving other countries of jobs and foreign exchange. This particular form of poaching, however, has not been widely regarded as out of bounds in the official world of international relations. Accordingly, where protests over its effects have arisen, they have generally been initiated by private interests. For instance, labor unions in the countries losing jobs because of the poaching efforts of other countries have been especially sensitive to such efforts.[18]

By the early 1970s, many governments were trying to use their control over the subsidiaries of multinational networks to push up the prices of exports, especially exports of raw materials. In some of these price-setting efforts, the aim of the governments was not necessarily to take an added cut of the profits of the enterprises, but rather to increase the size of the pie available for sharing between governments and enterprises; the target, in short, had become the buyers in the importing countries.[19] In oil, bauxite, copper, and bananas, among other commodities, the efforts of the developing countries to use multinational enterprises as a conduit for raising prices in the buying countries became quite explicit, so that the enterprises came to be described as the developing countries' tax collectors.

As the decade of the 1970s has rolled on, however, it has grown increasingly clear that various restraints are limiting the extent to which nations can use multinational enterprises as a passive conduit for promoting their national interests. For example, when several states put pressure on the same multinational enterprise, the pressures are sometimes directly in conflict. When all the affiliated mines of a multinational copper company are being importuned to increase their exports and when the only available market in the short run is the company's own smelters, something has got to give. When a subsidiary in one country is told to export more components and a subsidiary in another country is told to import fewer components, the elements of an impasse are present. When the inevitable limits have been reached, multinational enterprises have often been projected into the position of arbitrating the conflicting commands of the sovereign states.

The function of the multinational enterprise as informal arbiter was especially apparent at the peak of the oil crisis in 1973 and 1974, when the multinational oil companies in effect found themselves operating as the world's oil rationers. After the crisis, the function continued; at that stage, however, the multinational enterprises shifted their function from doling out the scarce oil to doling out the limited markets. As Iran, Iraq, Abu Dhabi, Algeria, Libya, and Indonesia simultaneously demanded that their sales grow and that prices not be reduced, the oil companies found themselves in the inescapable position of juggling conflicting claims. Care had to be taken to handle the conflicting claims with sensitive appreciation of the varying degrees of tolerance of the different states. And when reductions in output did occur, the best possible face had to be put upon them. Characteristically, therefore, cutbacks in production were announced by the exporting states as their voluntary decision, tangible evidence of their determination, in fraternal association with other oil-exporting states, to restrict output and hold up prices.

One feature of the multinational enterprises' role as arbiter in this case has to be underlined, however. If the market were genuinely atomistic and competitive, these enterprises would not have had a chance to assume the arbiter's role. In that case, in order to achieve their purpose, the exporting countries themselves would have been required to develop effective agreements that partitioned the market among themselves. As it was, the ability of the multinational enterprises to act as rationers was reinforced by their various oligopolistic characteristics: their limited number and large size, their producing partnerships and other links, and their vertical integration.

In any case the tug-of-war among rival national interests carried on via the networks of the multinational enterprises combines two important elements. First, the struggle has some of the earmarks of the beggar-thy-neighbor economic policies that preoccupied governments in other eras. Beggar-thy-neighbor policies, it is true, have generally been associated with other kinds of destructive rivalry among governments, notably with tariff wars and with competitive devaluations, but the principle has been fundamentally the same: each government, trying to increase its own share and prepared to achieve its goal at the expense of the others, makes its small contribution to the destruction of a system that could conceivably be useful to all of them. In the fields of trade policy and exchange-rate policy governments eventually recognized the destructive potential of their rivalry and made some effort to limit the game. The General Agreement on Tariffs and Trade has provided some sort of framework for curbing trade wars, and the International Monetary Fund has offered a structure for dealing with the exchange-rate problem. But the beggar-thy-neighbor consequences of the rivalrous regulation of the multinational enterprise have not yet attracted much notice.

The very structure of the multinational enterprise that exposes it to the conflicting pressures of national governments also invests it with a special opportunity, namely, the opportunity for enlisting the powers of one government in order to help its negotiating position with another. The standard socialist indictment of the multinational enterprise, of course, dwells heavily on this point, identifying the interests of a multinational enterprise closely with those of the parent's government; but as was suggested earlier, the evidence of the ability of an enterprise to command that support is quite equivocal.

It almost goes without saying that when the parent firm of a multinational enterprise asks its government for support in promoting its interests through a foreign subsidiary, that government has some predisposition to lend its support. The embassies of industrialized countries, in fact, provide a formidable set of facilities designed to promote and protect "their" enterprises by offering guidance, opening doors, and running interference. The commitment of different governments in the performance of that task, however, varies enormously.

One variable of importance affecting the nature of the home country's support for its multinational enterprises is the size and structure of the home economy.

The Netherlands, for example, is home for only a handful of multinational enterprises with important overseas holdings: Unilever in consumer goods, Royal Dutch/Shell in oil, AKZO in drugs, Philips in electronics. These firms are rarely in competition with other Dutch enterprises abroad. When the Dutch government weighs the problems of, say, Philips in Brazil, therefore, it does not have to give much weight to the effects of any given line of policy on other Dutch companies. This does not mean that the governments of small countries are more favorably disposed than those of large countries to act on behalf of their home-based enterprises. At times, quite the opposite attitude is in evidence.[20] It means simply that one complicating factor—the need to weigh the implications of any chosen policy upon other national interests abroad—is generally not very important in the choice of action.

The contrast with the United States in this respect is overwhelming. When the U.S. government is asked to support an enterprise overseas, it usually finds itself obliged to weigh the implications of its response in a dozen different directions. That obligation, in practice, has proved to be no small restraint. It goes a long way toward explaining, for instance, a quite distinctive and persistent aspect of U.S. policy with regard to the overseas projects of U.S.-based oil companies. Repeatedly, U.S. policy has taken on the burden of promoting the position of its "independent" oil companies in foreign countries, even though the established major oil companies were quite prepared to perform. This line of policy was a plank in the official U.S. campaign of the 1920s to squeeze U.S. companies into the Middle East; it reappeared as a plank in the U.S. position when the Iran oil consortium was created in 1954. In those instances, as well as in others, it reflected the fact that any U.S. administration failing to take into account the enormous diversity of the U.S. oil industry exposed itself to political disaster.[21]

Although the diversity of U.S. interests may sometimes be reflected in the complex internal structure of a single industry, as in the case of oil, more often it makes itself felt in other ways. When Exxon's International Petroleum Company was seized by the Peruvian government in 1968, the efforts of the U.S. government to get adequate compensation for the enterprise had to be tempered by an awareness that several hundred other U.S. enterprises spread out over a dozen different industries had a $600 million stake in Peru and these were strongly against a hard-line U.S. approach.[22]

The complexity of the U.S. position in situations such

as the IPC expropriation derives also from the wide range of U.S. political interests. Since the second World War the foreign policies of the United States have made it a party to virtually every major international dispute. Accordingly, its foreign relations have taken on convolutions unmatched by any other country. In the Peruvian case, as the U.S. government was aware, the IPC problem was being watched carefully throughout Latin America; its outcome was subtly or overtly linked with a dozen other issues, including the hemisphere's attitude toward Cuba, the Canal Zone, and offshore fishing rights.[23]

The equivocal quality of the support that the U.S. government gave its oil companies in their negotiations in Tehran in 1971 also seems to have been the result of such a linkage; here, the State Department was eager to keep Iran on its side in the complex game of containing the Soviet Union's role in the Middle East.[24] The linkage factor, too, was what forced the United States in 1976 to support the embargo on chrome ore from Southern Rhodesia, in spite of the interests of its enterprises. By that time, the expanding influence in Africa of the Soviet Union, China, and Cuba had propelled the problems of that area into the mainstream of U.S. policies. As a result, the risks to the United States of responding to the interests of its individual enterprises had risen sharply.

The U.S. government's chronic inability to use the claws of its foreign-aid legislation to help U.S.-based enterprises abroad can also be attributed mainly to the linkage problem. The Hickenlooper amendment, adopted in 1962, directs the president to terminate foreign aid to any country that nationalizes a U.S. property and fails to provide adequate compensation to its former owner. Except in one trivial case, no U.S. president has actually exercised that power; presidents have preferred instead to take refuge in procedural delays, informal compromises, and other available loopholes. In each case, the risks of suspending aid seemed too high.[25]

The same outcome appears in numerous other con-

texts in U.S. history. One careful study of the quarrels between the United States and Canada over the past half-
century or so concludes that when the interests of U.S. enterprises have been involved in the conflict, the U.S. government has not proved to be of much help. "The pressures of democratic politics," say the authors of the study,
"usually favor the smaller state in the bargaining process,
because for them, politicization from below tends to lead
to tough negotiating behavior and coherent stands by
government, whereas for the United States such politicization leads to fragmentation of policy." [26]

To understand the behavior of governments in the
support of their enterprises, however, variables other
than size and diversity have to be introduced.

For example, Japan's strong support of the overseas
ventures of its enterprises during the 1960s and early
1970s can probably be explained by its uncomplicated
priorities during the period. These placed overwhelming
emphasis on securing foreign markets and access to raw
materials, but they also were a reflection of a style and
structure of governance at home. The foreign initiatives of
individual enterprises could be coordinated through a
powerful Ministry of International Trade and Industry;
any domestic interests that felt injured by such coordinated programs could usually be held in line by the joint
power of the bureaucracy and the ruling political party. [27]

The French case can be seen in a similar light. Coordination in this instance was helped by various institutions, notably the French bureaucracy. Most important in
setting the behavioral patterns of the bureaucracy has
been that its leaders are recruited from a little group of eli-
tist institutions, the *grandes écoles*, of which the Ecole Na-
tionale d'Administration is the acknowledged leader. That
infrastructure has helped to fortify a succession of strong
presidents, beginning with de Gaulle, and a tradition of
tutelary ministries that were expected to set the main
policies for the various branches of French industry. [28]

These two elements could provide a coordinating mechanism to reconcile conflicting French objectives and provide a buffer against the complaints of dissenting French interests.[29]

The British case offers still another set of powerful conditioning variables rooted in national history and culture. American academics are widely assumed to be disqualified by birth from commenting about the social structure of Britain. Nevertheless, I feel safe in making a few generalizations, especially because they are widely supported by British scholars.[30] British administrations, like their French counterparts, are capable of contemplating the idea of national champions or chosen instruments without a sense of having breached any deep-seated principle of governance. Britain's leading computer firm, ICL, is recognized as an entity in a special category, to be dealt with on terms not necessarily available to other companies in Britain, foreign or domestic.[31] For its leading position in the manufacture of aircraft engines, Rolls Royce has been endowed with similar status. So, too, has British Petroleum, partly by reason of a government interest in the equity of the enterprise.

In the case of Britain, the relationship between the government bureaucracy and the bureaucracy of the enterprises is not nearly as close and personal as in the case of France, but preferential relations are still possible and acceptable. On the other hand, the probability that a leading British enterprise will demand the support of government in some critical and contentious matter involving a foreign country is somewhat constrained. In the give-and-take between business leaders and government leaders, the business leaders are invested with relatively low status, at least by comparison with the situation in continental Europe, the United States, and Japan.

The U.S. case, as usual, seems to exhibit its own special set of aberrant characteristics. The essence of the U.S. style of governance is, in Richard Hofstadter's words, "a perennial quest for a way of dividing, diffusing and checking power and preventing its exercise by a single interest." [32] That enduring trait, vividly illustrated by the extraordinary sequence of events in the Watergate affair,[33] was strengthened in the 1960s and 1970s by the grant of unprecedented rights to the U.S. public to examine public documents [34] and to sue government officials who seemed to be negligent in the performance of their duties.[35]

The diffuse structure of public power in the United States, according to numerous studies, has been accentuated by the nature of the country's political parties.[36] No strong ideological cement ties the politicians of any party together; from an ideological viewpoint, many leaders of the Democratic party could as easily be Republicans and vice versa. The party that occupies the White House or dominates the Congress is generally led by regional politicians, comparative strangers who happen to be sharing national power.

Since the ideological ties of any U.S. party are fairly weak, the ideological differences between the parties are not very sharp; unlike most countries in Europe, for instance, the United States has no working-class party, and U.S. business can take comfort in the fact that no important U.S. party is ideologically committed to its destruction. That, however, leaves plenty of room for the regulation and restraint of business, based on other kinds of interests: New England's interest in cheap crops and cheap power, for instance, versus the South's interest in high-priced crops and high-cost power. Since the party that occupies the White House or dominates the Congress does not stand for a relatively clear and unambiguous set of national goals, its policies are hard to predict and harder to keep on a consistent course.

The heterogeneous quality of the U.S. political parties is matched by the diffusion and variety of the American bureaucrats, a characteristic that distinguishes them sharply from their counterparts in other countries.[37]

Whereas bureaucrats of Britain, France, Japan, and most other industrialized countries are the product of a long process of conditioning that tends to turn them into a well-delineated professional group, high-level U.S. public administrators may be expected to come from almost anywhere, with almost any kind of training and background. A considerable proportion achieve their eminent public positions in midcareer, after many years as lawyers, teachers, businessmen, or journalists. Their ideologies are diverse and their loyalties diffuse.

None of the elements in the loosely structured apparatus of governance in the United States can be thought of as uninhibitedly hostile to big business, certainly not by the norms of Europe's political parties. Nevertheless, the political process has managed to produce policies and programs in the fields of antitrust action, corporate disclosure, corporate taxation, consumer protection, and environmental controls that equal or exceed those of Europe and Japan in their regulatory impact.

The nature of the curious interactive process in U.S. governance is well enough illustrated by the U.S. government's handling of recent disclosures that U.S. firms had been making secret payments of various sorts to friends, agents, and extortionists in foreign countries. In one sense, there was nothing new in these disclosures; it had long been assumed that enterprises of all nationalities were making such payments at home and abroad. French and Japanese firms, for instance, were notorious in some areas for their alleged propensity to buy their way through difficult situations. But it remained for the U.S. process to document the widespread assumption with regard to U.S. firms.

The process began with the unprecedented congressional investigation of the Watergate affair. Some of the disclosures attending that inquiry led another arm of the U.S. government, the Securities and Exchange Commission, to reconsider whether it had been discharging its statutory duty to compel corporations to make full disclosure of material information. As enterprises delivered up the information demanded by the SEC, the information moved effectively into the public domain. That result came about through the extraordinary provisions of the Freedom of Information Act, which laid the material open to the press and the public. Although the U.S. government is no more hostile to multinational enterprises than any other industrialized country, its processes have produced a restrictive policy unmatched elsewhere.

The performance of the U.S. government in matters relating to the multinational enterprise has often left observers in other countries both baffled and troubled. The bafflement has been produced by cases such as that just described, which do not seem to fit the widely held picture of the United States as champion of the multinational enterprise. The troubled reaction has been due mainly to the enormous latent power of the United States.

The gravity of a problem in international relations is not necessarily determined by the most probable outcome, that is, by the outcome ordinarily to be expected. More important than the expected outcome in a government's exercise of power are the latent possibilities. In the U.S. case, the rest of the world remains acutely aware of two disconcerting facts. First, the U.S. economy continues by a considerable margin to be the most powerful in the world. Second, despite its diffuse and loose-jointed apparatus of governance, the United States has proved capable of some extraordinary external thrusts, from the suppression of the Barbary pirates to the war in Vietnam. It may be that the CIA and the Marines have been harnessed by public opinion and that public opinion may perhaps be counted on to harness them again if ever they break free. Nevertheless, great powers such as the United States, history confirms, have an awful potential for mischief. To exist by the sufferance of a great power may be the unavoidable lot of smaller countries. But it is not one they can be expected to accept without casting about for some means to assert their independence.

9 | The Gap between Prospects and Policies

JUST a few years ago multinational enterprises were busily and profitably occupied in spreading their subsidiaries across the globe. Today the world is awash with actions and proposals that would restrain the multinational enterprise and alter its relation to nation-states.

We do not lack explanations for the shift in mood and direction. Yet most explanations ignore the real causes of the tension between multinational enterprises and nation-states, and most of the prescriptions for dealing with those causes are impractical or irrelevant.

Perhaps the most proximate source of tension has been the revolutionary shrinkage in international space over the past two or three decades, brought on by new modes of international communication, including the radiotelephone, jet airplane travel, and the computer. The shrinkage of space has narrowed the gap in consumer tastes between one country and the next, bringing nylon thread and Honda motobikes into the remotest corners of the world. And it has helped to reduce the differences among producers in different nations in their choices of machinery and industrial processes.

These developments are the basis for a new interdependence among nations, manifested in higher levels of international trade, a greater flow of technical services across borders, and larger movements of international capital. At the same time, the shrinkage of space has provided enterprises everywhere with a new impetus for spreading outward from their home bases. Worldwide operations have offered increased opportunities for enterprises to profit from innovations or trademarks or patents, to develop new economies of scale, and to reduce their risks by spreading their operations over a number of different countries.

At first, the largest enterprises in the industrialized countries, and especially the leading firms of the United States, were in the vanguard of the movement to foreign countries. Soon, however, firms from Europe and Japan were crowding at the heels of the leading U.S. firms. Eventually, smaller firms from everywhere followed close behind the large. Today the signs of multinational spread can be seen even among enterprises based in developing countries, such as the enterprises of Mexico, India, Brazil, and Taiwan.

The multinational spread of enterprises has generated powerful tensions and stirred sharp reactions, both in the developing countries and in the industrialized nations. Many leaders have associated the growth of multinational enterprises with some of the endemic ills of the modern industrialized world, such as the efforts of various countries to create hegemony, the presence of corruption in high places, the pervasive waste and inequities in the distribution of rewards, and the pollution and degradation of the environment.

The association between multinational enterprises and these universal ills has been natural enough, perhaps even unavoidable, in view of the prominence of leading multinational enterprises in the modern world. But the association is misleading in one critical respect. Hegemony, corruption, waste, inequity, and pollution are not the special hallmarks of the multinational form of enterprise. Although their degree and style differ from one country to the next, these disconcerting features of contemporary life are endemic in the Soviet Union and Eastern Europe, where multinational enterprises are virtually barred, and are prominent in Japan, India, Nigeria, and Mexico, where multinational enterprises are substantially restrained.

The tensions associated with the multinational enterprise arise from another source as well, namely, the growth of economic interdependence among national economies. As nations have been drawn together by various economic links, some national leaders have been alarmed by the restraints that these links impose upon national autonomy and national choice. Although the links seem indispensable for continued growth, they also have seemed at times to threaten some of the national goals for which the growth was intended, including national stability, egalitarianism, participation, and protection.

A state of interdependence, to be sure, may exist without the help of the multinational enterprise. It may be created by international trade, international licensing, and international borrowing conducted among parties operating at arm's length. Nevertheless, the multinational enterprise is commonly seen as the epitome of the trend toward interdependence. Multinational networks have special characteristics that heighten the sense of interdependence in the nations where the enterprises are implanted. Wherever such enterprises operate, the link between national economies is made tangible by the presence of an affiliate that forms part of a multinational network. Unavoidably, each affiliate includes the elements of a double personality. It is an entity created under the laws of the country in which it operates, responsive to the sovereign that sanctions its existence. Yet at the same time, as a unit in a multinational network, each affiliate must also be responsive to the needs and strategies of the network as a whole. The multiplicity of influences to which any affiliate of a multinational enterprise is potentially exposed preoccupies national leaders, creating fertile ground for speculation and a sense of foreboding about their effects on the national economy.

Even while national leaders have been disturbed by the growth of multinational enterprises, many of them have sensed that their own bargaining power has actually been increasing in their dealings with such enterprises. Some observers attribute this seeming shift in bargaining power to an increasing world demand for certain essential materials, such as oil or iron ore; some attribute it to an increasing political cohesion among those countries determined to face down the multinational enterprise.

I suggest, however, that the increase in the bargaining power of national governments, where it has occurred, is due mainly to the very factors that have created the growing state of interdependence. With the shrinkage of international space and the improvement of international communication, some of the capital, technology, or access to markets that multinational enterprises have offered to host countries has been matched by rival offers from other sources. Sometimes the rival has been another multinational enterprise, prepared to perform the same economic function, but sometimes the challenge has come from an independent licenser of technology or from a lender of funds. Wherever rival sources have appeared, their rivalry has diluted the unique strengths of any single enterprise and has weakened its bargaining position.

The realization by national leaders that their bargaining position might be increasing in individual cases has, however, proved cold comfort. Overall, the role of multinational enterprises as a class has been growing, not declining. And in their efforts to deal with that growth, national leaders have cast about for countermeasures that might hold the multinational enterprise in check.

Although the tensions associated with multinational enterprises have been similar from one country to the next, the leaders of the developing countries have for obvious reasons experienced far higher levels of tension than have leaders in the industrialized nations. The efforts of the developing countries to deal with these tensions, therefore, have had some distinctive characteristics.

One clear line of policy in many developing countries has been to provide public support to local public and private enterprises in their efforts to find untied sources of foreign capital and technology, so as to develop their own channels to local and foreign markets. With that objective in mind, governments have imposed special taxes on the income of foreign-owned subsidiaries, ceilings on license fees paid by local licensees to foreign licensers, limitations on foreigners' use of local credits, requirements for the sale of equity to local interests, and so on.

The vigor with which developing countries have applied such regulations has generally been influenced by the bargaining strength of the multinational enterprises they confronted. Multinational enterprises with nothing unique to offer or to withhold when the pressure was applied have been especially vulnerable. But those with special strengths have usually been able to count on seeing such regulations applied with caution and restraint.

Although governments of developing countries have been able to extract added benefits from some of the subsidiaries of foreign-owned enterprises, the uncertain progress in their struggle for autonomy has left important groups in these countries preoccupied and frustrated. Accordingly, even as these countries have pushed their efforts at the national level, they also have tried to improve their positions through joint international action. The multinational enterprise, therefore, has figured centrally in the broader north-south confrontation.

One international effort, well advertised as being highly effective, was manifested in the program of the Organization of Petroleum Exporting Countries. OPEC's role in the quadrupling of crude oil prices in 1973 and 1974 was widely interpreted as a sign of a vast shift in power. With the passing of time, however, early impressions of the extent of the shift have been modified. First, oil in the mid-1970s has proved to be a rare case, resting on a special set of economic factors. Second, OPEC's seeming success required first of all an undermining of the powers of the established leaders in the oil industry, a condition achieved mainly by the entry of additional international oil companies. Finally, the OPEC countries do not seem to have freed themselves from dependence on the leading international companies. OPEC, it appears, has not yet acquired the power to dominate the international oil markets by brute force alone.[1]

Another group effort, antedating OPEC, also is of interest in assessing the speed and direction of change. This effort was the adoption in 1969 of Decision 24 of the Andean Pact. The decision represented an extraordinarily bold effort on the part of five (later six) countries of Latin America to pool their economic power in a joint policy toward multinational enterprises. The policy itself seemed to break new ground in many different respects. In principle it denied to foreign-owned enterprises the advantages of the incipient free-trade area among the Andean Pact countries, unless they committed themselves to a divestiture program that would place majority ownership and control in local hands. Foreigners' participation in public utilities, the communication industries, banking, and the raw materials sectors was to be limited. The contractual ties between foreign parents and their local subsidiaries, such as licensing agreements and loans, were to be restricted in such a way as to prevent the draining off of added profits.

The actual application of these extraordinary provisions, however, has been quite limited.[2] Chile, for instance, disregarded the provisions during most of the period of its membership, then withdrew from the pact altogether. Other countries, including Colombia, have made the most of the decision's various loopholes. Peru, which once had seemed determined to enforce the extraordinary provisions, eventually veered away from a policy of strict enforcement. The multinational enterprises themselves have muted their early opposition to the decision, seemingly content on the whole to let the divided interests inside the signatory countries hold its restrictive provisions in check. Nothing is quite the same as it was before the decision was adopted, but neither is anything very different.

The developing countries have been pressing on still another international level, one that is more comprehensive and more nearly universal. In the various organs of the United Nations, the so-called Group of Seventy-seven—actually representing the hundred or so developing countries of the world—has established a common front on the subject of the multinational enterprise, one that is remarkable for its cohesiveness and strength. On issues relating to the multinational enterprise, political enemies have buried their differences and voted *en bloc*— Iraq with Syria, Ethiopia with Somalia, Sudan with Libya, India with Pakistan, Zaïre with Angola, Brazil with Cuba, and so on.

To achieve this unity, however, individual countries have had to disregard vast differences in ideology and interest within the group. Accordingly, the common position has been limited to a list of demands to be made on a common adversary. Capital, technology, and access to markets, the group agrees, should be provided by the industrialized countries on easier terms. The industrialized countries should recognize the inherent right of the developing countries to preferential terms in access to technology and should use governmental powers to compel their enterprises to offer such terms. Moreover, the industrialized nations should finance a large fund for the stabi-

lization of commodity prices, and they should acknowl-
edge their joint and several responsibilities to do
everything necessary to help in all other respects. Meanwhile, each developing country should remain free to take
any further measures that in its opinion would contribute
to its national objectives.[3]

Various U.N. organs have offered to the developing
countries new facilities intended to improve their position in dealing with multinational enterprises. The
Centre on Transnational Corporations, set up in 1975,
promises not only to contribute to the stream of information regarding such enterprises, but also to provide direct
technical assistance to developing countries faced with
difficult problems in regulation or bargaining.[4] And
standing in the wings are a half-dozen different projects
for imposing codes of conduct of various sorts upon the
multinational enterprises that operate in developing
countries.

So far, the collective demands of the developing
countries have been exceedingly general. Most of the
countries are aware that defining their interests more explicitly would risk exposing the underlying conflicts
within the borders of each country and among the leaders
in the group. The effect of their collective efforts so far is
thus mainly atmospheric, aimed at stiffening the systems
of national administration and national regulation in
some developing countries. Meanwhile, individual countries continue quietly to offer tax holidays and preferential exemptions from local regulations to many prospective foreign investors. At the same time, the multinational
enterprises continue to protect their positions in developing countries by appearing to be indispensable and,
where their indispensability is on the wane, by bolstering
their bargaining position through the development of
new capacities and new functions.

All told, the developing countries may gain a little
from these international efforts by moderately strength-

ening their negotiating position. Nevertheless, for most countries, interdependence in some form or other seems likely to grow, not to decline. Whether it is accompanied by a sense of inferiority and dependence or by a sense of equality and mutuality will turn mainly on the internal capabilities and self-perceptions of the leadership in each country.

The problems of the industrialized countries in dealing with multinational enterprises are not wholly dissimilar from those of the developing nations. Most industrialized countries find themselves balancing the economic contributions of these enterprises against the need for a sense of national control. Most industrialized countries, too, face the problem of reconciling the diverse interests of the various domestic groups affected by the operations of these enterprises. Now and then, the strains have been strong and visible.

Take the case of France in the 1960s. Under the leadership of General de Gaulle, the objective of holding the Anglo-Saxons, especially the Americans, at arm's length and forging an independent political course for France became a major national objective. France withdrew its contingent from NATO's armed forces, vetoed Britain's entry into the Common Market, and flirted ostentatiously with the Soviet Union. Yet all through that period, under a case-by-case licensing procedure administered by the French bureaucracy, the subsidiaries of firms from the United States, Britain, and the rest of Europe were being admitted liberally into the French economy.[5]

The reason for the disparity between France's objectives and France's policies was, quite simply, that the price of independence had grown so high. Recognizing the costs of an autarkic policy, France opened up its borders to the goods of its European neighbors and of other countries, including the United States. Even if France excluded foreign-owned subsidiaries, therefore, it would not be excluding their products; these could still enter the French market as imports. Besides, the establishment of foreign-owned subsidiaries inside France was useful in other ways. A Ford Motor Company proposal to set up a plant in Bordeaux mobilized a wave of support from local political interests, an offer by General Electric was used to rescue a sick Machines Bull, an offer by Honeywell, in turn, to rescue General Electric,[6] and so on.

The Canadian case carries similar overtones. From the 1950s on, the growing concern of many Canadians about the threat of being swamped by the oversized economy to the south has been evident in a steady stream of official and unofficial studies and reports.[7] Yet the most potent economic step taken by the Canadians until the 1970s was one calculated to expand the role of multinational enterprises in a key Canadian industry, not to contain it. This was Canada's initiative in 1965 supporting the North American Automotive Agreement, a project that integrated the Canadian subsidiaries of U.S. automobile firms more firmly and extensively into the U.S. market. The reason why Canada avoided a restrictive regime was the same as that of France. Any measures taken against the steady tide of foreign investment generally carried some risks to specific Canadian interests. The Canadian need for capital and technology, for instance, seemed insatiable. Besides, an irrepressible rivalry among Canada's semiautonomous provinces complicated the mix. Francophone Quebec, unwilling to be outdistanced by the anglophone areas, was eager to invite multinational enterprises into the province. And the relatively poor Maritime Provinces of Nova Scotia and Newfoundland were determined to capture a share of the prosperity of the provinces surrounding the Great Lakes. The consequent ambivalence and frustration of Canadian leaders injected a new tone of bitterness in their approach to U.S. relations.[8]

Although the United States is commonly thought of

as the main source and support of multinational enterprises, U.S. policies toward the multinational enterprise can be interpreted in much the same light. U.S.
measures in the field of capital export controls, trade, and
taxation, all affecting the multinational enterprise, have
had to be tailored to fit the inescapable fact that some internal interests of the United States see themselves as
served by restrictive measures in these areas while other
internal interests see themselves as hurt by such measures.

Multinational enterprises now play a large role in the
national economies of most industrialized countries. As
long as those countries maintain representative governments, the interests of those enterprises will—and, on
any theory of representative government, should—carry
considerable weight. In the decade or two just ahead,
those in the industrialized countries who see their interests in strengthening the individual states will continue
to struggle with those who see their interests in operating
globally. Part of the struggle will take place inside each
nation. But part will surface in international organizations.

The organs of the European Economic Community,
for instance, have struggled valiantly to secure the adoption of a European program tailored to meet special problems associated with the multinational structure. Among
other things, the proposals cover problems of taxation,
employment, competition, and disclosure.[9] But so far,
progress has been insignificant, as both the multinational
enterprises and the national governments have tended to
resist any relevant action.

The OECD, at first glance, seems to have made a little
more progress in taking the edge off some of the tensions
among industrialized countries which are associated with
the expansion of multinational enterprises. The OECD organization has helped to create a model bilateral tax treaty
and has developed consulting mechanisms that could
head off international disputes over the application of na-

tional security controls and antitrust laws. But observe how that result has been achieved. The bilateral tax treaties have consisted mainly of agreements by both sides to pull back from levies and practices that might pinch business enterprises too painfully. The antitrust consulting procedures have also led to a pulling back; they have reduced the probability that any country would unilaterally apply its national antitrust laws, but they have not introduced in the place of those laws an effective way of dealing with the problems of international restrictive business practices. As for the consultation procedures on security controls, these have in general mitigated the force and the reach of restrictive U.S. measures and have placed the foreign subsidiaries of U.S. firms nearer to a parity position with their foreign competitors; but they have not improved the international machinery for dealing with the security issue. The tension has been reduced mainly by nations' agreeing to pretend that no common international problem exists.

One OECD-sponsored exercise that has taken a more affirmative approach is a set of guidelines adopted by OECD governments in 1976, which OECD member governments "jointly recommended to multinational enterprises operating in their territories." [10] The adoption of the code is voluntary, and its application unenforceable. But the enterprises that adopt the recommended guidelines will presumably be entitled to an extra modicum of goodwill from host governments. Under the guidelines, the multinational enterprises will publish information about their global operations which is somewhat more ample than that such enterprises customarily provide, including, notably, some added data classified by product line and by geographical area. The enterprises will undertake to avoid practices that might have anticompetitive results, such as buying up competitors and imposing discriminatory prices on buyers. They will provide information that national tax authorities might require about the operations of their networks in other countries. And they will adhere to a set of practices in labor relations that for some firms might represent a change from existing practices. For instance, they will undertake to mitigate the effects of a plant shutdown, to avoid threats to shut down an existing facility, and to negotiate in good faith with employee groups.

On the whole, the code can be seen as a cautious, evolutionary step in a long process of accommodation of the needs of the nation-states and those of the enterprises. But it has almost ostentatiously avoided any recognition of one basic source of the tension, namely, that any affiliate in a multinational network must be responsive in some degree to the imperatives of a global strategy and that any such affiliate—whether parent or subsidiary—is exposed in some measure to the influences of more than one government. Codes on the OECD pattern, therefore, still leave largely unresolved most of the underlying problems.

If history could be counted on to move in reasonably straight lines, the outlook for managing the tensions between multinational enterprises and national interests would not be altogether foreboding.

First of all, some trends now visible could very well reduce the sharp differences in viewpoint between the developing countries and the industrialized countries. Some countries that currently place themselves in the developing category—Brazil, Mexico, Iran, India, and a half-dozen others—are changing rapidly. These may find themselves supporting, in their national interest, policies not unlike those of the industrialized nations. That shift will begin as local entrepreneurs in such countries increase their capacity for assembling capital and technology and for building up effective access to foreign markets. It will be increased as the local firms move ahead

with the establishment of their own foreign operating
subsidiaries. When that happens, it is true, the search of
these countries for their particular Holy Grail will be set
back—their sense of autonomy will be reduced and their
elbowroom will shrink. But a few nations have demonstrated their capacity gradually to abandon the goal of autonomy without undergoing trauma, as evidenced by the
relatively relaxed state of the Scandanavian countries, the
Netherlands, and Singapore.

Most developing countries, however, are unlikely to
give up their persistent search for autonomy and choice.
As long as they lack the internal resources to meet their
compelling need for capital, technology, and market access, they will continue to feel threatened by their need to
rely on foreign-owned enterprises. With an improvement
in the capacity of those countries for administration and
negotiation, the sense of tension may conceivably be held
in bounds. Moreover, a decline in tension could be accelerated a little if—or, perhaps, as—the role of the multinational enterprise is determined and constrained by nego-
tiated international commodity agreements on the raw
materials. In addition, managerial contracts and other
ambiguous arrangements with foreign enterprises may
also provide the governments of developing countries
with a sense of increased control over the multinational
enterprise. The real role of the multinational enterprise
may not decline in some critical respects, such as control
of the channels by which a developing country gains
access to foreign markets. But the tone and form of participation on the part of developing countries could change
sufficiently to take the sharp edges off the tension.[11]

As for the role of multinational enterprises among industrialized countries, any projection based on the assumption of gradual change has to confront two linked
problems: the outsized proportions of the U.S. economy
and the unfinished state and uncertain future of European
integration.

As long as the U.S. economy continues to enjoy the relative advantages associated with sheer size and diversity, it is difficult to picture a set of altogether tranquil relations among industrialized countries on problems connected with the multinational enterprise. In the field of high technology, the buying and financing power of the U.S. government will remain a constant irritant. The lesser vulnerability of the U.S. economy to the effects of transactions across its borders will add to the irritation. Finally, the increasing propensity of European and Japanese firms to set up subsidiaries in the U.S. market will add to the worries of governments in their home countries, as some of the managerial attention and financial resources of these firms are diverted to the U.S. market.

If the U.S. economy persistently gains advantages from its relative size and relative autonomy, Europe might conceivably be compelled to respond. In that case, defying the standard prediction of present-day observers, European governments might find themselves pushed to a state of integration capable of matching the advantages that the U.S. economy provides. That would require a much more unified European policy toward high technology, a unified monetary area, and a capacity for effective negotiation with outside countries.

If Europe should develop that capacity, a great deal would depend on how the capacity was used. Bargaining between a united Europe and an outsized America could produce some sort of consensus on critical issues and some new degree of tolerance for the parties' growing interdependence—or it could produce a new level of hostility among equally matched adversaries. If the new matching of power led to easier consensus among the industrialized countries, it could establish a basis for their renewed leadership in world affairs. In that case, leaders in the developing countries would probably see the partnership of the rich as foreshadowing a new hegemony. Accordingly, the tension associated with the operation of multinational enterprises would continue to be very high.

History, however, has a habit of following a crooked course. New factors, not in the gradualist's predictive model, are bound to appear. Although factors of this sort cannot all be foreseen, a few are already so tangible that they merit a word or two of speculation.

One of these new elements is the possibility that command economies, such as that of the Soviet Union, may find themselves compelled to create their own crop of multinational enterprises. No crystal ball can be expected reliably to project the full consequences of such a development. What is clear is that whenever the multinational enterprise is thought to be linked directly to the decision-making apparatus of any government, it becomes a particularly troublesome institution for other nations to abide. The saving grace that has led governments so far to tolerate the foreign subsidiaries of state-owned enterprises, such as the subsidiaries of British Petroleum, Renault, and Volkswagen, has been the obvious disarticulation of those enterprises from the apparatus of government. But how far that tolerance will go is a highly uncertain question.

Another source of disruption could originate in the United States. Studies of the attitudes of American leaders in the mid-1970s agree on a number of points. Such leaders seem to accept the fact that the nation-states of the world are headed for an increasing degree of interdependence and that the U.S. will be involved in that trend along with everyone else.[12] But another powerful element is found in U.S. thinking, a mood rather than a projection. There is a sense of pique and resentment, a feeling that the rest of the world is using the United States as a punching bag, to express its own inadequacies and frustrations. Many Americans are irritated, for instance, when the CIA is trotted out by foreign commentators as the likely cause of any misfortune, from poor crops and adverse trade balances to earthquakes and train derailments. The resentment is coupled with a strong sense among many U.S. leaders—a sense not altogether inconsistent with the evidence—that most countries need the cooperation of the United States more than the other way around.

For many Americans, therefore, it is tempting to consider a policy by which the United States uses its brute bargaining power unilaterally, through channels of its own choosing, and reduces its participation in institutions such as the General Agreement on Tariffs and Trade, the International Monetary Fund, the World Bank, the International Energy Agency, the various international commodity agreements, the Organization of American States, and the United Nations. The overseas interests of U.S. enterprises, according to this view, would be protected not by the forbearance and cooperation of host governments but by the economic and political clout of the United States, and whatever the effects might be on the welfare of the world at large, U.S. welfare might conceivably be improved.[13] If the United States should decide to adopt that line of policy, a new, volatile element would be thrown into the mix, and present projections about the multinational enterprise could prove to be very wide off the mark.

But the most likely sources of major discontinuities are in the developing world. On the whole, the developing countries do not have quite as much capacity for upsetting the institution of the multinational enterprise as do the leaders of the industrial world. For one thing, multinational enterprises still do over two-thirds of their business in the industrialized countries; for another, the multinational enterprises are still in a position to bargain more effectively with a hostile developing country than with a hostile industrialized nation.

One strong possibility is that the objective conditions that helped to propel the Group of Seventy-seven into a

position of seeming strength will reverse themselves. A
brief, spasmodic shortage in some key raw materials
during the early 1970s put the developing countries in a
position to bargain more effectively, using the strength
provided by their resources. But the history of
capital-intensive standardized products, such as oil, metals, and chemicals, also includes recurrent periods of surplus. And the decline in the concentration of the world's
industrial structure in these products, recounted in
Chapter 4, carries powerful implications for the future behavior of the markets in these products. Among other
things, it suggests a decline in the power of leading firms
to hold up prices if a period of oversupply should develop.

The number of producers in standardized products
has been growing at a rapid rate, and many of the added
producers, new to their markets, are found casting about
for dependable outlets. In the Middle East, Latin America, and elsewhere, state-owned enterprises are appearing
in petrochemicals, chemicals, aluminum, and copper, determined to establish a place in world markets. In some
cases, these enterprises are assiduously cultivating the
markets of socialist countries. But these enterprises are
usually aware that socialist countries make major decisions to import, export, or shift their trading partners
through a central mechanism; accordingly, the socialist
countries are capable of even more abrupt shifts in their
trading patterns than are capitalist countries.[14] As a result, not many of the new producers are willing to place
all their eggs in one socialist basket, and many have been
pushing to find outlets in capitalist countries as well.[15]

The risks that the new sellers may prove to be a
destabilizing market force are increased a little because a
considerable proportion of them are state-owned and
state-managed. In spite of an occasional exception such as
Saudi Arabia, the state enterprises of most countries commonly have stronger reasons than private enterprises for

continuing to operate at high levels of output in the face of a softening in world demand; mines operated by state-owned enterprises, for instance, cannot easily cut back on production if employment will be affected.

If sharp price declines actually develop, the declines no doubt will stimulate proposals for intergovernmental commodity agreements. But various factors are likely to interfere with the prompt consummation of effective agreements. One of these is simply the increasing number of producers. Another is the disparity in the viewpoints of the producers; the state-owned enterprises of the developing countries, freshly hatched with a mandate to achieve independence for their national economies, cannot be expected to see eye to eye with the old dominant leaders from the industrialized countries.

Moreover, in products such as aluminum and copper, producers headquartered in the developing countries face the disconcerting fact that the multinational enterprises established in the industrialized countries are making some progress toward sloughing off their reliance on supplies from "unsafe" sources. In oil and its derivatives, the outlook is more problematic; all depends on the effects that higher oil prices may have on the long-run demand for oil, as well as on the size and timing of production from the North Sea, the U.S. East Coast, the USSR, and other such sources.

In any event, if the threat of surplus develops, the instinct of the leaders headquartered in the industrialized areas will be to try to secure a favored position for their "safe" supplies within the markets they have historically controlled. Since most of them maintain processing and distribution networks on both sides of the Atlantic, their interests could easily lead them to press for a protected area whose outer bounds covered the markets of the industrialized world. Access to the area would be available first of all to the products originating inside it and, second, to favored suppliers from the developing countries.

The history of international commodity arrangements offers plenty of illustrations of patterns such as these. In sugar, for instance, the U.S. market has been linked by quotas mainly to Latin America, Britain has been linked mainly to the Commonwealth, and Europe mainly to former colonies in Africa. And in oil, the U.S. market has been regulated in times of surplus on a similar principle.

That threat, or something like it, is one major reason why Saudi Arabia, Iran, Kuwait, Yugoslavia, and others have been willing to consider entering into joint ventures with Western firms. As a strategy, this approach may very well pay off for the developing countries that pursue it. At the same time, however, these links will tend to differentiate the interests of the different suppliers from developing countries and will weaken their ability to maintain unity in an effective bargaining bloc.

If the negotiating position of the developing countries should visibly deteriorate, some of them may be tempted to deal with their problems by imposing a higher degree of central control upon the national economy, emulating the Soviet pattern. But the success of such a strategy depends on a strong capacity for organization and a strong technical nucleus, such as China is said to have, and so far these qualities are exceptional among the developing countries. In recent years Indonesia, Egypt, Ghana, and Peru, among others, have had to pull back from their highly centralized systems in order to allow their economies to operate. In pulling back, they have tried to make a place for foreign-owned enterprises to operate, on one basis or another, inside the national structure.

Because the alternatives are so costly and so uncertain, the developing countries that now limit the role of the multinational enterprises are unlikely altogether to exclude them. The ability of such enterprises to use and reuse their information, their access to markets, and their trade names from one country to the next may prove to be relatively unimpaired. Accordingly, the sense of nakedness and uncertainty on the part of many developing countries may well remain high.

Neither the multinational enterprise nor the nation-state shows much evidence of losing its vitality in the world economy. Multinational forms of enterprise are still emerging in various forms in response to every new advance in international communication and transportation. And national programs intended for social betterment are still being initiated at a prodigious rate. At the same time, very few of the programs and policies presently being proposed seem likely to reduce the tension between multinational enterprises and national interests. The developing countries are still concentrating on the strategy of getting more, to the exclusion of other objectives. The leaders of the industrialized countries have learned to talk about a new state of interdependence, but they have not yet assimilated the extraordinary implications of the conditions they profess to recognize. And the managers of multinational enterprises for the most part are still at the stage of hoping that the tension will somehow go away.

One necessary condition for constructive action is to sort out those problems only partially related to the multinational enterprise and to recognize that they cannot be dealt with effectively by any program targeted at the multinational enterprise alone. The problems that arise out of the growing interdependence of nations illustrate the point. No matter what benefits multinational enterprises may claim to bring to any country, they do contribute in various ways to reducing the economic meaning of national boundaries. Nevertheless, the multinational enterprise is not the prime cause of interdependence. The increased efficiency of international communication has created the trend, and the multinational enterprise is much more a manifestation of the trend than a cause. But there is a widespread belief to the contrary, and there is a resulting expectation in many countries that exorcising the multinational enterprise will greatly alleviate a gnawing sense of dependence and vulnerability. As long as that misapprehension exists, it will be difficult to focus on the problems that are genuinely due to the multinational structure of enterprise.

The same point can be made with regard to some of the other major worries that are widely shared by national leaders in many countries—the emptiness, the corruption, the inequities, and the ugliness that so often accompany the industrializing process. Here again, it is commonly assumed that these problems will be greatly reduced by a program of control over the multinational enterprise. Yet as I read the evidence, the disposition of any enterprise to corrupt, pollute, or waste has not been greatly affected by whether an enterprise is widely multinational or narrowly national, state-owned or privately owned.

Nevertheless, the world's policymakers are right when they identify certain problems directly with the multinational structure of enterprise. Most of these problems stem from the ineluctable fact that the multinational enterprise is exposed simultaneously to various national jurisdictions. Accordingly, any government in a position to seize some sensitive part of the anatomy of a multinational network has the potential for influencing the rest of the network as well: when Mexico demands that its foreign-owned automobile subsidiaries export their components to other markets, São Paolo and Detroit are bound to suffer. At the same time, any action or reaction that emanates from the headquarters of the multinational network, whether induced by government or not, generally has repercussions beyond the jurisdiction in which the headquarters sits.

The problem of multiple jurisdictions adds new complications to virtually every issue that nations would normally classify under the general heading of industrial policy. These issues include, for instance, policies aimed at creating jobs, reducing inequitable income differences between classes and regions, ensuring the availability of scarce national supplies and the benign functioning of markets, securing tax revenues, promoting consumer safety, protecting the environment, and safeguarding national security. The very breadth of the agenda causes policymakers to recoil.

Not only is the agenda unusually broad; it is also unusually sensitive. Subjects such as taxation, subsidy, competition, and security controls go to the heart of domestic politics. Inside any nation, the war between competing interests—between labor and capital or between rich taxpayer and poor taxpayer—is settled by a variety of devices: diktat, law, court process, or strike. When an international dimension enters the war among the interests, cutting across nations, no obvious machinery exists for settling the clash; the numerous transnational links that have developed among like-minded groups in different countries, such as the links between business groups and those between labor unions in different countries, are not yet strong enough to carry such heavy weight. Intuitively, therefore, national policymakers find themselves pulling back from an international approach to problems arising out of the multinationalizing trend.

Although the variety of subjects appropriate to the agenda is appalling, many of the subjects call for a somewhat similar international approach. One common need is to disentangle conflicting national jurisdictions, so that the unilateral actions of individual states will not have the effect, often inadvertent, of harming other states. That is what the OECD has sought to do, for instance, in its efforts to limit the extraterritorial reach of antitrust actions by national authorities. A second common need is to find a way of securing agreement among national authorities concerning the nature of the public action that may be needed.

Although these needs are obvious, very few countries are in a mood to discuss them in the terms I have suggested here. Certainly not the developing countries. One or another may be willing to bargain hard with individual enterprises or to struggle over the terms of a new international commodity agreement. But as a manifestation of their loyalty to the group, most developing countries are determined to display an unswerving public attitude of hostility toward multinational enterprises. This prevents the group from bargaining realistically over a new international regime governing the activities of such enterprises, because any such regime would entail new obligations on the part of the developing countries in addition to new rights and privileges.

To the extent that international cooperation is conceivable at this stage, therefore, it consists largely of cooperation among the industrialized countries. For them, the means of disentangling national jurisdictions would vary according to the subject matter. With some problems it might be sufficient for sovereign states to enter into agreements explicitly limiting their jurisdictional reach; security controls, for instance, could conceivably be dealt with in this way. But other areas will require a set of common rules that shape and limit the application of domestic law, as well as ongoing institutions to administer the rules. In the field of taxation, for instance, avoiding a destructive clash of jurisdictions would require some agreed-upon rules on how to calculate the profits of the multinational network, as well as rules on transfer prices and the allocation of central administrative costs.

But disentangling national jurisdictions will not be enough in many cases. Affirmative international action also may be required. In the field of restrictive business practices, for instance, nations will have to go beyond a commitment to keep from treading on one another's toes and will have to find the standards and the machinery for a collective response.

So far, the initiatives of governments have been trivial in relation to the issues. We cannot altogether overlook the modest initiatives of multinational organizations, such as the disclosure program of the U.N. Centre for Transnational Corporations and the OECD voluntary code. But these efforts are only marginally relevant to the problem of disentangling and redirecting national jurisdictions as they bear on the multinational enterprise. Besides, the effect of these initiatives is diluted by insistent confusion over their purpose—whether that purpose is to deal with the special problems associated with multinational enterprise or with the more general problems of an industrializing society.

In the end, some nations, even developing nations, may be persuaded to face the problem of uncoupling and remeshing their national jurisdictions in order to handle multinational-enterprise problems. If they do, progress is likely to come from the realization that failure to act will reintroduce, in a new and virulent form, the beggar-thy-neighbor policies so prevalent in international economic relations forty years ago. The realization that any government can exert influence on all the units of a multinational network opens up possibilities for economic aggression and counteraggression that have only begun to be exploited. Mexico's insistence that foreign-owned automobile plants in Mexico export their components to other markets could be countered by the insistence of other governments that their affiliates be designated as exporters. The demand of home governments that parents assess their foreign subsidiaries for a share of the network's central costs of research and administration could be countered by the insistence of other governments that no such payments be made. This conl;ict of national wills could produce a stalemate for governments. Meanwhile, the cutting edges of the conflicting jurisdictions, pushing

into the structure of multinational enterprises, could produce in such enterprises a pattern of erratic and evasive
action that no government intended and that served no
nation's interests.

In times past, nations have sometimes managed to
head off a threatening escalation in beggar-thy-neighbor
policies. Thanks to various international agreements, for
instance, tariff wars and competitive devaluations no
longer pose quite the threat that they did in decades past.
To be sure, the challenge of finding an acceptable international regime for the multinational enterprise is more formidable in many ways than the challenge posed by tariff
wars and competitive devaluations. Moreover, at this
juncture, it is hard to detect among the leaders of government and of business any disposition to begin serious
work on building an acceptable international regime. But
the time for constructive response has not yet run out.
And these leaders may yet prove subject to persuasion
that the existing strands of national and international policy create a situation that could inflict lasting injury on all
the interests concerned.

Notes

Index

Notes

CHAPTER 1. THE MULTINATIONAL ENTERPRISE AS SYMBOL

1. American Telephone and Telegraph Co., *The Telephone in America* (New York, 1971), p. 15; P. C. Mabon, *Mission Communications: The Story of Bell Laboratories* (Murray Hill, N.J.: Bell Telephone Laboratories, 1975), pp. 30, 37, 71.

2. Rein Turn, *Computers in the 1980s* (New York: Columbia University Press, 1974), pp. 53–59.

3. The data are from various editions of *World Air Transport Statistics,* published by the International Air Transport Association.

4. The data on operating expenses are based on U.S. experience, reported in the U.S. Civil Aeronautics Board annual, *Handbook of Airline Statistics.*

5. *The State of Food and Agriculture, 1974* (Rome: Food and Agriculture Organization, 1975), pp. 139–145.

6. *Statistical Yearbook 1972* (Paris: UNESCO, 1973), pp. 47–48; World Bank, *Trends in Developing Countries* (Washington, 1973), chap. 3–6.

7. For Brazilian data, see John Wells, "Underconsumption, Market Size and Expenditure Patterns in Brazil," *Bulletin of the Society for Latin American Studies,* no. 26 (March 1976), pp. 28–39.

8. R. T. Kudrle, *Agricultural Tractors: A World Industry Study* (Cambridge, Mass.: Ballinger, 1975), pp. 141–152.

9. A. J. Surrey and J. H. Chesshire, *The World Market for Electric Power Equipment* (Brighton: University of Sussex, 1972), pp. 22, 31.

10. See Nathan Rosenberg, "Introduction," in Nathan Rosenberg, ed., *The American System of Manufactures* (Edinburgh: Edinburgh University Press, 1969); Christopher Freeman, "Process Plant: Innovation and the World Market," *National Institute Economic Review,* no. 45 (August 1968), pp. 40, 50.

11. See, for instance, General Agreement on Tariffs and Trade (GATT), *International Trade, 1974/1975* (Geneva, 1975), p. 2; also R. N. Cooper, *The Economics of Interdependence* (New York: McGraw-Hill, 1968), pp. 59–63; Assar Lindbeck, "The Changing Role of the Nation State," *Kyklos* 28 (1975): 23–46.

12. See, for instance, Organization for Economic Cooperation and Development (OECD), *The Chemical Industry, 1967–68* (Paris, 1968), pp. 35–37; OECD, *Policy Perspectives for International Trade and Economic Relations* (Paris, 1972), p. 147; and GATT, *International Trade, 1967* (Geneva, 1968), pp. 31–75.

13. Compiled from various International Monetary Fund sources.

14. UNCTAD, *Proceedings,* 3d Sess., New York, 1973, TD/180, 111: 113–116.

15. For a review of Indian experience, see National Council of Applied Economic Research, *Foreign Technology and Investment* (New Delhi, 1971).

16. For India, the trend is well described in Ranadav Banerji, *Exports of Manufacturers from India: An Appraisal of the Emerging Pattern* (Tübingen: J. C. B. Mohr [P. Siebeck], 1975). See also GATT, *International Trade, 1973* (Geneva, 1974), pp. 104–140.

17. Banerji, *Exports of Manufactures from India,* p. 116.

18. *Forbes,* July 1, 1974, pp. 39–43. See also *The Economist,* February 16, 1976, special survey on international banking; Federal Reserve Bank of New York, *Monthly Review,* June 1973, pp. 140–154; and testimony of A. F. Brimmer in U.S., Congress, House, Committee on Banking, Currency and Housing, Subcommittee on Financial Institutions Supervision, Regulation and Insurance, *Financial Institutions and the Nation's Economy,* 94th Cong., 1st Sess., 1975.

19. These figures and those in the sentence that follows were compiled by the Harvard Multinational Enterprise Project.

20. Federal Reserve Board, reproduced in A. F. Brimmer and F. R. Dahl, "Growth of American International Banking: Implications for Public Policy," *Journal of Finance* 30, no. 2 (May 1975): 345.

CHAPTER 2. THE MULTINATIONAL ENTERPRISE: A CLOSE-UP VIEW

1. In the case of U.S. firms, multinational enterprises have been about three times the size of national enterprises on the average, according to unpublished data of the Harvard Multinational Enterprise Project.

2. Compiled by the Harvard Multinational Enterprise Project. Other studies have produced similar results. See, for example, Tom Houston, "Dimensions of U.K. Transnational Business," in S. P. Sethi

and R. H. Holton, eds., *Management of Multinational Operations* (New York: Free Press, 1974), table 4, p. 56.

3. See, for example, R. E. Caves, "International Corporations: The Industrial Economics of Foreign Investment," *Economica* 38, no. 149 (February 1971): 12–17.

4. F. M. Scherer, *Industrial Market Structure and Economic Performance* (Chicago: Rand McNally, 1970), p. 68. Also, R. P. Rumelt, *Strategy, Structure, and Economic Performance* (Boston: Division of Research, Harvard Business School, 1974), chap. 2.

5. See B. R. Scott, "The Industrial State: Old Myths and New Realities," *Harvard Business Review* 51, no. 2 (March–April 1973): 139–141; also A. D. Chandler, Jr., "The Multi-Unit Enterprise," in H. F. Williamson, ed., *Evolution of International Management Structures* (Newark, Del.: University of Delaware Press, 1975), pp. 225–254.

6. M. Y. Yoshino, *Japan's Multinational Enterprises* (Cambridge, Mass.: Harvard University Press, 1976), pp. 5–9, 95.

7. W. T. Hogan, *The 1970s: Critical Years for Steel* (Lexington, Mass.: D. C. Heath, 1972), p. 88.

8. J. L. Enos, "Invention and Innovation in the Petroleum Refining Industry," in R. R. Nelson, ed., *Rate and Direction of Inventive Activity* (Princeton: Princeton University Press, 1962), pp. 311–312.

9. Seev Hirsh, "The United States Electronics Industry in International Trade," in L. T. Wells, Jr., ed., *The Product Life Cycle and International Trade* (Boston: Division of Research, Harvard Business School, 1972), p. 49.

10. A. W. Lake, "Multinational Firms and the U.K. Pharmaceutical Industry: A Study of Innovation and Imitation," working paper, National Bureau of Economic Research, 1975, p. 5; B. M. Bloom, "The Rate of Contemporary Drug Discovery," in B. M. Bloom and G. E. Ullyot, eds., *Drug Discovery: Science and Development in a Changing Society* (Washington: American Chemical Society, 1971), pp. 176–184.

11. Compiled by the Harvard Multinational Enterprise Project.

12. Federal Reserve Board data, in testimony of A. F. Brimmer, U.S., Congress, House, Committee on Banking, Currency and Housing, Subcommittee on Financial Institutions Supervision, Regulation and Insurance, *Financial Institutions and the Nation's Economy*, 94th Cong., 1st and 2d Sess., 1975–1976, pt. 1, pp. 383–434.

13. Ibid., pt. 2, pp. 994–1098.

14. See, for instance, *The Banker* 125, no. 597 (November 1975): 1327–61.

15. Gert Rosenthal, "The Role of Private Foreign Investment in the Development of the Central American Common Market" (in press), table 27.

16. These data and others are reported in L. T. Wells, Jr., "The Internationalization of Firms from the Developing Countries," in C. P. Kindleberger, ed., *Multinationals from Small Countries* (Cambridge, Mass.: M.I.T. Press, 1977).

17. K. Balakrishnan, "Indian Joint Ventures Abroad: An Analysis of the Geographical and Industry Patterns," mimeographed (Ahmadabad: Indian Institute of Management), presented in New Delhi, March 1976.

18. R. J. Barnet and R. E. Müller, *Global Reach* (New York: Simon and Schuster, 1974), p. 361.

19. This point has been emphasized by various economists; see, for instance, C. P. Kindleberger, *American Business Abroad* (New Haven: Yale University Press, 1969), pp. 11–13.

20. D. T. Brash, *American Investment in Australian Industry* (Cambridge, Mass.: Harvard University Press, 1966), pp. 195, 117; D. Van den Bulcke, "Les entreprises étrangères dans l'industrie belge," study of the Seminaire d'Economie Appliqué, University of Ghent (Ghent, 1971), pp. 272–297; A. E. Safarian, *Foreign Ownership of Canadian Industry* (Toronto: McGraw-Hill, 1966), pp. 86–88; M. D. Steuer et al., *The Impact of Foreign Direct Investment on the U.K.* (London: Her Majesty's Stationery Office, 1973), pp. 138–147; R. S. Deane, *Foreign Investment in New Zealand Manufacturing* (Wellington: Sweet and Maxwell, 1970), pp. 183–188; Gérard Garnier, "Pouvoirs de décision des filiales québécoises d'entreprises américaines," *Etudes Internationales* 2, no. 1 (March 1971): 36, 40–42; C. O. Bertero, "Drugs and Dependency in Brazil: An Empirical Study of Dependency Theory" (Ph.D. diss., Cornell University, 1972), pp. 139–140; see also S. M. Robbins and R. B. Stobaugh, *Money in the Multinational Enterprise: A Study of Financial Policy* (New York: Basic Books, 1973).

21. International Labor Organization, *Social and Labor Practices of Some European-Based Multinationals in the Metal Trades* (Geneva, 1976), ppm 75–83, 115; International Textile, Garment, and Leather Workers Federation, "Multinational Corporations and Trade Unions" (Brussels, 1975), p. 80; Van den Bulcke, "Les entreprises étrangères," pp. 281–298; M. J. Jedel and Duane Kujawa, "Management and Employment Practices of Foreign Direct Investors in the U.S.," mimeographed, submitted to the U.S. Department of Commerce, Washington, March 1976, pp. 37–38.

22. Ulrich E. Wiechmann, "Marketing Management in Marketing-Intensive Firms" (D.B.A. diss., Harvard Business School, 1974), pp. 164–166; R. J. Aylmer, "Who Makes Marketing Decisions in Multinational Firms?" *Journal of Marketing* 3 (October 1970): 25–30.

23. Henri de Bodinat, "Influence in the Multinational Corporation" (D.B.A. diss., Harvard Business School, 1975), chap. 6.

24. L. G. Franko, *The European Multinationals* (London: Harper & Row, 1976), p. 199.

25. The studies are summarized in Chandler, "The Multi-Unit Enterprise," pp. 225–254.

26. Scott, "The Industrial State," p. 139.

27. For insight into the power and persistence of cultural differences in business management, see David Granick, *Managerial Comparisons of Four Developed Countries: France, Great Britain, United States, and Russia* (Cambridge, Mass.: M.I.T. Press, 1972); Heinz Hartmann, ed., "German Management," *International Studies of Management and Organization* 3, nos. 1–2 (Spring–Summer 1973).

28. See Kozo Yamamura, "A Compromise with Culture: The Historical Evolution of Large Japanese Firms," in Williamson, *Evolution of International Management Structures*, pp. 159–185, as well as the qualifying comments by H. T. Patrick, ibid., pp. 186–192.

29. Yoshino, *Japan's Multinational Enterprises*, pp. 122, 167–178; Yoshihiro Tsurumi, *The Japanese Are Coming* (Cambridge, Mass.: Ballinger, 1976), chap. 8; J. E. Roemer, *U.S.-Japanese Competition in International Markets* (Berkeley: University of California Press, 1975), chap. 4.

30. For a discussion of the use of such holdings by British companies, see J. M. Stopford and K. O. Haberich, "Policies for Ownership and Control of Foreign Manufacturing Affiliates," mimeographed, London Business School [1975].

31. J. M. Stopford and L. T. Wells, Jr., *Managing the Multinational Enterprise* (New York: Basic Books, 1972), p. 108.

32. Franko, *The European Multinationals*, p. 197.

CHAPTER 3. ENTERPRISE STRATEGIES: THE TECHNOLOGY FACTOR

1. See A. K. Severn and M. M. Lawrence, "Direct Investment, Research Intensity, and Profitability," *Journal of Financial and Quantitative Analysis* 29 (March 1974): 181–190; B. N. Wolf, "Size and Profitability among U.S. Manufacturing Firms: Multinational versus Primarily Domestic Firms," *Journal of Economics and Business* 28, no. 1 (Fall 1975): 15–22.

2. D. C. Mueller and J. E. Tilton, "Research and Development Costs as a Barrier to Entry," *Canadian Journal of Economics* 2, no. 4 (November 1970): 570–579.

3. Edwin Mansfield, *Economics of Technological Change* (New York: W. W. Norton, 1968), pp. 69–98; John Jewkes, David Sawers, and Richard Stillerman, *The Sources of Invention* (New York: St. Martin's Press, 1958), pp. 162–166; A. A. Romeo, "Interindustry and Interfirm Differences in the Rate of Diffusion and Innovation," *Review of Economics and Statistics* 57, no. 3 (August 1975): 311–319; W. J. Adams,

"Firm Size and Resource Activity: France and the U.S.," *Quarterly Journal of Economics* 84, no. 3 (August 1970): 386–409. F. M. Scherer, *Industrial Market Structure and Economic Performance* (Chicago: Rand McNally, 1970), pp. 352–362.

4. For a summary of such studies based on U.S. experience, see U.S., Congress, Joint Economic Committee, Subcommittee on Economic Growth, *Technology, Economic Growth and International Competitiveness*, by Robert Gilpin, 94th Cong., 1st Sess., 1975, pp. 35–40. For an account of the European experience, see L. G. Franko, *The European Multinationals* (London: Harper & Row, 1976), pp. 27–44.

5. Nathan Rosenberg, "The Direction of Technological Change: Inducement Mechanisms and Focussing Devices," *Economic Development and Cultural Change* 18, no. 1, pt. 1 (October 1969): 17–18; also Sumner Myers and Donald Marquis, *Successful Industrial Innovations*, NSF-69-17 (Washington: National Science Foundation, 1969), p. 31; Report of the Central Advisory Council, *Technological Innovation in Britain* (London: Her Majesty's Stationery Office, 1969), p. 3.

6. Edwin Mansfield et al., *Research and Innovation in the Modern Corporation* (New York: W. W. Norton, 1971), pp. 40–42.

7. For an indication of the difficulties associated with creating impact in communication, see T. J. Allen, "The Differential Performance of Information Channels in the Transfer of Technology," in W. H. Gruber and D. G. Marquis, eds., *Factors in the Transfer of Technology* (Cambridge, Mass.: M.I.T. Press, 1969), pp. 137–154; also E. M. Rogers and F. F. Shoemaker, *Communication of Innovations* (New York: Free Press, 1971).

8. See J. M. Utterbeck et al., "The Process of Innovation in Five Industries in Europe and Japan," *IEEE Transactions in Engineering Management*, February 1976, pp. 3–9.

9. The process and the related literature are nicely described in R. R. Nelson and S. G. Winter, "In Search of a Useful Theory of Innovation," in Karl Stroetman, ed., *Innovation, Economic Change, Technological Policy* (Basel: Birkhauser Verlag, 1976).

10. D. B. Creamer, *Overseas Research and Development by United States Multinationals, 1966–1975* (New York: The Conference Board, 1976).

11. For U.S. firms, R. C. Ronstadt, "R & D Abroad: The Creation and Evolution of Foreign Research and Development Activities of U.S.-Based Multinational Enterprises" (D.B.A. diss., Harvard Business School, 1975), pp. 193–208, reproduced by Xerox University Microfilms, Ann Arbor. For Sweden, H.-F. Samuelsson, "National Scientific and Technological Potential and the Activities of Multinational Corporations: The Case of Sweden," mimeographed, Report to the OECD Committee for Scientific and Technological Policy, 1974.

12. Another illustration of the occasional exception to the predominant pattern is the U.S.-based drug companies' practice of introducing their new drugs first in the United Kingdom, largely because of the inhibiting effects of U.S. law on the introduction of drugs. A. W. Lake, "Foreign Competition and the U.K. Pharmaceutical Industry," proposed working paper, National Bureau of Economic Research, March 1976.

13. Compiled by the Harvard Multinational Enterprise Project

14. Almarin Phillips, *Technology and Market Structure: A Study of the Aircraft Industry* (Lexington, Mass.: D. C. Heath, 1971), p. 104; Aerospace Industries Association of America, *Aerospace Facts and Figures* (New York: *Aviation Week and Space Technology*, 1971–1972), p. 38.

15. T. G. Parry, "Firms of International Production and Home Industry Characteristics: The U.S. Manufacturing Sector," University of Reading Discussion Paper, no. 19 (Reading, Eng., April 1975), pp. 3, 10–12.

16. See, for instance, Joseph Ben-David, *Fundamental Research and the Universities* (Paris: Organization for Economic Cooperation and Development, 1968), p. 21; *Gaps in Technology: Comparison between Member Countries in Education, R & D, Technological Innovation, International Exchanges* (Paris: OECD, 1970), p. 184.

17. See, for instance, U.S., Congress, *Technology, Economic Growth and International Competitiveness.*

18. Ibid., p. 7; Michael Boretsky, "Concerns about the Present American Position in International Trade," in *Technology and International Trade* (Washington: National Academy of Engineering, 1971), pp. 34–35.

19. R. E. Miller, *Innovation, Organization, and Environment: A Study of Sixteen American and West European Steel Firms* (Sherbrooke, Quebec: University of Sherbrooke, 1971), pp. 127–128; Walter Adams and J. B. Dirlam, "Big Steel, Invention, and Innovation," *Quarterly Journal of Economics* 80, no. 2 (May 1966): 169–174; OECD, *Gaps in Technology: Non-Ferrous Metals* (Paris, 1969), pp. 68–82; M. Hohenberg, *Chemicals in Western Europe, 1850–1914: An Economic Study of Technical Change* (Chicago: Rand McNally, 1967), pp. 109–113, 117–125.

20. For the computer industry, see Y. S. Hu, *The Impact of U.S. Investment in Europe: A Case Study of the Automotive and Computer Industries* (New York: Praeger, 1973), pp. 68–71. For telecommunications, see James Martin, *Future Development in Telecommunications* (Englewood Cliffs, N.J.: Prentice-Hall, 1971).

21. See "Sweeping the Sea Floor, *The Economist*, September 15, 1973, p. 70; David Jones, "North Sea Oil," *Worldwide Projects and Installations*, March–April 1973, pp. 14–20; D. L. Wright and Dale Crane, "Laser Becomes a Component for Mass-Market Application," *Electronics* 47, no. 12 (June 13, 1974): 91–95.

22. On the increasing problems of scale associated with new aircraft development, see M. S. Hochmuth, "Aerospace," in Raymond Vernon, ed., *Big Business and the State: Changing Relations in Western Europe* (Cambridge, Mass.: Harvard University Press, 1974), pp. 145–169. On the introduction of Britain's carbon-fiber innovation, see "Mr. Nicholson's Other Headache," *The Economist,* October 9, 1971, p. 76.

23. J. E. Parker, *The Economics of Innovation: The National and Multinational Enterprises in Technological Change* (London: Longmans, 1974), p. 41; OECD, *Gaps in Technology: Electronic Computers* (Paris, 1969), pp. 66–67.

24. B. I. Cohen, Jorge Katz, and W. T. Beck, "Innovation and Foreign Investment Behavior of the U.S. Pharmaceutical Industry," Working Paper, no. 101 NBER, August 1975; V. A. Mund, "The Return on Investment of the Innovative Pharmaceutical Firm" in J. D. Cooper, ed., *The Economics of Drug Innovation* (Washington: American University Press, 1970), pp. 130, 133.

25. For statistics comparing the U.S. government programs and the U.S. market with those of the EEC. countries, see "Action Programme for the European Aeronautical Sector," *Bulletin of the European Communities,* Supplement 11/75, October 3, 1975.

26. "Harrier Jump-Jet: Yanks Take Over," *The Economist,* October 11, 1975, p. 98; also "Departure Delayed," ibid., May 1, 1976, p. 85.

27. For some of the difficulties encountered in the European programs, see P. S. Johnson, *Cooperative Research in Industry: An Economic Study* (New York: John Wiley and Sons, 1973); *The Conditions for Success in Technological Innovation* (Paris: OECD, 1971), p. 115; U.K. Sixth Report from the Expenditure Committee, Session 1971–72, *Public Money in the Private Sector* (London: Her Majesty's Stationery Office, July 1972).

28. Nicolas Jéquier, "Computers," in Vernon, *Big Business and the State,* p. 209.

29. Ibid.; Hochmuth, "Aerospace," ibid., pp. 145–169.

30. H. R. Nau, *National Politics and International Technology* (Baltimore: Johns Hopkins University Press, 1974), p. 151. See also P. L. Joskow, "The International Nuclear Industry Today," *Foreign Affairs* 54, no. 4 (July 1976): 788–803.

31. See "That's Unidata, That Was," *The Economist,* September 13, 1975, p. 56.

32. "French Computers," ibid., May 17, 1975, p. 87.

33. "After Concorde: Shall We Dance?," ibid., April 3, 1976, pp. 111–112.

34. See, for instance, "Nucléaire: un quatrième américain entre dans la course en Europe," *Entreprise,* September 21, 1972, p. 89;

"Computers: A Survey," *The Economist,* September 13, 1975, pp. 5–9.

35. Franko, *The European Multinationals,* pp. 219–220.

36. See, for instance, the following cases from Intercollegiate Case Clearing House, Harvard Business School: "United Electric Berhad (B)" (9-571-620), "Philippine Association of Flour Millers" (9-512-031), "Esso Pakistan (A)" (9-575-618), and "The ITT Global Advertising Campaign" (9-573-676).

37. For a survey of the literature, see G. K. Helleiner, "The Role of Multinational Corporations in the Less-Developed Countries' Trade in Technology," *World Development* 3, no. 4 (April 1975): 161–189. For a discussion of technology and the means by which it is transferred to developing countries, see W. A. Chudson and L. T. Wells, Jr., "The Acquisition of Technology from Multinational Corporations by Developing Countries," ST/ESA/12, prepared for the United Nations Department of Economic and Social Affairs (New York, 1974). See also David Morawetz, "Employment Implications of Industrialization in Developing Countries: A Survey," *Economic Journal* 84, no. 335 (September 1974): 491–542.

38. For tractors, see R. H. Mason, "Technology Transfer and Adaptation of Production Processes by Foreign Agribusiness Firms in Developing Countries," mimeographed, Conference on Foreign Agribusiness, University of Iowa, May 22–25, 1972; for automobiles, Jack Baranson, *International Transfer of Automobile Technology to Developing Countries,* UNITAR Research Report, no. 8 (New York, 1971), pp. 57–61.

39. "Detroit's Low-Gear Drive in Asia," *Far Eastern Economic Review* 85, no. 28 (July 15, 1974): 58–61.

40. See, for example, Fernando Fajnzylber and T. Martínez Tarragó, *Las empresas transnacionales: expansión a nivel mundial y proyección en la industria mexicana* (Mexico City: Fondo de Cultura Económica, 1976), p. 153.

41. The increase in capital intensity which often accompanies expanded production can be explained in engineering terms. See, for example, W. P. Strassmann, *Technological Change and Economic Development: The Manufacturing Experience of Mexico and Puerto Rico* (Ithaca: Cornell University Press, 1968), pp. 157–166; David Felix, "The Technological Factor in Socio-Economic Dualism: Toward an Economy-of-Scale Paradigm for Development Theory," mimeographed, 1976, pp. 10–14; S. A. Morley and G. W. Smith, "The Choice of Technology: Multinational Firms in Brazil," Rice University, Program of Development Studies, no. 58 (Houston, Fall 1974); Howard Pack; "The Substitution of Labor for Capital in Kenyan Manufacturing," *Economic Journal* 86, no. 341 (March 1976): 50–52.

42. Indicative of the wide range of conclusions, covering all possi-

bilities, are D. J. Lecraw, "Choice of Technology in Low-Wage Countries: The Case of Thailand" (Ph.D. diss., Harvard University, 1976), pp. 89–91); R. H. Mason, *The Transfer of Technology and the Factor Proportions Problem: The Philippines and Mexico,* UNITAR Research Report, no. 10 (New York, 1972); Pack, "The Substitution of Labor for Capital in Kenya," pp. 56–57; Francis Stewart, "Technology and Employment in Less-Developed Countries," *World Development* 2, no. 3 (March 1974): 38–39.

43. See, for example, W. A. Yeoman, "Selection of Production Processes for the Manufacturing Subsidiaries of U.S.-Based Multinational Corporations" (D.B.A. diss., Harvard Business School, 1968). See also, L. T. Wells, Jr., "Economic Man and Engineering Man: Choice and Technology in a Low-Wage Country," *Public Policy* 21, no. 2 (Summer 1973): 331; James Keddie, "Adoptions of Production Techniques by Industrial Firms in Indonesia" (Ph.D. diss., Harvard University, 1975), esp. pp. 136–137, 143–152; D. J. Lecraw, "Choice of Technology in Low-Wage Countries," pp. 105–106; L. J. White, "Appropriate Technology and a Competitive Environment: Some Evidence from Pakistan," *Quarterly Journal of Economics* 90, no. 4 (November 1976): 575–589. For an explicit example, see R. B. Stobaugh et al., *Nine Investments Abroad and Their Impact at Home* (Boston: Division of Research, Harvard Business School, 1976.)

44. Felix, "The Technological Factor," pp. 21–22.

45. J. N. Bhagwati and T. N. Srinivasan, *Foreign Trade Regimes and Economic Development: India* (New York: NBER, 1975), pp. 212–227, discusses Indian research and development efforts in some detail.

46. "Mexico: The Drive to Export Home-Grown Know-How," *Business Week,* August 30, 1976, p. 40. For an illustration from the refrigeration industry, see L. T. Wells, Jr., "The Internationalization of Firms from the Developing Countries," in C. P. Kindleberger, ed., *Multinationals from Small Countries* (Cambridge, Mass.: M.I.T. Press, 1977). One of the objectives of a new Third World Center established in Mexico City is to speed this trend.

47. A. U. Khan, "Mechanization Technology for Tropical Agriculture," in Nicolas Jéquier, ed., *Appropriate Technology: Problems and Promises* (Paris: OECD Development Centre, 1976), pp. 213–230.

48. M. K. Garg, "The Scaling-down of Modern Technology: Crystal Sugar Manufacturing in India," ibid., pp. 156–170.

CHAPTER 4. ENTERPRISE STRATEGIES: THE DRIVE FOR STABILITY

1. The advantages of scale is a subject of endless debate among economists. For a summary of the conventional wisdom, see H. J. Goldschmid, H. M. Mann, and J. F. Watson, eds., *Industrial Concentration: The New Learning* (Boston: Little, Brown, 1974).

2. See *Bell Journal of Economics* 6, no. 1 (Spring 1975), esp. the articles of Robert Wilson and A. M. Spence, for a roundup of the existing theory. See also K. J. Arrow, *The Limits of Organization* (New York: W. W. Norton, 1974), esp. pp. 39, 42, 58. For a more institutionally oriented analysis, see P. R. Lawrence and J. W. Lorsch, *Organization and Environment* (Boston: Harvard Business School, 1967), as well as Raymond Vernon, "Organization as a Scale Factor in the Growth of Firms," in J. W. Markham and G. F. Papanek, eds., *Industrial Organization and Economic Development* (Boston: Houghton Mifflin, 1970).

3. Jacob Viner, *Dumping: A Problem in International Trade* (Chicago: University of Chicago Press, 1923), pp. 51–93.

4. See, for instance, Ervin Hexner, *International Cartels* (Chapel Hill: University of North Carolina Press, 1946); G. W. Stocking and M. W. Watkins, *Cartels in Action* (New York: Twentieth Century Fund, 1946); L. G. Franko, *The European Multinationals* (London: Harper & Row, 1976), pp. 74–104.

5. Summarized in Kingman Brewster, Jr., *Antitrust and American Business Abroad* (New York: McGraw-Hill, 1958), pp. 26–30.

6. H. B. Price, *The Marshall Plan and Its Meaning* (Ithaca: Cornell University Press, 1955), pp. 107–108, 139, 156, 333; U.S. International Cooperation Administration, *European Productivity and Technical Assistance Programs: A Summing Up (1948–1958)* (Paris [1958?]), pp. 6–7; W. A. Brown, Jr., and Redvers Opie, *American Foreign Assistance* (Washington: Brookings Institution, 1953), pp. 240–241; W. R. Sharp, *International Technical Assistance Programs and Organization* (Chicago: Public Administration Clearing House, 1952), pp. 39–44. See also Nobuo Noda, *How Japan Absorbed American Management Methods* (Tokyo: Asian Productivity Organization, 1969), pp. 22–23.

7. For oil, see M. A. Adelman, *The World Petroleum Market 1946–1969* (Washington: Resources for the Future, 1971); for tin, Zuhayr Mikdashi, *A Comparative Analysis of Selected Mineral Exporting Industries*, mimeographed (Vienna, March 1971); for aluminum, ibid., as well as "La grande bataille de l'aluminium," *Entreprise*, December 6, 1969, pp. 51–71; for copper, F. E. Banks, *The World Copper Market: An Economic Analysis* (Cambridge, Mass: Ballinger, 1974).

8. "Alcan Goes More International," *The Economist*, September 6, 1969, p. 48.

9. See esp. F. T. Knickerbocker, *Oligopolistic Reaction and Multinational Enterprises* (Boston: Harvard Business School, 1973).

10. Quoted in "Ford Regroups for the Minicar Battle," *New York Times*, December 14, 1975, sec. 3, pp. 1, 9.

11. F. T. Knickerbocker, "Competition among Multinational Enterprises" (unpublished).

12. Knickerbocker, *Oligopolistic Reaction*, pp. 166–178. Knicker-

bocker does not address the behavior of standardized products as a class, but the conclusion is implicit in his findings.

13. E. M. Graham, "Oligopolistic Imitation and European Direct Investment in the United States" (D.B.A. diss., Harvard Business School, 1974), pp. 175–177. Graham attributes this motive for establishing U.S. subsidiaries to, among others, Olivetti, ICI, Volvo, and Nixdorf.

14. For statistical analyses consistent with this hypothesis, see Graham, "Oligopolistic Imitation"; E. B. Flowers, "Oligopolistic Reaction in European Direct Foreign Investment in the United States" (doctoral diss., Georgia State University, 1975).

15. The classic source for an institutional description of the process is still Yair Aharoni, *The Foreign Investment Decision Process* (Boston: Harvard Business School, 1966).

16. Graham, "Oligopolistic Imitation," pp. 121–154.

17. For a careful treatment of this phenomenon with somewhat different emphases, see Franko, *The European Multinationals*, chap. 4.

18. Derived from data in J. W. Vaupel and J. P. Curhan, *The World's Multinational Enterprises* (Boston: Harvard Business School, 1973), pp. 347–348.

19. For a careful analysis of the factors associated with acquisitions, see Michael Dubin, "Foreign Acquisitions and the Spread of the Multinational Firm" (D.B.A. diss., Harvard Business School, 1976).

20. See, for instance, Thomas Horst, *At Home Abroad: A Study of the Domestic and Foreign Operations of the American Food-Processing Industry* (Cambridge, Mass.: Ballinger, 1974), pp. 89–121, 127–129.

21. K. D. George and T. S. Ward, *The Structure of Industry in the EEC* (Cambridge: Cambridge University Press, 1975), p. 51.

22. D. G. Rhys, *The Motor Industry: An Economic Survey* (London: Butterworth, 1972), pp. 177–178; James Ensor, *The Motor Industry* (London: Longmans, 1971), pp. 32–36.

23. Commission of the European Communities, *Third Report on Competition Policy* (Brussels, May 1974), pp. 117–124. See also J. R. Pickering, *Industrial Structure and Market Conduct* (London: Martin Robertson, 1974), pp. 12–20; F. Jenny and A.-P. Webber, *Concentration et politique des structures industrielles* (Paris: La Documentation Française, 1974). For a study suggesting somewhat similar trends in Japan, see Yoshikaza Miyazaki, "The Japanese Structure of Big Business," *Japanese Economic Studies*, Fall 1973, pp. 3–61.

24. Commission of the European Communities, *Third Report on Competition Policy*, pp. 123–128.

25. "Driving Foreign Cars," *The Economist*, October 7, 1972, p. 95.

26. An account of the importance of the remaining barriers inside

the EEC is found in Franko, *The European Multinationals,* chap. 6. See also Barbara Farnsworth, "Advertising in Europe," *European Community,* March 1976, pp. 29–34.

27. Commission of the European Communities, *Fifth Report on Competition Policy* (Brussels, April 1976), and prior reports.

28. Bernardo Sepulveda Amor et al., *Las empresas transnacionales en México* (Mexico City: El Colegio de México, 1974), pp. 4, 15.

29. U.S., Congress, Senate, Committee on Foreign Relations, Subcommittee on Multinational Corporations, *Multinational Corporations in Brazil and Mexico: Structural Sources of Economic and Noneconomic Power,* by R. S. Newfarmer and W. F. Mueller, 94th Cong., 1st Sess., 1975, pp. 148–149.

30. J. V. Sourrouille, *El impacto de las empresas transnacionales sobre el empleo y los ingresos: el caso de Argentina,* Working Paper, no. 7, International Labor Organization (Geneva, April 1976), pp. 55, 61.

31. See M. Y. Yoshino, *Japan's Multinational Enterprises* (Cambridge, Mass.: Harvard University Press, 1976), pp. 70–71. See also Yoshihiro Tsurumi, *The Japanese Are Coming* (Cambridge, Mass.: Ballinger, 1976), chap. 3.

32. David Felix, "The Technological Factor in Socio-Economic Dualism: Toward An Economy-of-Scale Paradigm for Development Theory," mimeographed, 1976, pp. 19–23.

33. Yoshino, *Japan's Multinational Enterprises,* p. 73; Tsurumi, *The Japanese Are Coming,* chap. 10.

34. For another study with a different approach but a similar conclusion, see J. R. Weston, "Are Multinational Corporations Using Market Power to Overprice?" in C. H. Madden, ed., *The Case for the Multinational Corporation: Six Scholarly Views* (New York: Praeger, 1977).

35. R. T. Kudrle, *Agricultural Tractors: A World Industry Study* (Cambridge, Mass.: Ballinger, 1975).

36. See studies of R. B. Stobaugh, Mira Wilkins, E. T. Penrose, Zuhayr Mikdashi, et al., in Raymond Vernon, ed., *The Oil Crisis* (New York: W. W. Norton, 1976). See also Neil Jacoby, *Multinational Oil* (New York: Macmillan, 1974); E. R. Fried and C. L. Schultze, eds., *Higher Oil Prices and the World Economy* (Washington: Brookings Institution, 1972); Adelman, *The World Petroleum Market;* Commission of the European Communities, *Report by the Commission on the Behaviour of the Oil Companies in the Community during the Period from October 1973 to March 1974* (Brussels, December 10, 1975).

37. For more detailed accounts, see, for instance, Mira Wilkins, *The Maturing of Multinational Enterprise* (Cambridge, Mass.: Harvard University Press, 1974), p. 365; J. P. C. Carey and A. G. Carey,

"Libya—No Longer 'Arid Nurse' of Lions," *Political Science Quarterly*
76, no. 1 (March 1961): 59–60; L. H. Schatzl, *Petroleum in Nigeria*
(Ibadan: Oxford University Press, 1969), pp. 3–4.

CHAPTER 5. ENTERPRISE STRATEGIES:
THE STRUGGLE AGAINST ENTROPY

1. For a careful survey and test of the generality of the product
cycle as a feature of international trading performance, see W. B.
Walker, "Industrial Innovation and International Trading Performance," mimeographed, University of Sussex Science Policy Research
Unit, October 30, 1975.

2. While some European and Japanese automotive firms overcame
the increasing barriers and successfully challenged the American
leaders, the national firms in Latin America that had originally started
under heavy local protection generally did not succeed. See R. O.
Jenkins, "The Dynamics of Dependent Industrialization in the Latin
American Motor Industry" (D.Phil. diss., University of Sussex, 1974).

3. Reported in R. B. Stobaugh and P. L. Townsend, "Price Fore-
casting and Strategic Planning: The Case of Petrochemicals," *Journal of
Marketing Research* 12 (February 1975): 19–29. See also Walker, "International Innovation," pp. 20–34.

4. G. K. Helleiner, "Manufactured Exports from Less-Developed
Countries and Multinational Firms," *Economic Journal* 83, no. 329
(March 1973): 21–47; Michael Sharpston, "International Sub-Contract-
ing," *Oxford Economic Papers* 27, no. 1 (March 1975): 101.

5. See R. W. Moxon, "Offshore Production in the Less-Developed
Countries by American Electronics Companies" (D.B.A. diss., Har-
vard Business School, 1973). A closely related finding is that of W. A.
Yeoman, "Selection of Production Processes for the Manufacturing
Subsidiaries of U.S.-Based Multinational Corporations" (D.B.A. diss.,
Harvard Business School, 1968), which is further confirmed by D. J.
Lecraw, "Choice of Technology in Low-Wage Countries: The Case of
Thailand" (Ph.D. diss., Harvard University, 1976). All three studies in-
dicate that multinational enterprises tend to adopt cost-saving produc-
tion techniques most extensively in those lines in which price compe-
tition is strongest.

6. "Offshore Lure Fades for Electronics Firms," *Industry Week*,
May 21, 1973, pp. 18–20.

7. See, for instance, "Brazil: A New Brand of Imperialism," *Business Week*, August 11, 1973, p. 52.

8. M. Y. Yoshino, *Japan's Multinational Enterprises* (Cambridge,
Mass.: Harvard University Press, 1976), pp. 69–72; Yoshihiro Tsurumi,
The Japanese Are Coming (Cambridge, Mass.: Ballinger, 1976), chaps.
3, 7.

9. Lecraw, "Determinants of Capital Intensity in Low-Wage Countries," pp. 139–142.

10. See Ranadav Banerji, *Exports of Manufactures from India: An Appraisal of the Emerging Pattern* (Tübingen: J. C. B. Mohr [P. Siebeck], 1975), pp. 235–237.

11. See Terutomo Ozawa, "Peculiarities of Japan's Multinationalism: Facts and Theories," Banca Nazionale del Lavoro, *Quarterly Review* 28, no. 115 (December 1975): 404–426.

12. Yoshino, *Japan's Multinational Enterprises*, pp. 72–77.

13. For a detailed description of the entropic process in the case of electric power, see M. S. Wionczek, "Electric Power: The Uneasy Partnership," in Raymond Vernon, ed., *Public Policy and Private Enterprise in Mexico* (Cambridge, Mass.: Harvard University Press, 1964), pp. 21–110.

14. J. I. Dominguez, *Cuba: Order and Revolution in the Twentieth Century* (Cambridge, Mass.: Harvard University Press, 1977), chap. 3.

15. See R. E. Evenson, J. P. Houck, Jr., and V. W. Ruttan, "Technical Change and Agricultural Trade: Three Examples—Sugarcane, Bananas, and Rice," in Raymond Vernon, ed., *The Technology Factor in International Trade* (New York: National Bureau of Economic Research, 1970), pp. 415–478.

16. The data have to be interpreted with some caution because they are based upon records collected by the Harvard Multinational Enterprise Project in the late 1960s. Subsidiaries that had dropped out of the multinational network prior to that time could readily have gone unreported, leading to an understatement of the rate of withdrawals in earlier years. For a careful study of withdrawals in earlier periods, see R. L. Tornedon, *Foreign Disinvestment by U.S. Multinational Corporations: Eight Case Studies* (New York: Praeger, 1975).

CHAPTER 6. THE STRAIN ON NATIONAL OBJECTIVES:
THE INDUSTRIALIZED COUNTRIES

1. See J. N. Behrman, *National Interests and the Multinational Enterprise: Tensions among the North Atlantic Countries* (Englewood Cliffs, N.J.: Prentice-Hall, 1970), pp. 105–111, for a review of cases of this sort.

2. See, for instance, D. R. Leyton-Brown, "Governments of Developed Countries as Hosts to Multinational Enterprises: The Canadian, British, and French Policy Experience" (Ph.D. diss., Harvard University, 1973), pp. 101–105.

3. "Socialist Angola's Main Economic Prop: Gulf Oil," *New York Times*, May 30, 1976, sec. 4, p. 4.

4. Jonathan Galloway, "The Military-Industrial Linkages of U.S.-

Based Multinational Corporations," *International Studies Quarterly* 16, no. 4 (December 1972): 491–510.

5. Raymond Vernon and M. I. Goldman, "U.S. Policies on the Sale of Technology to the USSR," mimeographed, Department of Commerce memorandum, August 23, 1974, pp. 8–9, 19, 36–39, 54.

6. H. R. Nau, *National Politics and International Technology* (Baltimore: Johns Hopkins University Press, 1974), p. 136.

7. Ibid., pp. 154–155.

8. Michael Hodges, *Multinational Corporations and National Government: A Case Study of the United Kingdom's Experience 1964–1970* (Lexington, Mass.: D. C. Heath, 1974), pp. 242–257. See also U.K., Fourth Report from the Select Committee of Science and Technology, Session 1970–71, *The Prospects for the United Kingdom Computer Industry in the 1970s*, vol. 1 (London: Her Majesty's Stationery Office, October 1971). For a general statement of the U.K. position, see William Wallace, *The Foreign Policy Process in Britain* (London: Royal Institute of International Affairs, 1975), pp. 140–149.

9. See Nicolas Jéquier, *Les télécommunications et l'Europe* (Lausanne: Centre de Recherches Européenes, 1976), esp. chaps. 2, 3.

10. For a review of the aircraft consortia, see "Action Programme for the European Aeronautical Sector," *Bulletin of the European Communities*, Supplement 11/75, October 3, 1975, p. 16.

11. See M. S. Hochmuth, *Organizing the Transnational* (Leiden: Sijthoff, 1974). See also Roger Williams, *European Technology: The Politics of Collaboration* (New York: John Wiley and Sons, 1973); W. J. Feld, *Transnational Business Collaboration Among Common Market Countries* (New York: Praeger, 1970); Christopher Layton, *European Advanced Technology* (London: Allen and Unwin, 1969); P. M. Goldberg, "The Evolution of Transnational Companies in Europe" (Ph.D. diss., Sloan School of Management, M.I.T., 1971), pp. 218–224.

12. As a crude indication of the importance of costs such as these, see David Teece, "The Multinational Corporation and Resource Cost of International Technology Transfer" (Ph.D. diss., University of Pennsylvania, 1975). For twenty-six projects involving the creation of capital installations, the intangible costs associated with the projects came to 19 percent of total costs on average, ranging in individual projects from 4 percent to 59 percent.

13. See, for instance, "La vérité sur Aerospatiale," *Entreprise*, September 13, 1974, p. 68, describing the troubles of Concorde and the Airbus; "Concorde: Double Your Losses," *The Economist*, March 23, 1974, pp. 70–71; "Centrales nucléaires: un pari au-dessus de nos forces," *Entreprise*, January 30, 1975, pp. 54–60; Nau, *National Politics and International Technology*, pp. 180–181 on the ORGEL consortium; Williams, *European Technology*, pp. 152–153 on the ESRO consortium.

14. See, for instance, John Fayerweather, "Elite Attitudes toward Multinational Firms: A Study of Britain, Canada, and France," *International Studies Quarterly* 16, no. 4 (December 1972): 475, 483.

15. John Gennard and M. D. Steuer, "The Industrial Relations of Foreign-Owned Subsidiaries in the United Kingdom," *British Journal of Industrial Relations* 9, no. 2 (July 1971): 143–159.

16. Marc Beckers et al., *La Belgique face aux investissements étrangers: une approche sociologique* (Louvain: University of Louvain, 1973), pp. 64–65, cited in E. M. Kassalow, "Multinational Corporations and Their Impact on Industrial Relations," mimeographed, presented at the International Conference on Trends in Industrial and Labour Relations, Montreal, May 1976, p. 9.

17. For a summary of such cases, see Kassalow, "Multinational Corporations," pp. 13–15.

18. "U.A.W. President Cautions VW," *New York Times*, July 13, 1974, p. 30.

19. The literature on this subject proliferates. Kassalow, "Multinational Corporations," offers a good summary. See also Charles Levinson, *International Trade Unionism* (London: Allen and Unwin, 1972); I. A. Litvak and C. J. Maule, "The Union Response to International Corporations," *Industrial Relations* 11, no. 1 (February 1972): 62–71; H. R. Northrup and R. L. Rowan, "Multinational Collective Bargaining Activity: The Factual Record in Chemicals, Glass, and Rubber Tires," *Columbia Journal of World Business*, Spring 1974, pt. 1, pp. 112–126, and Summer 1974, pt. 2, pp. 49–64; H. R. Northrup and R. L. Rowan, "Multinational Bargaining in Metals and Electrical Industries: Approaches and Prospects," *Journal of Industrial Relations* 17, no. 1 (March 1975): 1–29; Duane Kujawa, ed., *International Labor and the Multinational Enterprise* (New York: Praeger, 1975).

20. Hans Gunter, "Trade Unions and Industrial Policies," in S. J. Warnecke and E. N. Suleiman, eds., *Industrial Policies in Western Europe* (New York: Praeger, 1975), pp. 108–111.

21. See, for instance, *The Effects of U.S. Corporate Foreign Investment 1970–1973* (New York: Business International Corporation, 1975); *The Role of the Multinational Corporation in the United States World Economies* (Washington: Emergency Committee for American Trade, 1972); J. H. Dunning, "The Multinational Enterprise: The Background," in J. H. Dunning, ed, *The Multinational Enterprise* (London: Allen and Unwin, 1971), pp. 19–21; also H.-F. Samuelsson, "National Scientific and Technological Potential and the Activities of Multinational Corporations: The Case of Sweden," mimeographed, report to the Organization for Economic Cooperation and Development, Committee for Scientific and Technological Policy, 1974.

22. But see the objection to this way of formulating the question,

in R. J. Barnet and R. E. Müller, *Global Reach* (New York: Simon and Schuster, 1974) p. 301. Public policymakers, according to the Barnet-Müller argument, have no need to compare multinational enterprises with the available alternatives; all they need to know is that they find the existing condition unacceptable.

23. For instance, R. H. Frank and R. T. Freeman, "Multinational Corporations and Domestic Employment," mimeographed, a study made for the U.S. Department of Labor, 1975. See also, L. C. Thurow, "International Factor Movements and the American Distribution of Income," *Intermountain Economic Review* 7, no. 1 (Spring 1976): 13–25; U.S., Congress, Senate, Committee on Foreign Relations, Subcommittee on Multinational Corporations, *Direct Investment Abroad and the Multinationals: Effects on the U.S. Economy*, by P. B. Musgrave, 94th Cong., 1st Sess., 1975; Thomas Horst, "The Impact of U.S. Investment on U.S. Foreign Trade," mimeographed, January 1974.

24. International Labor Organization, *The Impact of Multinational Enterprises on Employment and Training* (Geneva, 1976), pp. 22–24.

25. See, for instance, R. Touleman and J. Flory, *Une politique industrielle pour L'Europe* (Paris: Presses Universitaires de France, 1974), pp. 166–181.

26. Yoshihiro Tsurumi, *The Japanese Are Coming* (Cambridge, Mass.: Ballinger, 1976), chap. 11.

27. A. F. Brimmer, "Direct Investment and Corporate Adjustment Techniques under the Voluntary U.S. Balance of Payments Program," *Journal of Finance* 21, no. 2 (May 1966): 266–282; John Ellicott, "United States Controls on Foreign Direct Investment: The 1969 Program," *Law and Contemporary Problems* 34, no. 1 (Winter 1969): 47–63.

28. G. C. Hufbauer and F. M. Adler, *Overseas Manufacturing Investment and the Balance of Payments*, Tax Policy Research Study No. 1, U.S. Treasury Department, Washington, 1968; W. B. Reddaway et al., *Effects of U.K. Direct Investment Overseas* (Cambridge: At the University Press, 1967).

29. For a statistical test consistent with that conclusion and covering the capital spending of U.S.-owned subsidiaries in six industrial countries from 1960 to 1971, see Donald Macaluso and R. G. Hawkins, "The Avoidance of Restrictive Monetary Policies in Host Countries by Multinational Firms," University of Reading Discussion Paper, no. 25, February 1976.

30. M. T. Stanley and J. D. Stanley, "The Impact of U.S. Regulation of Foreign Investment," *California Management Review* 15, no. 2 (Winter 1972): 56–64. See also F. H. Klopstock, "Impact of Euromarkets on the United States Balance of Payments," *Law and Contemporary Problems* 34, no. 1 (Winter 1969): 157–171.

31. A. F. Brimmer, "Multinational Banks and the Management of

Monetary Policy in the United States," mimeographed, presented at a joint session of the 85th Annual Meeting of the American Economic Association and the 31st Annual Meeting of the American Finance Association, Toronto, December 28, 1972, pp. 24–41.

32. The evidence is summarized in J. S. Aronson, "The Impact of American Commercial Banks on the International Monetary System: 1958–1976" (Ph.D. diss., Harvard University, 1976), chap. 5.

33. N. S. Fieleke, "The 1971 Flotation of the Mark and the Hedging of Commercial Transactions between the United States and Germany," *Journal of International Business Studies*, Spring 1973, pp. 43–60.

34. One of these studies is reported in U.S., Congress, Senate, Committee on Foreign Relations, Subcommittee on Multinational Corporations, *Multinational Corporations in the Dollar Devaluation Crisis: Report on a Questionnaire*, 94th Cong., 1st Sess., 1975. The second, so far unpublished, was made by R. M. Rodriguez in the Harvard Multinational Enterprise Project. See also the findings of an earlier study, generally consistent: S. M. Robbins and R. B. Stobaugh, *Money in the Multinational Enterprise: A Study of Financial Policy* (New York: Basic Books, 1973), pp. 119–142.

35. For summaries of national practices, see J. F. Chown, *Taxation and Multinational Enterprises* (London: Longmans, 1974). See also "Criteria for the Allocation of Items of Income and Expense between Related Corporations in Different States, Whether or Not Parties to Tax Conventions," *Cahiers de droit fiscal international* 56, no. 6 (1971); "Allocation of Expenses in International Arm's-Length Transactions of Related Companies," ibid., 60, no. 6 (1975).

36. G. C. Hufbauer and J. R. Nunns, "Tax Payments and Tax Expenditures on International Investment and Employment," *Columbia Journal of World Business* (Summer 1975), p. 13.

37. C. F. Bergsten et al., *American Multinationals and American Interests* (Washington: Brookings Institution), forthcoming.

38. G. D. Henderson and Peter Miller, "Proposals for Allocation of Deductions between Foreign and U.S. Source Income," *Tax Law Review* 29 (Summer 1974): 597–749.

39. U.S., Congress, *Direct Investment Abroad*, p. 16.

40. R. B. Stobaugh, *U.S. Taxation of U.S. Manufacturing Abroad: Likely Effects of Taxing Unremitted Profits* (New York: Financial Executives Research Foundation, 1976).

41. An econometric analysis suggestive of the same conclusion appears in Thomas Horst, "American Taxation of Multinational Corporations," September 1975, unpublished.

42. For Germany, see L. G. Franko, *The European Multinationals* (London: Harper & Row, 1976), pp. 149–150; for the United States, Bergsten et al., *American Multinationals and American Interests*.

43. J. S. Arpan, *International Intracorporate Pricing* (New York: Praeger, 1971), pp. 65–67; T. D. Duchesneau, *Competition in the U.S. Energy Industry* (Cambridge, Mass.: Ballinger, 1975), p. 132; U.S., Congress, Senate, Committee on Government Operations, Permanent Subcommittee on Investigations, *Investigation of the Petroleum Industry*, 93rd Cong., 1st Sess., 1973, pp. 7–8.

44. M. A. Adelman, *The World Petroleum Market* (Baltimore: Johns Hopkins University Press, 1972), pp. 78–89.

45. See, for instance, U.S., Congress, Senate, Committee on the Judiciary, *Petroleum Industry Competition Act of 1976*, 94th Cong., 2d Sess., 1976, pp. 67–70.

46. D. P. Swann, *Antitrust Policy in Europe* (London: *The Financial Times*, 1973), p. 23.

47. G. H. Küster, "Germany," in Raymond Vernon, ed., *Big Business and the State* (Cambridge, Mass.: Harvard University Press, 1974), pp. 74–76; H. Adler, Jr., and M. J. Belman, "Antimerger Enforcement in Europe," *Journal of International Law and Economics* 8, no. 1 (June 1973): 31–51.

48. E. N. Suleiman, "Industrial Policy Formulation in France," in S. J. Warneke and E. N. Suleiman, eds., *Industrial Policies in Western Europe* (New York: Praeger, 1975), pp. 27–29; Jack Hayward, "Employers Associations and the State in France and Britain," ibid., p. 144.

49. See, for example, W. C. Duncan, *U.S.-Japan Automobile Diplomacy* (Cambridge, Mass.: Ballinger, 1973); also R. E. Smith, "Cartels and the Shield of Ignorance," *Journal of International Law and Economics* 8, no. 1 (June 1973): 56.

50. See D. R. Leyton-Brown, "Governments of Developed Countries as Hosts," p. 117 et passim; also W. L. Fugate, "An Overview of Antitrust Enforcement and the Multinational Corporation," *Journal of International Law and Economics* 8, no. 1 (June 1973): 1–9.

51. For details, see W. V. Rapp, *Japan's Industrial Policy* (Tokyo: Committee For Economic Development, 1974).

52. Romano Prodi and Alberto Clô, "Europe," in Raymond Vernon, ed., *The Oil Crisis* (New York, W. W. Norton, 1976), pp. 91–97; Horst Mendershausen, *Coping with the Oil Crisis* (Baltimore: Johns Hopkins University Press, 1976), pp. 18–31.

53. For a more detailed account, see especially essays by E. T. Penrose, R. B. Stobaugh, and Mira Wilkins in Vernon, *The Oil Crisis;* also Commission of the European Communities, *Report by the Commission on the Behaviour of the Oil Companies in the Community during the Period from October 1973 to March 1974* (Brussels, December 10, 1975); R. J. Lieber, *Oil and the Middle East War*, Harvard Studies in International Affairs, no. 35 (Cambridge, Mass.: Harvard Center for International Affairs, 1976), pp. 16–18.

54. Ulf Lantzke, "The OECD and Its International Energy Agency," in Vernon, *The Oil Crisis*, p. 226.

55. See, for instance, D. J. C. Forsyth, *U.S. Investment in Scotland* (New York: Praeger, 1972), p. 6; D. Van den Bulcke, "Les entreprises étrangères dans l'industrie belge," a report of the Seminaire d'Economie Appliqué, University of Ghent (Ghent, 1971), pp. 165–178; G. N. Yannopoulous and J. H. Dunning, "Multinational Enterprises and Regional Development: An Exploratory Paper," University of Reading Discussion Paper, no. 21, April 1975.

56. Franko, *The European Multinationals*, pp. 183–184.

57. See, for example, Michel Beaud et al., *Une multinationale française: Pechiney Ugine Kuhlmann* (Paris: Editions du Seuil, 1975), pp. 130–155.

58. Although the statistics are ambiguous, authoritative views strongly support the generalization. See S. P. Huntington, "The Democratic Distemper," *Public Interest*, no. 41 (Fall 1975), p. 15; A. H. Miller, "Political Issues and Trust in Government: 1964–1970, *American Political Science Review* 68, no. 3 (September 1974): 951–973; Norman Nie, Sidney Verba, and John Petrovic, *The Changing American Voter* (Cambridge, Mass.: Harvard University Press, 1976), pp. 277–280; William Watts and L. A. Free, *State of the Nation* (New York: Universe Books, 1975), p. 271.

CHAPTER 7. THE STRAIN ON NATIONAL OBJECTIVES:
THE DEVELOPING COUNTRIES

1. The literature on the emergence of local business classes in developing countries is growing fairly rapidly. See, for instance, Aaron Lipson, *The Colombian Entrepreneur in Bogotá* (Coral Gables, Fla.: University of Miami Press, 1969); J. F. Leal, *La burguesia y el estado mexicano*, 2d ed. (Mexico City: Ediciones El Caballito, 1974). See also Tabe Noboru, *Indian Entrepreneurs at the Cross Road: A Study of Business Leadership* (Tokyo: Institute of Developing Economies, 1970); G. P. Hart, *Some Socio-Economic Aspects of African Entrepreneurship*, Institute of Social and Economic Research, Rode University, Occasional Paper, no. 16 (Grahamstown, 1972); B. R. Finney, *Big Men and Business: Entrepreneurship and Economic Growth in the New Guinea Highlands* (Honolulu: University of Hawaii Press, 1973); Flavia Derossi, *The Mexican Entrepreneur* (Paris: OECD Development Centre, 1971).

2. This conclusion is much disputed by intellectuals in developing countries, who tend to view the local business class as passive adjuncts of foreign business interests. For a typical statement of that conclusion, see Osvaldo Sunkel, "Big Business and 'Dependencia': A Latin American View," *Foreign Affairs* 50, no. 3 (April 1972): 527.

3. For historical treatments of this phenomenon in czarist Russia, see J. P. McKay, *Pioneers for Profit* (Chicago: University of Chicago Press, 1970), pp. 238–239, 376–377; for Cuba before Castro, J. I. Dominguez, *Cuba: Order and Revolution in the Twentieth Century* (Cambridge, Mass.: Harvard University Press, 1977), chap. 3; for Mexico, Raymond Vernon, *The Dilemma of Mexico's Development* (Cambridge, Mass.: Harvard University Press, 1963), pp. 154–175.

4. For a concise and well-balanced summary of such theories, see S. J. Rosen and J. R. Kurth, eds., *Testing Theories of Economic Imperialism* (Lexington, Mass.: D. C. Heath, 1974), esp. the contributions of K. W. Deutsch and Andrew Mack.

5. For a modern version of Leninist theory, incorporating current economic concepts, see L. G. Countinbo, *The Internationalization of Oligopoly Capital* (Ann Arbor, Mich.: Xerox University Microfilms, 1975).

6. For a review of some of these cases, see S. J. Rosen, "The Open Door Imperative and U.S. Foreign Policy," in Rosen and Kurth, *Testing Theories of Imperialism,* pp. 117–142. See also L. H. Thunell, *International Business and Political Risk* (New York: Praeger, 1977).

7. For a sensitive presentation of the point, see Octavio Paz, *Posdata* (Mexico City: Siglo Veintiuno, 1970).

8. For a thoughtful analysis of the link between multinational enterprises and the problems of industrialization in Mexico, see Fernando Fajnzylber and T. Martínez Tarragó, *Las empresas transnacionales: expansión a nivel mundial y proyección en la industria mexicana* (Mexico City: Fondo de Cultura Económica, 1976), pp. 139–148.

9. The available studies for Latin America which distinguish reactions to foreign investors according to social and economic class are summarized and interpreted in Jorge I. Dominguez, *Public Opinion on International Affairs in Less Developed Countries,* forthcoming. Dominguez' discussion draws on about a dozen studies that cover the principal Latin American countries and relate mainly to the period from 1960 to the early 1970s.

10. Quoted in Pierre Benaerts, *Les origines de la grande entreprise allemande* (Paris: Tierot [circa 1930]), p. 353, called to my attention by C. P. Kindleberger.

11. McKay, *Pioneers for Profit.*

12. For an authoritative summary of the studies of exports by multinational enterprises from developing countries, see John Dunning, "U.K. Multinational Enterprises and Trade Flows of Larger Developing Countries," mimeographed (London: Economists Advisory Group, 1974), chap. 2.

13. "Brazil Has Second Thoughts about Multinationals," *Multinational Business,* no. 3 (September 1975), pp. 18–27.

14. D. B. Keesing and P. A. Plesch, "Recent Trends in Manufactured Exports from Developing Countries," mimeographed, World Bank Report, March 1975, p. 10.

15. F. U. Adams, *Conquest of the Tropics* (Garden City, N.Y.: Doubleday, Page, 1914), p. 61.

16. Mira Wilkins, *The Maturing of Multinational Enterprise* (Cambridge, Mass.: Harvard University Press, 1974), pp. 98–99.

17. For a meticulously annotated description of these discussions, see Lorenzo Meyer, *México y los Estados Unidos en el conflicto petrolero (1917–1942)* (Mexico City: El Colegio de México, 1972), pp. 151–239.

18. On Iraq's negotiations in the 1930s, see U.S., Congress, Senate, Select Committee on Small Business, Subcommittee on Monopoly, *The International Petroleum Cartel,* by the U.S. Federal Trade Commission, 82nd Cong., 2d Sess., 1952, pp. 91–95. See also Franklin Tugwell, *The Politics of Oil in Venezuela* (Stanford: Stanford University Press, 1975), pp. 40–44; Edwin Lieuwen, *Petroleum in Venezuela: A History* (Berkeley: University of California Press, 1954), pp. 93–97; Abdul Amir Q. Kubbah, *Libya: Its Oil Industry and Economic System* (Baghdad: The Arab Petro-Economic Research Centre, 1964), pp. 64–97.

19. For a careful account of the process, see D. N. Smith and L. T. Wells, Jr., *Negotiating Third World Mineral Agreements: Promises as Prologue* (Cambridge, Mass.: Ballinger, 1975), esp. chaps. 1, 7.

20. R. F. Mikesell, *Foreign Investment in Copper Mining* (Baltimore: Johns Hopkins University Press, 1975), introduction.

21. The original study by Raúl Prebisch appears in *The Economic Development of Latin America and Its Principal Problems* (New York: United Nations, 1950). A recent review of the relationship is reported in "U.N. Unit Reports on Prices Survey: Issue Is Effect of Shifts on Poor-Land Economies," *New York Times,* May 28, 1975, p. 19. Other studies include Werner Baer, "Economics of Prebisch and ECLA," *Economic Development and Cultural Change* 10, no. 2, pt. 1 (January 1962): 169–182; Alfred Maizels, *Industrial Growth and World Trade* (Cambridge: Cambridge University Press, 1963), p. 42, 79; Theodore Morgan, "Terms of Trade between Primary Products and Manufacturers," *Economic Development and Cultural Change* 8, no. 1 (October 1959): pp. 1–23; Simon Kuznets, "Foreign Trade: Long Term Trends," ibid., 15, no. 2 (January 1967): 56–61; C. P. Kindleberger, "The Terms of Trade and Development," *Review of Economics and Statistics* 40, supplement (February 1958): 72–90; W. A. Lewis, "Aspects of Tropical Trade: 1883 and 1965" *Wiksell Lecture 1969* (Stockholm: Almqvist and Wiksell, 1969).

22. See R. B. Stobaugh, "Systematic Bias and the Terms of Trade," *Review of Economics and Statistics* 49, no. 4 (November 1967): 617–619, which demonstrates that the characteristic behavior of chemical product prices has been one of rapid decline and that the conventional price indexes for such products are heavily biased upward. See also, I. B. Kravis and R. E. Lipsey, *Competitiveness in World Trade* (New York: National Bureau of Economic Research, 1971), pp. 186–191.

23. E. T. Penrose, *The Large International Firm in Developing Countries: The International Petroleum Industry* (London: Allen and Unwin, 1968), p. 193.

24. D. L. McNicol, "The Two Price Systems in the Copper Industry," *Bell Journal of Economics* 6, no. 1 (Spring 1975): 50–73. McNicol concludes tentatively that the price mechanism used by the leaders in the industry is explained partly by their fear that buyers will shift to other metals if prices get too high and partly by their desire to capture a larger share of the monopoly rent from buyers.

25. A glimpse of the practical complexities that developing countries find in securing high and stable earnings in the mining industry is provided in R. L. Curry, "Problems in Export-Based Public Revenue Collections in Zambia and Liberia," *Journal of World Trade Law* 9, no. 6 (November–December 1975): 678–690.

26. For an illuminating study, see R. L. Sklar, *Corporate Power in an African State: The Political Impact of Multinational Mining Companies in Zambia* (Berkeley: University of California Press, 1975), esp. pp. 76–91.

27. See esp. Lars Nieckels, *Transfer Pricing in Multinational Firms* (New York: John Wiley & Sons, 1976); S. M. Robbins and R. B. Stobaugh, *Money in the Multinational Enterprise: A Study of Financial Policy* (New York: Basic Books, 1973), pp. 91–92.

28. Mixed practices are reported by G. L. Reuber et al., *Private Foreign Investment in Development* (Oxford: Clarendon Press, 1973), pp. 145–158; and D. T. Brash, *American Investment in Australian Industry* (Cambridge, Mass.: Harvard University Press, 1966), pp. 217–220. See also Jack Baranson, *Automotive Industries in Developing Countries* (Baltimore: Johns Hopkins Press, 1969), p. 37. Sanjaya Lall, in "Transfer-Pricing by Multinational Manufacturing Firms," *Oxford Bulletin of Economics and Statistics* 35, no. 3 (August 1973): 173–195, argues that transfer pricing detrimental to less-developed countries is likely but offers little empirical evidence to support his argument.

29. C. V. Vaitsos, *Intercountry Income Distribution and Transnational Enterprises* (Oxford: Clarendon Press, 1974), pp. 47–48. The study also covers some rubber and electronics products but with much less spectacular results. Similar results for the pharmaceutical industry in Argentina, albeit of a less startling kind, are presented in J. M. Katz,

Oligopolio, firmas nacionales y empresas multinacionales: la industria far-macéutica argentina (Buenos Aires: Siglo Veintiuno, 1974), p. 33.

30. Estes Kefauver, *In a Few Hands: Monopoly Power in America* (New York: Pantheon, 1965), pp. 8–79; Monopolies Commission, *Chlordiazepoxide and Diazepam* (London: Her Majesty's Stationery Office, 1973).

31. H. K. May, "Defects in Constantine Vaitsos' Analysis of Transfer Pricing," mimeographed, December 18, 1975.

32. The earnings and royalty fee percentages are based on a 1966 benchmark survey conducted by the U.S. Department of Commerce, superimposed on other Commerce Department data for 1973 and 1974: "U.S. Direct Investments Abroad—1966," mimeographed, supplement to U.S. Department of Commerce, *Survey of Current Business.* The profits on intermediate products are notional, based on an analysis in Robbins and Stobaugh, *Money in the Multinational Enterprise,* p. 169, which estimates the outside limits that a parent firm might achieve by financial policies designed to maximize profits from subsidiaries.

33. Ibid., pp. 75–96, 145–148.

34. A reflection of these tendencies is seen in M. F. J. Prachowny and J. D. Richardson, "Testing a Life-Cycle Hypothesis of the Balance-of-Payments Effects of Multinational Corporations," *Economic Inquiry* 13 (March 1975): 81–98. The study, covering U.S.-owned foreign manufacturing subsidiaries, purports to show that the younger subsidiaries generate lesser balance-of-payment flows to the United States than the older (and sometimes even negative ones). See also M. Z. Brooke and H. L. Remmers, *The Strategy of Multinational Enterprise* (New York: Elsevier, 1970), pp. 169–170, 173.

35. See Vaitsos, *Intercountry Income Distribution,* p. 85; Lall, "Transfer-Pricing," p. 183; and Y. Sabolo, R. Trajtenberg, and J. P. Sajhau, "The Impact of Transnational Enterprises on Employment in the Developing Countries," International Labor Organization, Working Paper (Geneva, 1976), pp. 33–35. Also Bernardo Sepulveda and Antonio Chumacero, *La inversion extranjera en México* (Mexico City: Fondo de Cultura Económica, 1973).

36. In 1968, the most recent year for which data are available, only 12 percent of the foreign profits reported by U.S. taxpayers showed up in the tax-haven countries, according to a private communication from the U.S. Treasury Department. But the figure was probably much higher in some industries, including the pharmaceuticals industry.

37. For a simplified description of these alternatives, see Raymond Vernon and L. T. Wells, Jr., *Economic Environment of International Business,* 2d ed. (Englewood Cliffs, N.J.: Prentice-Hall, 1976), pp. 94–110.

38. Based on U.S. Department of Commerce, "Direct Investments

Abroad—1966." Similar results are reported from another source for Brazilian and Mexican manufacturing subsidiaries for 1966 and 1972—a little higher for Brazil, a little lower for Mexico. See U.S., Congress, Senate, Committee on Foreign Relations, Subcommittee on Multinational Corporations, *Multinational Corporations in Brazil and Mexico: Structural Sources of Economic and Noneconomic Power,* by R. S. Newfarmer and W. F. Mueller, 94th Cong., 1st Sess., 1975, derived from data in Appendix A.

39. See Osvaldo Sunkel, "Big Business and 'Dependencia': A Latin American View," *Foreign Affairs* 50, no. 3 (April 1972): 528; R. J. Barnet and R. E. Müller, *Global Reach* (New York: Simon and Schuster, 1974), p. 165; Ivan Illich, "Outwitting the 'Developed' Countries," *New York Review of Books* 13, no. 8 (November 6, 1969): 20–22.

40. Gert Rosenthal, "The Expansion of the Transnational Enterprise in Central America," presented in Queretaro, Mexico, 1975, unpublished.

41. A poignant illustration of how intellectuals in the developing countries live with these dilemmas appears in Norman Girvan, "The Impact of Multinational Enterprises on Employment and Income in Jamaica," International Labor Office, preliminary report (Geneva, April 1976), p. 23. Girvan, who is unequivocally hostile to multinational enterprises in developing countries, notes that in the export-oriented industries they make use of processes that are highly labor-intensive. He explains that tendency by observing that multinational enterprises "are better endowed to exploit cheap labor. . ."

42. One of the more ambitious studies so far is P. P. Streeten and Sanjaya Lall, *Evaluation of Methods and Main Findings of UNCTAD Study of Private Overseas Investment in Selected Less-Developed Countries,* United Nations, TD/b/c.3/111, 1973. The study covers 159 manufacturing projects in six countries of the developing world. The authors strongly disfavor foreign-owned subsidiaries as compared with alternative means for securing foreign capital and technology. Their assumptions and calculations nonetheless lead them to conclude that a little over 60 percent of the projects had positive effects on the social income of the host country. So politicized is the debate, however, that the findings were reported with the reverse emphasis: "Nearly 40 percent . . . have negative effects. . ."

43. See, for instance, Reserve Bank of India, *Foreign Collaboration in Indian Industry* (Bombay, 1968), p. 104.

44. This figure, like every other in the paragraph, is vulnerable. It is too high when compared with typical Eurodollar borrowing rates and probably too low if allowance is made for plow-back of earnings by equity investors.

45. For instance, for a firm whose value added was equal to 40

percent of its sales and a capital/output ratio of unity. These assumptions are roughly consistent with the available data on the manufacturing subsidiaries of multinational enterprises.

46. See Streeten and Lall, *Evaluation of Methods,* p. 27.

47. Charles Cooper, "Science, Technology and Production in the Underdeveloped Countries: An Introduction," *Journal of Development Studies* 9, no. 1 (October 1972): 5–6. See also National Council of Applied Economic Research, *Foreign Technology and Investment* (New Delhi, 1971), p. 48; and Frances Stewart, "Technology and Employment in Less-Developed Countries," *World Development* 2, no. 3 (March 1974): 41–43.

48. See, for instance, W. A. Chudson and L. T. Wells, Jr., "The Acquisition of Technology from Multinational Corporations by Developing Countries," prepared for the United Nations Department of Economic and Social Affairs (New York, 1974), ST/ESA/12, pp. 11–12.

49. T. W. Allen, *Policies of ASEAN Countries toward Direct Foreign Investment* (New York: SEADAG, Asia Society, 1975).

50. Reported in R. H. Mason, "Technology Transfer and Adaptation of Production Processes by Foreign Agribusiness Firms in Developing Countries," mimeographed, Conference on Foreign Agribusiness, University of Iowa, May 22–25, 1972, p. 6. See also S. J. Burki et al., "Public Works Programs in Developing Countries: A Comparative Analysis," World Bank Working Paper, no. 224, February 1976, p. 21, which classifies Bangladesh, India, Jamaica, Pakistan, Trinidad-Tobago, and Tunisia as fostering labor-displacing policies in manufacturing technology. See also C. P. Timmer et al., *The Choice of Technology in Developing Countries,* Harvard Studies in International Affairs No. 32 (Cambridge, Mass.: Harvard Center for International Affairs, 1975).

51. See, for instance, Anne Krueger, *The Benefits and Costs of Import Substitution in India* (Minneapolis: University of Minnesota Press, 1975), p. 39.

52. On the state of industrial research and innovation in China, see Hans Heymann, Jr., *China's Approach to Technology Acquisition,* pt. 3 (Santa Monica, Calif.: RAND, February 1975); Genevieve Dean, "A Note on the Sources of Technological Innovation in the PRC," *Journal of Development Studies* 9, no. 1 (October 1972): 189–199; Carl Riskin, "Small Industry and the Chinese Model of Development," *China Quarterly* no. 46 (April–June 1971), pp. 245–273; Jon Sigurdson, "The Role of Small-Scale and Rural Industry and Its Interaction with Agriculture and Large-Scale Industry in China," mimeographed, Economic Research Institute, Stockholm School of Economics, July 1974. Several other important studies, not yet published or quotable, also have been available to me.

53. Sanjaya Lall, "The Patent System and the Transfer of Technology to Less-Developed Countries," *Journal of World Trade Law* 10, no. 1 (January-February 1976); S. J. Patel, "The Patent System and the Third World," *World Development* 2, no. 9 (September 1974): 3–14; Daniel Chudnovsky, *Aspectos económicos de la importación de tecnología en la Argentina en 1972* (Buenos Aires: Instituto Nacional de Tecnología Industrial, November 1974); Peter O'Brien, "Developing Countries and the Patent System: An Economic Appraisal," *World Development* 2, no. 9 (September 1974):27–36.

54. For an elaborate proposal to modify the patent grants of developing countries, see J. H. Barton, "Technology Transfer and LDCs: A Proposal for a Preferential Patent System," *Stanford Journal of International Studies* 6 (Spring 1971): 27–50. See also E. T. Penrose, "International Patenting and the Less-Developed Countries," *Economic Journal* 83, no. 331 (September 1973): 768; H. G. Maier, "International Patent Conventions and Access to Foreign Technology," *Journal of Law and Economic Development* 4, no. 2 (Fall 1969): 207–231; Douglas Greer, "The Case against Patent Systems in Less-Developed Countries," *Journal of International Law and Economics* 8, no. 2 (December 1973): 223–266.

55. On the uncertain protection afforded by patents, see F. M. Scherer, "Antitrust and Patent Policy," mimeographed, Seminar on Technological Innovation, sponsored by the U.S. National Science Foundation and the government of the Federal Republic of Germany, Bonn, April 1976.

56. R. D. Robinson, *National Control of Multinational Corporations: A Fifteen-Country Study* (New York: Praeger, 1976).

57. See J. M. Stopford and L. T. Wells, Jr., *Managing the Multinational Enterprise* (New York: Basic Books, 1972), pp. 121–122; Reuber et al., *Private Foreign Investment in Development*, pp. 163–164. On export restrictions, see J. R. de la Torré, Jr., "Export of Manufactured Goods from Developing Countries," (D.B.A. diss., Harvard Business School, 1970), pp. 93, 96; Reserve Bank of India, *Foreign Collaboration in Indian Industry*, pp. 106–107.

58. This point, of course, is implicit in much of the extensive *dependencia* literature of Latin America. For recognition of the point elsewhere, see Sung-Hwan Jo, "The Impact of Multinational Firms on Employment and Incomes: The Case Study of South Korea" (Geneva: International Labor Organization, July 1976), p. 61.

59. One of the few well-researched glimpses into this question is provided in Sklar, *Corporate Power in an African State*, pp. 179–216.

60. For a discussion of the investment incentive programs, see Reuber et al., *Private Foreign Investment in Development*, pp. 123–132. See also *Obstacles and Incentives to Private Foreign Investment*

1967–1968, vol. 2 (New York: National Industrial Conference Board, 1969).

CHAPTER 8. TRANSNATIONAL PROCESSES AND NATIONAL GOALS

1. C. D. Kepner, Jr., and J. H. Soothill, *The Banana Empire: A Case Study of Economic Imperialism* (New York: Russell and Russell, 1935), pp. 336–341. See also C. V. Crabb, Jr., *American Foreign Policy in the Nuclear Age,* 3d ed. (New York: Harper & Row, 1972), pp. 325–327, 330–331; R. J. Barnet, *Intervention and Revolution* (New York: World, 1968), pp. 229–236.

2. U.S. v. United Fruit Co. The complaint was filed in 1954, amended in 1956, and closed by consent decree in 1958.

3. U.S., Congress, Senate, Select Committee on Small Business, *Monopoly and Cartels,* pt. 1, 82d Cong., 2d sess., 1952, Appendix III.

4. David Wise and Thomas Ross, *The Invisible Government* (New York: Random House, 1964), p. 110; Andrew Tully, *CIA: The inside Story* (New York: William Morrow, 1967), pp. 88–89; C. J. V. Murphy, "Uncloaking the CIA," *Fortune,* June 1975, p. 90.

5. J. I. Dominguez, *Cuba: Order and Revolution in the Twentieth Century* (Cambridge, Mass.: Harvard University Press, 1977), chap. 3.

6. U.S., Department of State, *Foreign Legislation Concerning Monopoly and Cartel Practices,* a report to the Subcommittee on Monopoly of the Select Committee on Small Business (Washington: 1952), pp. 176–178.

7. See, for instance, Andrew Mack, "Comparing Theories of Economic Imperialism," in S. J. Rosen and J. R. Kurth, eds., *Testing Theories of Economic Imperialism* (Lexington, Mass.: D. C. Heath, 1974), pp. 35–56; B. J. Cohen, *The Question of Imperialism: The Political Economy of Dominance and Dependence* (New York: Basic Books, 1973). See also I. A. Litvak and C. J. Maule, "Nationalization in the Caribbean Bauxite Industry," *International Affairs,* January 1975, pp. 43–59.

8. For the U.S. role in Chile, see U.S., Congress, Senate, Committee on Foreign Relations, Subcommittee on Multinational Corporations, *Multinational Corporations and United States Foreign Policy, Hearings on the International Telephone and Telegraph Company and Chile 1970–71,* pt. 1, 2, 93d Cong., 1st Sess., 1973; also, U.S., Congress, Senate, Select Committee to Study Governmental Operations, *Foreign and Military Intelligence, Final Report of the Select Committee to Study Governmental Operations with Respect to Intelligence Activities,* book 1, 94th Cong., 2d sess., 1976, pp. 15–256.

9. For Japan, M. Y. Yoshino, *Japan's Multinational Enterprises,* (Cambridge, Mass.: Harvard University Press, 1976), pp. 53–59; for France, Commissariat Général du Plan, *Cinquieme plan de dévelop-*

pement économique et social (1966–1970), p. 60; and *Sixième plan* (Paris: Union Générale d'Editions, 1971), p. 16.

10. Ibid., p. 16.

11. I. A. Litvak and C. J. Maule, "Canadian–United States Corporate Interface and Transnational Relations," *International Organization* 28, no. 4 (August 1974): 711–731. Also J. N. Behrman, *National Interests and the Multinational Enterprise: Tensions among the North Atlantic Countries*, (Englewood Cliffs, N. J.: Prentice-Hall, 1970), pp. 114–127.

12. For a summary, see J. M. Starrels, "The Dilemmas of Governmental Intervention: Chrysler, the Labour Government, and Britain," presented at the Annual Meeting, American Political Science Association, Chicago, September 2, 1976.

13. "U.S. to Urge Pact in U.N. to Combat Corporate Bribes," *New York Times*, March 6, 1976, pp. 1, 37; R. M. Smith, "Corporate Bribery Files," *New York Times*, March 21, 1976, Sec. 4, p. 6.

14. In the debate over an OECD code in 1976, for instance, Sweden unsuccessfully pressed for mandatory disclosure on these lines. "24 Nations Set Up a Corporate Code," *New York Times*, May 27, 1976, pp. 1, 7.

15. For an account of Canada's support of its uranium companies in refusing to provide data to a U.S. grand jury on alleged market-rigging by Canadian firms, see "Canadian Firm Signs Uranium Supply Pact with Four U.S. Utilities," *Chemical Marketing Reporter*, July 19, 1976, pp. 7, 33.

16. R. O. Keohane and J. S. Nye, Jr., *Power and Interdependence: World Politics in Transition* (Boston: Little, Brown, 1977), chap. 7; Carl Beigie, "The Automotive Agreement of 1965: A Case Study in Canadian-American Economic Affairs," in R. A. Preston, ed., *The Influence of the United States on Canadian Development* (Durham, N.C.: Duke University Press, 1972), p. 118; U.S., Congress, Senate, Committee on Finance, *United States–Canadian Automobile Agreement, Hearings on H.R. 9042*, 89th Cong., 1st Sess., September 1965, pp. 53–56.

17. Oliver Oldman, "Tax Policies of Less Developed Countries with Respect to Foreign Income and Income of Foreigners," in R. M. Bird and Oliver Oldman, eds., *Readings on Taxation in Developing Countries* (Baltimore: Johns Hopkins University Press, 1967), pp. 202–205.

18. B. C. Roberts, "Multinational Enterprise and Labor," in P. B. Doeringer, ed., *Industrial Relations in International Perspective*, forthcoming. "Chasing the Rabbit," *Wall Street Journal*, April 22, 1976, pp. 1, 27.

19. U.S., Congress, Joint Economic Committee, Subcommittee on Economic Growth, *Outlook for Prices and Supplies of Industrial Raw Ma-*

terials, 93rd Cong., 2d Sess., July 1974, pp. 5–6, 13–14, 118, 140, 160–163, 172, 179–181.

20. See I. A. Litvak and C. J. Maule, "Canadian Investment Abroad: In Search of a Policy," *International Journal* 31, no. 1 (Winter 1975–76): 170–173.

21. Raymond Vernon, "The Influence of the U.S. Government upon Multinational Enterprises: The Case of Oil," in Antoine Ayoub, *The New Petroleum Order* (Quebec: Les Presses de l'Université Laval, 1976), pp. 44–79.

22. For an excellent account of the U.S. handling of the International Petroleum case in Peru, see J. P. Einhorn, *Expropriation Politics* (Lexington, Mass.: D. C. Heath, 1974).

23. A very different—but not necessarily conflicting—interpretation of the U.S. role in the IPC case is to be found in A. F. Lowenthal, "The United States and Latin America: Ending the Hegemonic Presumption," *Foreign Affairs* 55, no. 1 (October 1976): 205n.

24. Mira Wilkins, "The Oil Companies in Perspective," in Raymond Vernon, ed., *The Oil Crisis* (New York: W. W. Norton, 1976), p. 167, notes the lukewarm character of the State Department's support without referring to the underlying cause.

25. C. H. Lipson, "Corporate Preferences and Public Policies: Foreign-Aid Sanctions and Investment Protection," *World Politics* 28, no. 3 (April 1976): 396–421. By a fine twist of argument, Lipson concludes that the multinational enterprises do dominate U.S. policymaking after all, since the decision of the U.S. government not to act reflected the dominant preference of such enterprises.

26. Keohane and Nye, *Power and Interdependence,* p. 206.

27. M. Y. Yoshino, *The Japanese Marketing System: Adaptations and Innovations* (Cambridge, Mass.: M.I.T. Press, 1971), pp. 251–274.

28. S. S. Cohen, *Modern Capitalist Planning: The French Model* (Cambridge, Mass.: Harvard University Press, 1969).

29. An account of the links between the French bureaucracy and the French oil industry and of the parallel relation in Britain will appear in Louis Turner, *Oil Companies and the World System,* to be published under the auspices of the Royal Institute of International Affairs, London.

30. A solid review of the literature, mainly from British and American sources, appears in E. R. Epstein, "The Social Role of American Business Enterprise in Britain: An American Perspective," in three parts; the first part appears in *Journal of Management Studies* 13, no. 3 (October 1976): 213–233.

31. Nicolas Jéquier, "Computers," in Raymond Vernon, ed., *Big Business and the State: Changing Relations in Western Europe* (Cam-

bridge, Mass.: Harvard University Press, 1974), pp. 203, 214–219.

32. *The Paranoid Style in American Politics and Other Essays* (New York: Alfred A. Knopf, 1966), p. 205. See also R. A. Dahl, *Pluralist Democracy in the United States: Conflict and Consent* (Chicago: Rand McNally, 1967), p. 24; S. P. Huntington, "Political Modernization: America vs. Europe," *World Politics* 18, no. 3 (April 1966): 378–414; Bernard Bailyn, *Ideological Origins of the American Revolution* (Cambridge, Mass.: Harvard University Press, 1967), pp. 55–93, 273–301.

33. Potter Stewart, "Or of the Press," *Hastings Law Journal* 26, no. 3 (January 1975): 631–637.

34. G. L. Waples, "The Freedom of Information Act: A Seven-Year Assessment," *Columbia Law Review* 74 (June 1974): 895–959.

35. R. B. Stewart, "The Reformation of American Administrative Law," *Harvard Law Review* 88, no. 8 (June 1975): 1667.

36. For typical studies of this well-researched subject, see L. D. Epstein, *Political Parties in Western Democracies* (New York: Praeger, 1967), pp. 193–198; R. A. Alford, *Party and Society: The Anglo-American Democracies* (Chicago: Rand McNally, 1973), pp. 94–122, 219–248, 309–318; W. N. Chambers, "Parties and Nation-Building in America," in Joseph LaPalombara and Myron Weiner, eds., *Political Parties and Political Development* (Princeton: Princeton University Press, 1966), p. 83.

37. J. A. Armstrong, *The European Administrative Elite* (Princeton: Princeton University Press, 1973), esp. pp. 201–223, 244; T. B. Bottomore, *Elites and Society* (Middlesex, Eng.: Penguin Books, 1964), pp. 87–88; R. K. Kelsall, *Higher Civil Servants in Britain* (London: Routledge & Kegan Paul, 1955), esp. pp. 118–145; A. M. Craig and D. H. Shively, eds., *Personality in Japanese History* (Berkeley: University of California Press, 1970), p. 26; Reinhard Bendix, *Higher Civil Servants in American Society* (Boulder: University of Colorado Press, 1949), pp. 22–32. See also C. W. Mills, *The Power Elite* (New York: Oxford University Press, 1956), pp. 239–241.

CHAPTER 9. THE GAP BETWEEN PROSPECTS AND POLICIES

1. For a strongly dissenting evaluation, which assigns a much stronger role to OPEC, see D. A. Rustow and J. F. Mugno, *OPEC: Success and Prospects* (New York: Council on Foreign Relations, 1976).

2. For a summary of the operations of the pact during its first few years, see *Andean Pact: Definition, Design, and Analysis* (New York: Council of the Americas, 1973).

3. UNCTAD, *The Manila Declaration and Program of Action*, Fourth Session, Nairobi, May 5, 1976.

4. Statement of K. A. Sahlgren, Executive Director, U.N. Centre on Transnational Corporations, March 19, 1976, Lima, Peru.

5. See Gilles Bertin, "Foreign Investment in France," in I. A. Litvak and C. J. Maule, eds., *Foreign Investment: The Experience of the Host Countries* (New York: Praeger, 1970), pp. 105–122.

6. Y. S. Hu, *The Impact of U.S. Investment in Europe: A Case Study of the Automotive and Computer Industries* (New York: Praeger, 1973), p. 143.

7. For instance, Walter Gordon, *A Choice for Canada* (Toronto: McClelland and Stewart, 1966); *Report of the Standing Committee on External Affairs and National Defense*, No. 33 (Ottawa: Queen's Printer, 1970); *Report of the Task Force on the Structure of Canadian Industry* (Ottawa: Queen's Printer, 1968).

8. See, for instance, Abraham Rotstein, "Canada: The New Nationalism," *Foreign Affairs* 55, no. 1 (October 1976): 97–118.

9. See, for instance, "The Protection of Workers in Multinational Companies," *European Communities*, European Documentation Trade Union Series, 1976/1.

10. "The OECD Guidelines in Brief," *Business International* 23, no. 24 (June 11, 1976): 2; "New OECD Guidelines for Multinationals Agreed," *Multinational Business*, no. 2, June 1976, pp. 33–36.

11. D. N. Smith and L. T. Wells, Jr., *Negotiating Third World Mineral Agreements: Promises as Prologue* (Cambridge, Mass.: Ballinger, 1975), pp. 37–53.

12. See B. M. Russett and E. C. Hanson, *Interest and Ideology: The Foreign Policy Beliefs of American Businessmen* (San Francisco: W. H. Freeman, 1975), p. 96.

13. For surveys of U.S. leadership opinion that closely reflect this mood, see *FPA Outreacher*, Foreign Policy Association, New York, 1976; also Russett and Hanson, *Interest and Ideology*, pp. 77, 271.

14. See, for instance, G. J. Stoller, "Patterns of Stability in Foreign Trade: OECD and COMECON, 1950–1963," *American Economic Review* 57, no. 4 (September 1967): 879–888; also C. W. Lawson, "An Empirical Analysis of the Structure and Stability of Communist Foreign Trade 1960–68," *Soviet Studies* 26, no. 2 (April 1974): 224–238.

15. See, for instance, L. G. Franko, "Multinational Enterprises in the Middle East," *Journal of World Trade Law* 10, no. 4 (August 1976): 307–333; Ralph Landau and A. I. Mendolia, "An American View of Chemical Investment Patterns in the Era of High Energy Costs," *Chemistry and Industry*, December 6, 1975, p. 1011; "Large Projects in Mideast Getting Second Look," *Business Japan*, August 1976, p. 23; and R. B. Stobaugh, "The Evolution of Iranian Oil Policy" in George Lenczowski, ed., *The Crown of the Pahlevis: Modernity and Tradition in Iran* (Stanford: Hoover Institution Press, 1976).

Index